the Unofficial Guide®

DISNEY
Cruise Line

Photo: Laurel Stewart

Len Testa with Erin Foster and Laurel Stewart

Helmsman Mickey greets guests in the *Magic*'s lobby. (Photo: Laurel Stewart)

Cabanas buffet, found on the *Magic*, *Dream*, and *Fantasy*, is a great spot for breakfast and lunch. (Photo: Laurel Stewart)

The big finale of the *All Aboard* welcome show on the *Magic* (Photo: Scott Smith)

Getting started with the excellent Midship Detective Agency interactive adventure game on the *Dream* (Photo: Laurel Stewart)

Belle drops in to tell stories during *Disney Dreams—An Enchanted Classic*. (Photo: bright_shadows56)

Donald's Pool on the *Fantasy*. You can see the AquaDuck waterslide and Mickey's Pool in the background. (Photo: Laurel Stewart)

The *Magic*'s new Twist 'n' Spout waterslide (Photo: Len Testa)

Dumbo and Timothy Q. Mouse busy themselves sprucing up the stern of the *Fantasy*. (Photo: Laurel Stewart)

The AquaDuck waterslide is found on the *Dream* and *Fantasy*. (Photo: Laurel Stewart)

The AquaDuck waterslide (*Dream* and *Fantasy*) provides thrills aplenty for kids and grown-ups alike. (Photo: Laurel Stewart)

The *Fantasy*'s AquaLab splash area (Photo: Ricky Brigante)

The *Fantasy*'s adult pool at night (Photo: Laurel Stewart)

The *Magic*'s Quiet Cove Pool at night (Photo: Laurel Stewart)

The *Magic*'s new Oceaneer Club
(Photo: Len Testa)

Back dining room at Remy, the best restaurant on the *Dream* (Photo: Len Testa)

Each DCL ship has an Italian restaurant called Palo; the versions on the *Dream* (shown) and the *Fantasy* are the prettiest. (Photo: Len Testa)

The version of Vibe teen club on the *Magic* and *Wonder* (left) is markedly different in theme and decor from the version on the *Dream* and *Fantasy* (right).
(Photos: left, Laurel Stewart; right, Joe Tolley)

typical Deluxe Inside Stateroom. This one is om the *Wonder.* (Photo: Len Testa)

Deluxe Oceanview Stateroom with Verandah on the *Dream* (Photo: Scott Sanders/disneycruise lineblog.com)

g-city vistas unfold behind the bar at Skyline ounge on the *Dream*. (Photo: Laurel Stewart)

687 is the *Dream*'s upscale sports bar. (Photo: Laurel Stewart)

The *Dream*'s Walt Disney Theatre hosts the ship's live shows. (Photo: Laurel Stewart)

The *Magic*'s Brazilian-themed restaurant, Carioca's (Photo: Len Testa)

Selection of port wines at Palo on the *Wonder* (Photo: Laurel Stewart)

The *Fantasy*'s Enchanted Garden restaurant has a ceiling whose lighting changes from day to night. (Photos: Laurel Stewart)

Castaway Cay's Pelican Plunge: a floating platform of fun (Photo: Scott Smith)

Castaway Cay's Mount Rustmore makes for a fun photo opportunity. (Photo: Laurel Stewart)

One of Castaway Cay's white-sand beaches (Photo: Laurel Stewart)

Mayan ruins are part of DCL's Western Caribbean itineraries. (Photo: Chad Klotzle)

Stern-side view of the *Fantasy* in port (Photo: Laurel Stewart)

The *Wonder* in port at Nassau
(Photo: Laurel Stewart)

Daytime view of one
of the *Magic*'s funnels
(Photo: Laurel Stewart)

THE
unofficial GUIDE®
ᵀᴼDisney Cruise Line

Other Unofficial Guides

THE *unofficial* GUIDE®

TO Disney Cruise Line

LEN TESTA with ERIN FOSTER
and LAUREL STEWART

keen
communications

Please note that prices fluctuate in the course of time and that travel information changes under the impact of many factors that influence the travel industry. We therefore suggest that you write or call ahead for confirmation when making your travel plans. Every effort has been made to ensure the accuracy of information throughout this book, and the contents of this publication are believed to be correct at the time of printing. Nevertheless, the publishers cannot accept responsibility for errors or omissions, for changes in details given in this guide, or for the consequences of any reliance on the information provided by the same. Assessments of attractions and so forth are based upon the author's own experience; therefore, descriptions given in this guide necessarily contain an element of subjective opinion, which may not reflect the publisher's opinion or dictate a reader's own experience on another occasion. Readers are invited to write the publisher with ideas, comments, and suggestions for future editions.

Published by:
Keen Communications, LLC
P.O. Box 43673
Birmingham, AL 35243

Editors: Ritchey Halphen and Amber Kaye Henderson

Cover and color insert design: Scott McGrew

Text design: Vertigo Design and Annie Long

Cartography and illustrations: Steve Jones

Indexer: Ann Cassar / Cassar Technical Services

For information on our other products and services or to obtain technical support, please contact us from within the United States at 888-604-4537 or by fax at 205-326-1012.

Keen Communications, LLC, also publishes its books in a variety of electronic formats. Some content that appears in print may not be available in electronic formats.

ISBN-10: 1-628-09018-9; ISBN-13: 978-1-62809-018-5

Distributed by Publishers Group West

Manufactured in the United States of America

5 4 3 2 1

CONTENTS

LIST *of* MAPS *and* DIAGRAMS

ABOUT *the* AUTHORS

LEN TESTA is the coauthor of *The Unofficial Guide to Walt Disney World; The Unofficial Guide to Disneyland; The Unofficial Guide to Walt Disney World with Kids; The Unofficial Guide Color Companion to Walt Disney World; Mini-Mickey: The Pocket-Sized Unofficial Guide to Walt Disney World;* and *The Unofficial Guide to Britain's Best Days Out: Theme Parks and Attractions.* A computer scientist, Len created both the *Unofficial Guides* touring plan software and the **touringplans.com** website. The father of a teenage daughter, he lives in Greensboro, North Carolina.

As a charter member of the official Disney Parks Moms Panel, **ERIN FOSTER** has researched and written answers to more than 10,000 guest questions about Disney travel. In a quest to consume absolutely everything Disney Destinations has to offer, Erin has visited Walt Disney World, Disneyland, Disneyland Paris, and Hong Kong Disneyland. (Somebody send her to Tokyo Disneyland—please!) Her travels also include Disney Cruise Line voyages throughout the world and Adventures by Disney journeys on four continents. She is a regular contributor to the **touringplans.com** blog and **disneyfoodblog.com** and has been a guest on many other Disney-related websites and podcasts, including **allears.net,** PassPorter Moms, Be Our Guest, Disney Wedding Blog, WDW Today, and WDW Radio. Erin lives near New York City with her husband and three teenage daughters.

LAUREL STEWART has contributed to *The Unofficial Guide to Walt Disney World* and *The Unofficial Guide Color Companion to Walt Disney World* and works for **touringplans.com.** Despite not enjoying sand, seawater, or direct sunlight, she's always up for a cruise. Laurel was born in the Bahamas and lives in North Carolina.

ACKNOWLEDGMENTS

IT TOOK A LIFEBOAT FULL OF PEOPLE to produce this book and its companion Web content. David Davies created our website for Disney Cruise Line (DCL) information, wrote the Fare Tracker tool, and lent an expert eye to the proofreading of the text. Scott Sanders from **disney cruiselineblog.com** keeps us updated on the latest DCL news. Also, thanks to Emily and Isabelle Sanders for testing the waterslides with us.

DCL kids' club research was done by Alex Duncan, "Captain" Kieran Duncan, Jacklyn Scirica, and Hannah Testa. Kelsey and Kathy Lubetich bravely navigated the waters and lumberjacks of Alaska for that coverage. Thanks also to Tammy Whiting of Storybook Destinations, Beci Mahnken and Stephanie Hudson of Mouse Fan Travel, and Sue Pisaturo and Lynne Amodeo of Small World Vacations for their help in determining cruise-pricing trends.

—*Len Testa and Laurel Stewart*

I WOULD LIKE TO THANK my husband, Jeff, who was the first person to hire me as a writer, and my daughters, Charlie, Josie, and Louisa, who make me go on the scary rides. Additional thanks to the women and men of the Disney Parks Moms Panel, whose passion for all things Disney is a constant inspiration.

—*Erin Foster*

INTRODUCTION

ABOUT THIS GUIDE

WHY "UNOFFICIAL"?

THE MATERIAL HEREIN originated with the authors and has not been reviewed, edited, or approved by the Walt Disney Company, Inc., or Disney Cruise Line (DCL). To the contrary, we represent and serve you, the consumer: If a ship serves mediocre food or has subpar entertainment, we say so. Through our independence, we hope that we can make selecting a cruise efficient and economical and help make your cruise experience on-target and fun.

Toward that end, our *unofficial* guide offers the following:

- Our recommendations for which ship to choose for your first cruise
- How to find the perfect itinerary, including specific cruises and dates
- When to book your cruise to get the cheapest fares
- What to pack, including travel documents for you and your children
- Color photos from throughout the ships, plus deck and stateroom diagrams
- Unbiased reviews of onboard restaurants, live entertainment, and nightlife
- The best family activities, including children's clubs, family games, outdoor sports, and more
- Where and when to meet Disney characters on board
- Full coverage of Disney's private island, Castaway Cay, along with ports and shore excursions

DISNEY CRUISE LINE:
An Overview

IN 1998, THE WALT DISNEY COMPANY LAUNCHED—literally—its own cruise line with the 2,400-passenger *Disney Magic.* An almost identical ship, the *Disney Wonder,* entered service in 1999. Two larger ships, the *Disney Dream* and the *Disney Fantasy,* joined the fleet in 2011 and 2012, respectively.

In starting a cruise line, Disney put together a team of respected industry veterans, dozens of the world's best-known ship designers, and its own unrivaled creative talent. Together, they created the Disney ships, recognizing that every detail would be critical to the line's success.

The result? They've succeeded, starting with the ships' appearance: simultaneously classic and innovative. Exteriors are traditional, reminiscent of the great ocean liners of the past, but even here you'll find a Disney twist or two. Inside, the ships feature up-to-the-minute technology and are full of novel ideas for dining, entertainment, and cabin design. Even Disney's exclusive cruise terminal at Port Canaveral, Florida, is part of the overall strategy, aiming to make even embarking and disembarking enjoyable.

For Port Canaveral and Miami cruises, Disney's private island, **Castaway Cay,** was chosen to avoid the hassle of tendering. As for dining, Disney practically reinvented the concept for cruises when it introduced rotational dining (see Part Seven), where each evening you dine in a different restaurant with a different motif, but your waiters and dining companions move with you.

The foundation of DCL's business is built on Bahamian and Caribbean cruises out of Port Canaveral, about 90 minutes from Walt Disney World, and Miami. Disney also offers Alaskan, Californian, Canadian, and European cruises, as well as repositioning cruises. Other departure ports include San Diego, California; San Juan, Puerto Rico; Barcelona, Spain; Vancouver, Canada; and Venice, Italy.

unofficial **TIP**
Because the ships' decor and entertainment are based almost entirely on Disney films and characters, we don't recommend a DCL cruise to anyone who isn't at least mildly fond of Mickey and the gang.

All Bahamian cruises originating in Port Canaveral and Miami make at least one port call at Castaway Cay. DCL's Alaskan and European itineraries are well conceived and interesting; by comparison, its Bahamian and Caribbean itineraries are unimaginative and prosaic, but they are good for first-time cruisers.

DCL'S TARGET MARKET

DISNEY CRUISES ARE TAILORED to families who are new to cruising. But like the theme parks, the cruise line is a Disney product for kids of all ages.

Disney Cruise Line Ships in a Nutshell

	Disney Magic	Disney Wonder	Disney Dream	Disney Fantasy
YEAR LAUNCHED	1998	1999	2011	2012
CAPACITY				
PASSENGERS (maximum)	2,713	2,713	4,000	4,000
CREW	950	950	1,458	1,458
TOTAL	3,663	3,663	5,458	5,458
PASSENGER DECKS	11	11	14	14
STATEROOMS				
INSIDE	256	256	150	150
OCEANVIEW	362	362	199	199
OUTSIDE VERANDAH	259	259	901	901
TOTAL	877	877	1,250	1,250
THEME	Art Deco	Art Nouveau	Art Deco	Art Nouveau

To cater to varied constituencies, some facilities, services, activities, and programs are designed specifically for adults without kids, including seniors and honeymooning couples. For example, in addition to the themed restaurants, each ship has at least one alternative restaurant, swimming pool, and nightclub for adults only, as well as entertainment for all the family. Disney continues trying to enhance the adult experience with such facilities as adults-only cafés, adult-oriented sports bars, and areas for teens.

Initially, cruise experts questioned whether Disney could fill its ships when kids are in school, but Disney determined that if 1–2% of the estimated 40 million annual visitors to its resorts and parks bought a Disney cruise vacation, the ships would sell out. Disney was right—now, after more than 15 years of success, no one is questioning them.

Disney offers a "seamless vacation package" to those who want to combine a stay at Walt Disney World with a cruise departing from Florida. DCL passengers are met at the airport by Disney staff and transported to the terminal in easily identifiable buses. When your cruise is packaged with a stay at most Disney hotels, into both your land and sea portion of your vacation at once.

COMPETITORS AND PRICES

DCL USES ITS REPUTATION for high quality, service, and entertainment to dispel novices' doubts about cruise vacations. Disney's main competitor seems to be **Royal Caribbean International,** which offers Caribbean, Mediterranean, and Alaskan cruises similar to Disney's, with most of the same departure and destination ports. The two cruise lines often have ships departing within days—sometimes hours—of each other, headed mostly to the same places.

While the itineraries may be similar, remember when comparing prices that Disney offers larger cabins than Royal Caribbean. An inside cabin for an Alaska sailing on the *Disney Wonder,* for example, is about 11% larger than a similar cabin on Royal Caribbean's *Radiance of the Seas:* 184 square feet versus 165 square feet. Oceanview staterooms on both ships are 214 and 170 square feet, respectively, or about 25% larger on the Disney ship.

In addition, Disney's fares include unlimited fountain soda, plain coffee, tea, and water (bottled versions cost extra), while Royal Caribbean charges around $22 per person per day for the same (though it includes bottled water, orange juice, and nonalcoholic cocktails too), or about $154 for a family of four for a seven-night cruise.

When it comes to the bottom line, however, the fact is that Disney charges a premium for its cruise product. For example, on seven-night Eastern Caribbean cruises out of Port Canaveral during the second half of 2013, Disney's prices were $4,000–$7,300 for one inside cabin, depending on the specific date; Royal Caribbean's prices were $2,200–$5,400, or 20–70% less than Disney for very similar cruises. (All cruise prices assume two adults and two children ages 12 and 6 in one cabin.)

We initially thought that Disney was charging more for these cruises because their Orlando theme parks provide a built-in audience for Port Canaveral sailing; the port is, after all, within 90 minutes of Walt Disney World. But Disney is more expensive for ports far away from its theme parks: We spot-checked Disney's seven-night Alaska cruises out of Vancouver for 2013 and 2014 and found that they run anywhere from 60% to 100% more than Royal Caribbean's—a difference of $1,700–$2,400 per cruise. That kind of money buys a lot of ice.

One area where Disney seems to be price-competitive with Royal Caribbean is on seven-night Mediterranean cruises out of Barcelona, Spain. Fares for random dates in 2013 and 2014 show Disney cruises were only about 10% higher, on average, than Royal Caribbean.

HOW *to* CONTACT *the* AUTHORS

MANY WHO USE THE UNOFFICIAL GUIDES write to us with questions, comments, or their own strategies for planning and enjoying travel. We appreciate all such input, both positive and critical. Readers' comments are frequently incorporated into revised editions and have contributed immeasurably to their improvement. Please write to:

Len, Erin, and Laurel
The Unofficial Guide to Disney Cruise Line
P.O. Box 43673
Birmingham, AL 35243
unofficialguides@menasharidge.com

When you write, put your address on both your letter and envelope; the two sometimes get separated. It's also a good idea to include your phone number. If you e-mail us, please tell us where you're from. Remember, as travel writers, we're often out of the office for long periods of time, so forgive us if our response is slow. *Unofficial Guide* e-mail isn't forwarded to us when we're traveling, but we'll respond as soon as possible after we return.

READER SURVEY

OUR WEBSITE HOSTS A QUESTIONNAIRE you can use to express opinions about your Disney cruise, at **touringplans.com/disney-cruise-line/survey.** The questionnaire lets every member of your party, regardless of age, tell us what he or she thinks about attractions, restaurants, and more.

If you'd rather print out and send us the survey, mail it to **Reader Survey, *The Unofficial Guides*, P.O. Box 43673, Birmingham, AL 35243.**

PART ONE

DOLLARS *and* SENSE

WHAT'S INCLUDED *in* YOUR DISNEY CRUISE FARE

A DISNEY CRUISE ISN'T CHEAP. Given the cost, you might be wondering how much more you'll have to pay once you're aboard the ship. Here's a quick rundown of what is and isn't included in your cruise fare. We've included some rough estimates of the optional items to help with budgeting.

FOOD

INCLUDED: LOTS OF FOOD All meals, including snacks, are free at all of the ship's restaurants except for Remy and Palo. You can order as much food as you like.

NOT INCLUDED: FANCY RESTAURANTS Meals at Remy and Palo require an additional charge of $75 and $25, respectively, for dinner; Palo also charges $25 for its brunch, while Remy's brunch is $50. Wine is an extra charge beyond those prices, at each meal.

INCLUDED: MOST ROOM-SERVICE ITEMS Your fare includes room-service meals, except as noted below. Room service is a great option for when you don't feel like dressing up for dinner.

NOT INCLUDED: PACKAGED SNACKS AND BOTTLED DRINKS Beverages such as bottled water ($3), soda not served as part of meal service or from the self-service dispensers on the pool deck ($3), beer ($6), and wine ($8 and up) cost extra, as do packaged snacks such as popcorn and peanuts. Tips are another additional charge.

INCLUDED: ALL-YOU-WANT SOFT DRINKS AND ICE CREAM Complimentary soda, coffee, water, and hot and iced tea are unlimited at meals, and beverages served from drink dispensers on deck are also free of charge. Self-serve ice cream from the onboard dispensers is free.

Continued on page 9

The 10 Best Bangs for Your Buck (and One Freebie) on a Disney Caribbean Cruise

1. Rainforest at Senses Spa (*Dream* and *Fantasy*) At around $25 per day, this is a must-do. Only a limited number of passes are sold per cruise, so make a point of buying your pass soon after boarding. Because of the limits on how many passes are sold (we've heard 20 per cruise), there are many times when you'll have the entire Rainforest to yourself. This is the ultimate in quiet relaxation for adults, and a total bargain at that. The package is also available at Senses Spa on the *Magic* and Vista Spa on the *Wonder* (about $16 per day), but the smaller Rainforest area means that you're more likely to have company, and the number of showers and saunas is a little disappointing if you've ever experienced the spa on the larger ships. Try the body scrubs (extra charge) at least once.

2. Porters for your bags The $2–$5 per bag you'll tip your porter both boarding and returning home through Customs is money well spent. These guys work hard and make our lives so much easier. When boarding, not having to handle your own bags is one less hassle in a hectic process. When you leave the ship, it helps you end your cruise on a high note.

3. Bicycles on Castaway Cay These wheels cost $10 per hour and make getting around the island a breeze. But more than that, they're fun for the whole family. Between riding out to the observation tower (off the airstrip) for a great view of the island and getting to your destination on the island faster than the tram can get you there, this decision is as easy as riding a . . . well, you know.

4. Snorkeling on Castaway Cay A mask, flippers, and life vest will set you back $29 per adult and $14 per kid. The sea life is copious in the lagoon, and the hidden treasures Disney has added under water are a delight. Go in the morning and again in the afternoon. Hours of entertainment isn't usually this cheap when Disney's name is attached.

5. Palo A quiet, no-rush brunch or dinner for adults with great service and food for $25 plus gratuity? Heck, yeah! Let's face it: Your kids are probably ready to spend some time away from you, too. Come for the food; linger for the atmosphere. Dress up and remember that a meal this good would cost several times as much on shore.

6. Adult-beverage tastings For around $15, you're treated to several wines, liquors, or cocktails. (*Remember:* No one is spitting out the spirits, and they can sneak up on you, so try to eat something first.) We've been lucky enough to be the only participants on a few occasions, allowing us to really interact with the guides. Our favorite is the Champagne tasting, but we haven't been let down by any of them. One author discovered a new favorite wine during a tasting at Meridian on the *Fantasy*. Another time, we were asked, "How would you like to try the most expensive whiskey we sell?" Our reply: "Yes, please!"

7. Castaway Ray's Stingray Adventure This is both less expensive and better organized than stingray encounters in other ports. It's a winner with kids ($36) and adults ($45). There's no time wasted getting back and forth to your port adventure because it's on Castaway Cay—just show up at the ray area at your appointed time, and have fun.

8. Flounder's Reef Nursery (*Wonder*)/It's a Small World Nursery Parents of children younger than age 3 can enjoy some downtime and let the excellent staff watch their little ones for $9 per hour for the first child and $8 per hour per additional child in the same family. Feedback from parents is extremely positive.

9. Coffee The "coffee" at the beverage stations can best be described as a tepid, vaguely coffee-flavored substance that will make you question your will to live. Pony up for the real thing at Cove Café, Vista Café, or the coffee bar at the buffets. Sure, it's around $3–$5 plus tip, but that's less than you'd pay at Starbucks, and it doesn't make you regret your caffeine habit. Ask for a Café Fanatic rewards card and get every sixth coffee drink free. (For us, that's sometime early in day two of any cruise.) Didn't fill all the punches on your card? Hang on to it for your next cruise.

10. Castaway Cay 5K This port adventure is free, and you get the moral superiority of knowing you've gotten in your exercise for the day while being among the first to exit the ship at the island. There are race bibs and plastic medals, and the whole family can join in. Try to beat your Castaway Cay personal best every time you come to the island.

11. Gratuities DCL ships are full of energetic young men and women, many of whom are far away from home, who make your trip magical. In addition to tipping our servers and stateroom attendants generously—yes, that means more than the recommended amount—we also start our trip off right by meeting our baristas and bartenders on the first day and night of the cruise and treating them well. We don't do it because we expect anything extra (though being known as good customers never hurts), but because we get fantastic service. And don't forget these folks when you're filling out your comment cards at the end of the cruise. It's always good to help a deserving person's career when you can.

Continued from page 7

NOT INCLUDED: BOTTLED WATER, ALCOHOLIC BEVERAGES, AND FANCY COFFEES Bottled water, beer, wine, and cocktails cost extra. A wine package is available. You'll also pay out-of-pocket for specialty coffees, espresso, cappuccinos, and teas from bars and cafés (such as the Cove Café). A 15% gratuity is automatically added to bar and beverage tabs. Adults 21 and older may also bring their own wine and liquor aboard in their carry-on luggage; a $20 corking fee applies if you bring your own wine or Champagne to a full-service restaurant on board.

ENTERTAINMENT AND ACTIVITIES

INCLUDED: LOTS OF ENTERTAINMENT There's no extra charge for live performances, movies, and character greetings.

NOT INCLUDED: BINGO, SOME ONBOARD SEMINARS, AND MOVIE SNACKS A few activities, such as bingo, cost money to play. Beverage seminars, which typically offer several kinds of spirits for sampling, cost $15–$25 depending on the alcohol. Likewise, at the movie theater, candy bars and such cost extra.

INCLUDED: GYM FACILITIES Covered in your fare is use of the fitness center, including free weights and other fitness equipment. The center also has changing rooms with showers and sauna.

NOT INCLUDED: SPA AND SALON SERVICES Spa treatments (including massages, facials, steam rooms, and upscale showers) cost from $115 to upwards of $500 per person, per treatment. Salon services range from $50 to $70 for manicures and pedicures, and from $35 to around $75 for hairstyling, depending on hair length.

INCLUDED: POOLS, GAMES, AND MOST SPORTS These include all of the pools and waterslides and activities such as miniature golf, basketball, ping-pong, and shuffleboard. Board games are available at no charge in some lounges.

NOT INCLUDED: VIDEO GAMES The video arcades on the ships charge 25¢–$2 per game.

INCLUDED: CASTAWAY CAY BEACHES AND RESTAURANTS Food, lounge chairs, and beach umbrellas are free, as is Castaway Cay's 5K road run.

NOT INCLUDED: CASTAWAY CAY RECREATION AND ALCOHOL Disney Cruise Line (DCL) charges for bike rentals ($10 per hour), snorkeling ($14–$29 for one day, $18–$36 for two days), and use of boats ($14–$27 per half-hour) and watercraft ($95 per hour for one rider, $160 per hour for two riders). The same goes for private cabanas—a whopping $400 or $529 per day—and alcoholic drinks at Castaway Cay's bars.

KID STUFF

INCLUDED: KIDS' CLUBS (AGES 3 AND UP) These include the Oceaneer Club/Oceaneer Lab for kids ages 3–12, the Edge club for tweens ages 11–14, and the Vibe club for teens ages 14–17.

NOT INCLUDED: CHILD CARE FOR KIDS UNDER 3 The Flounder's Reef and It's a Small World Nurseries charge $9 per hour for the first child and $8 per hour for a second child in the same family.

MISCELLANEOUS

INCLUDED: CALLS TO ANYWHERE ON THE SHIP Use of the ships' Wave Phones is free.

NOT INCLUDED: SHIP-TO-SHORE CALLS AND INTERNET Ship-to-shore calls from onboard phones cost $8 per minute. Each stateroom has a standard phone with voice mail, plus a Wave Phone, a mobile phone you may use free of charge on the ship and Castaway Cay for calls, voice mail, and text messaging (only from Wave Phone to Wave Phone).

Rather than charge cruisers for their Internet usage based on how long they're online, Disney Cruise Line charges based on the amount of bandwidth used. The following is a list of the packages available, with our recommendations:

PLAN	DATA (MB)	COST	NOTES
Pay as You Go	1	25¢	Use if you have a one-off need for the Internet to check or send e-mail
Small	100	$19 (19¢/ minute)	For guests who will need to check e-mail from time to time, but do not need to surf the Internet during their cruise
Medium	300	$39 (13¢/ minute)	For guests who wish to use social media to let their friends know how much fun they are having on board via photos
Large	1,000	$89 (9¢/ minute)	For guests who are unable to leave their work at home or who wish to stream music (note that many movies will take up more than the 1GB allowance, and a high-def movie can be up to four times this much)

Other items not included:

PHOTOS Disney offers packages of prints or CDs similar to its Memory Maker packages at Walt Disney World. Pricing begins at around $150 for a package of 10 prints and up to $280 for a package of all your onboard photos on a CD as well as printed. Onboard photographers will also shoot pictures for free with your own camera.

SHORE EXCURSIONS Known in DCL-speak as port adventures, these cost anywhere from $10 (for a 1-hour bike rental on Castaway Cay) to $1,900 (for a private catamaran tour of St. Maarten).

LAUNDRY It costs $2 to wash and $2 to dry a load of clothes. Soap, fabric softener, and dryer sheets are available for $1 each, per load. Dry cleaning is also available for an additional fee.

GRATUITIES Disney automatically adds gratuities of around $12 per person per day to your onboard account. A 15% gratuity is automatically added to bar and beverage tabs. See page 51 for more information.

TRANSPORTATION TO THE PORT Round-trip service between Walt Disney World and Port Canaveral costs $70 per person, and transportation between any city's cruise terminal and airport also costs about that much. See the section starting on page 37 for more details.

▌ CRUISING *with* KIDS

WE'LL START BY SAYING that there's a good chance your kids will have a great time.

As parents, we know that one of the most difficult parts of planning a vacation with kids is ensuring that they're entertained throughout the trip. For us, this usually means making sure that every travel day has at least a couple of things specifically designed to appeal to our kids and their friends—things we'd prefer didn't involve shopping or sitting passively in front of a screen.

It can be exhausting to plan this way (and we're *professionals*!). In fact, we think this is one of the main reasons why a trip to Disney World is so appealing to parents: Disney's theme parks provide a nearly constant and wide-ranging set of entertainment options for kids and adults. A family that hasn't planned a thing can show up and find something fun to do. Disney cruises work the same way—family activities, including trivia contests, scavenger hunts, and shuffleboard, are scheduled throughout the day, on virtually every day of every sailing.

If you think your kids would benefit from spending some time with their peers, Disney provides organized activities throughout the day for children ages 3–17. Some activities for younger children get started as early as 7 a.m., while activities for older teens can run until 2 a.m. Off the ships, Castaway Cay offers dedicated beach and recreation spots for families, teens, and tweens, plus a splash area for little ones. There are shore excursions created just for families too.

Disney is also keeping up with two recent trends in the cruise industry. The first is setting aside more space per ship for kids' clubs.

unofficial **TIP**
See page 133 for our advice on cruising with teens and tweens.

On the newer *Dream* and *Fantasy*, these clubs take up substantially more space than on older DCL ships. Second, Disney frequently runs concurrent, age-appropriate activities within the same club. For example, the Oceaneer Club accepts children ages 3–12; however, Disney may group together the younger kids for a game with marshmallows in one area of the club while the older kids sing karaoke in another.

Our own children have found Disney's children's activities more fun than hanging around with us on the ship. It may be a cliché, but it's true: We saw the kids only during meals, at bedtime, or when we specifically scheduled things to do as a family. Thanks to the Web, our kids are still in contact with the friends they've made on their cruises, even though some are an ocean away.

CRUISING *without* KIDS

GIVEN DISNEY'S REPUTATION FOR FAMILY-FRIENDLY enter-tainment, it's natural for those who travel without children to wonder if DCL is a good choice for adult cruisers. Happily, just as with the Disney parks, there's something for folks of all ages to enjoy on a Disney cruise. Disney ships have an adults-only pool and coffeehouse, the spa is limited to guests age 18 and up (with the exception of the Chill teen spa on the *Dream* and *Fantasy*), and some of the entertainment districts are limited to cruis-ers age 18 and up every night after around 9 p.m. For those wanting to dine in an adults-only atmosphere, Remy (*Dream* and *Fantasy* only) and Palo (see Part Seven) are likewise restricted to those age 18 and older. Castaway Cay has an adult beach with its own dining, bar, and cabanas (which must be reserved in advance). We recommend traveling when school is in session if you're looking for a more adult-oriented vacation, and the good news is that these times tend to be far less expensive.

unofficial **TIP**
DCL seems to be very popu-lar for girls' trips because of its safe atmosphere.

If your idea of a fun cruise is a party boat, then DCL probably isn't for you. There's no casino, and honestly the nightlife is more mild than wild. But we've traveled several times with only adults in our party and had a fantastic time. Spend some time at the spa, get to know the bartenders and baristas at the various bars and lounges, skip the shows, dine at Palo or Remy (or both!), and enjoy some downtime.

WHERE *to* FIND MORE INFORMATION

DISNEY CRUISE LINE'S OFFICIAL WEBSITE is **disneycruise .disney.go.com.** Here, you can see which itineraries are served by each ship; search for cruises by destination, month, and length; and see prices for various kinds of staterooms. Once you've made a reserva-tion, you can book shore excursions, restaurants, and children's activi-ties through the site.

PassPorter's Disney Cruise Line and Its Ports of Call guidebook ($21.95 for the basic edition) provides a good overview of DCL. The deluxe edition ($47.95) includes paper worksheets that you can use to plan everything from a cruise budget to a daily schedule. The book's companion website, **passporter.com,** has user-led discussion forums, where folks from all over can ask questions and provide answers to almost any cruise-related scenario.

Another good online resource is **disneycruiselineblog.com,** which posts almost-daily updates, including everything from new-itinerary rumors to new shopping merchandise on board. The site also has a neat feature that lets you see the current location of every ship in the Disney fleet.

Despite the somewhat confusing name, the **Disney Parks Moms Panel** (**disneyworldforum.disney.go.com**) features Disney Cruise Line specialists. These folks are veterans of many DCL voyages and have received training from DCL cast members. They're able to answer any individual Disney cruise–planning question, big or small.

Popular general Disney sites with dedicated DCL forums include **disboards.com, forums.wdwmagic.com, micechat.com,** and, for Brits, **thedibb.co.uk** (*DIBB* stands for "Disney Information Bulletin Board").

PART TWO

PLANNING YOUR CRUISE

CHOOSING *an* ITINERARY

DISNEY CRUISE LINE OFFERS ALMOST 50 SEPARATE ITINERARIES, ranging from 2-night weekend getaways to 15-night voyages between two oceans using the Panama Canal. The cruise you select is likely to be determined by how much vacation time you have, the ship on which you want to sail, the cost, and the ports that interest you.

ITINERARY RECOMMENDATIONS FOR FIRST-TIME CRUISERS

WE THINK THE IDEAL ITINERARY for first-time cruisers is four or five nights aboard the *Dream* or *Fantasy*. Why? They're newer ships, with better restaurants, bars, and spas; interactive areas such as the Midship Detective Agency; more space for kids' activities; and more space on deck for pools and lounging.

An ideal cruise for first-timers also includes two stops at Castaway Cay, Disney's private island (see Part Ten). You'll need one visit to become familiar with the island and its features; by the second day, you'll be more relaxed, knowing that you're taking advantage of the best the island has to offer.

Unfortunately, there are only two sailings scheduled for the *Dream* that meet those criteria, in October and November 2014. The next-best alternative is a 7-Night Eastern Caribbean cruise aboard the *Fantasy*, with three days at sea plus stops at St. Maarten; San Juan, Puerto Rico; and Castaway Cay. Three days at sea allows you plenty of time to relax and explore the ship. Dozens of these cruises are available, so finding one should be easy at any time of year.

unofficial **TIP**
The average Disney cruise lasts five nights, sails somewhere in the Caribbean, and stops at Disney's Castaway Cay island in the Bahamas.

GENERAL RECOMMENDATIONS

IF YOU'RE TRYING TO DECIDE among Eastern Caribbean, Western Caribbean, and Bahamian cruises, you only have two questions to answer: First, are you interested in exploring the culture of the ports you're visiting? Second, if so, are you more interested in Caribbean towns or Mayan history?

If the answer to the first question is no—if your perfect vacation involves lying on a beach, taking the kids snorkeling, scuba diving, or swimming with dolphins—you can do that in every port from Barbados to Cozumel. Pick any itinerary that includes Castaway Cay and that also fits your schedule and budget, and you're set.

If you're interested in local color, choose between the Eastern and Western Caribbean itineraries. The Eastern itineraries offer the best ports to explore. **St. John** and **St. Thomas** are great stops, but Disney gives you only 5 or 6 hours there. **St. Maarten** is fun because it's Dutch.

On Western Caribbean cruises, **Costa Maya** and **Cozumel** are notable only for their inland tours of Mayan ruins. If those interest you more than Caribbean towns, pick a Western itinerary.

Now, lest you think we're making an "all those people look the same" argument in advising you how to choose between Bahamian and Caribbean itineraries, rest assured we're not. Rather, our advice is based on the observation that the cruise industry's overbooking of the same Caribbean ports has led to a certain sameness of experience virtually everywhere. As Julia Cosgrove, editor-in-chief of *Afar* magazine, observes, "There's no sense of 'I should go to this island as opposed to that because I'm going to get this deeper cultural experience by connecting with people in one place versus another.' "

Disney's seven- and nine-day Alaska itineraries are virtually identical, and all are served by the *Wonder*. Pick whichever itinerary suits your budget and schedule.

Disney's Mediterranean cruises are distinguished primarily by their length (4, 5, 7, 9, or 12 nights), departure port, and whether they visit Venice. The main distinction among the 12-night cruises is whether they include that visit to Venice: Three of the four itineraries do, with only the "A" itinerary skipping it. If you really want to see Venice, however, the 12-night "B" itinerary includes an overnight stop, which would allow you to stay out to the wee hours.

SAVING MONEY

YOU HAVE FOUR PRIMARY STRATEGIES for saving money on a Disney cruise:

1. **Book as early as possible.** Most cruise fares start low and begin to rise as the ship fills up. It's possible to save 10–20% by booking a year in advance.

2. **Book at the last minute.** Conversely, if your travel schedule is very flexible, savings of up to 25% off are possible when you book a cruise within two weeks of its sailing date. These deals are especially good if you live within a day's drive of the departure port, because you can avoid the last-minute price hikes on airline tickets. Offers including last-minute deals can be found on DCL's website (**disneycruise.disney.go.com**), as well as on our favorite money-saving site, **MouseSavers** (**mousesavers.com**), under "Disney Cruise Line."

3. **Book your next cruise while on board.** DCL offers discounts up to 10% off the lowest prevailing rates, occasionally along with onboard ship credits. Stop by the Future Cruise Sales Desk, usually on Deck 4 Midship, for details.

4. **Depart from a less popular port.** Disney offers aggressive discounts on cruises from ports that aren't in great demand. Disney cruises out of the poor-selling Galveston, Texas, port, for example, were discounted throughout most of 2013 and early 2014, when Disney left the port. Your travel agents should know which ports aren't selling as quickly as others. Armed with that information, you'll find it easy to compare transportation costs to the ports you're considering. (See Part Four for more tips on choosing a port.)

5. **Take advantage of onboard credit offers.** While pricing for cruise fares is consistent from Disney to independent travel agents to larger online sites such as Orbitz and Expedia, some agencies are able to sweeten the pot with generous onboard credits. We suggest that you shop around for the best packages.

unofficial **TIP**
When you're combing through the DCL website for discounts, look for stateroom categories with the codes **IGT, OGT,** and **VGT.** These indicate heavily discounted inside, outside, and verandah staterooms.

SURF *and* TURF, DISNEY-STYLE

COMBINING YOUR CRUISE WITH A WALT DISNEY WORLD VACATION

DISNEY SELLS PACKAGES THAT COMBINE A DISNEY CRUISE and a trip to Walt Disney World, for cruises departing from Port Canaveral. Called **Land and Sea** packages, the itineraries include the Bahamas, Eastern and Western Caribbean, and the *Magic*'s Eastbound Transatlantic cruise to Barcelona. Land and Sea packages include lodging at a Disney World resort; theme park admission, dining plans, and other extras can be added to the Disney World portion of the trip. Because of the lack of flexibility with a Land and Sea package through DCL, and due to better prices when booking à la carte, we recommend making reservations for each part of a theme park and cruise vacation separately. Regardless of whether you book land and sea together or separately, you will be able to arrange bus transportation between Port Canaveral and your Walt Disney World resort for a fee.

The most frequent question we're asked about combining a theme park and cruise vacation is whether to visit Disney World before or after the cruise. The majority of people who've done both say they were more relaxed on the cruise than at Walt Disney World, so they prefer to take the cruise after the park visit. Some families don't have a preference either way. A relatively small number prefer to see Walt Disney World second, because they prefer the faster pace of WDW after a cruise. Our recommendation, though, is to see the World first—chances are that your tired legs (and wallet) will appreciate some downtime at sea.

COMBINING YOUR CRUISE WITH AN ADVENTURES BY DISNEY TRIP

MANY EUROPEAN CRUISES out of Barcelona and Venice can be combined with a pre-cruise Adventures by Disney guided vacation. Your trip includes lodging, meals, and tours. See **adventuresbydisney.com** for more details (click "Destinations," then "Europe").

 # *The* BOOKING PROCESS

GETTING STARTED

ONCE YOU'VE SETTLED ON A SHIP, an itinerary, and dates, it's time to book your trip. You have three ways to do this:

1. Use the Disney Cruise Line website (**disneycruise.disney.go.com**).
2. Call DCL at ☎ 800-951-3532.
3. Use a travel agent.

There are advantages to each. The main advantage to booking yourself, either online or by phone, is that you can usually do it immediately. If you have booked a cruise before, have access to each traveler's information, don't have questions about the ship or itinerary, and want instant gratification, this may be your best option.

The advantage of using a travel agent is that he or she can save you time by doing most of the tedious data entry for you, and the agent may also offer onboard credits. Many agents have booked dozens, if not hundreds, of cruises, and have a single-page form for you to fill out, where you provide your preferences for everything from what time you prefer to board the ship to when you prefer to eat. Some travel agencies will also rebook your cruise automatically if a lower fare becomes available. A travel agent might also be able to save you money because he or she might have access to group space for a particular cruise. The traveler doesn't have to participate in any group activities but receives the price advantage of being part of the group booking.

DEPOSIT TERMS AND CANCELLATION POLICY

MOST CRUISE RESERVATIONS REQUIRE A DEPOSIT equal to 20% of the cruise's price (not including taxes) for each passenger age 3 and older on that reservation. Some DCL promotions, such as booking a follow-up cruise while you're already on a current cruise, require only a 10% deposit. Booking a future cruise while you're on the ship almost always includes an onboard credit for the cruise you're booking too.

DCL's full cancellation policy can be found online at the DCL website; click "Terms and Conditions" at the bottom of the home page. You can cancel a reservation in writing or by phone; also, moving the date of your cruise or changing the name of someone on your reservation is considered a cancellation.

If your cruise starts or ends in the United States and your cruise is fewer than 10 days long, your refund amount depends on how much advance notice you give Disney. The following table summarizes the criteria used:

IF YOU CANCEL THIS MANY DAYS BEFORE START OF CRUISE	DCL CHARGES THIS FOR CANCELLATION
45+ days (suites and concierge rooms)	Your entire deposit (typically 20%)
45–74 days (other than suites and concierge rooms)	Your entire deposit (typically 20%)
44–30 days	50% of trip price, per person
29–15 days	75% of trip price, per person
14 days or fewer	100% of trip price, per person

If your cruise starts and ends *outside* of the United States or lasts 10 days or more, the cancellation terms are as follows:

IF YOU CANCEL THIS MANY DAYS BEFORE START OF CRUISE	DCL CHARGES THIS FOR CANCELLATION
56+ days (suites and concierge rooms)	Your entire deposit (typically 20%)
119–56 days (other than suites and concierge rooms)	Your entire deposit (typically 20%)
55–30 days	50% of trip price, per person
29–15 days	75% of trip price, per person
14 days or fewer	100% of trip price, per person

For full details, go to the DCL website and click "Terms and Conditions" at the bottom of the home page.

THE DCL PLANNING CENTER

A KEY PART OF YOUR Disney Cruise Line booking is the Planning Center at the DCL website: **disneycruiseline.com/plan.** You can access the Planning Center only with a reservation number—available after you've paid your deposit and received your confirmation e-mail. In addition to the reservation number, you'll need access to the birth date of at least one member of your party. If you've cruised with Disney previously, you may also access your reservation without your reservation number through the Castaway Club section of the DCL site.

The Planning Center includes the following:

- **Reservation Summary** Basic info such as your stateroom number; dining-time assignment; names of the guests in your party; air transportation, ground transportation, and WDW hotel information, if you've booked any of these through Disney; and trip itinerary, including ashore and onboard times for port days. Remember that if your party has booked multiple staterooms, you'll have multiple reservation numbers. To reserve excursions or onboard activities, you'll need the correct reservation number for each member of your party, and you'll need to be in the Planning Center for the correct stateroom.

- **My Cruise Activities** Descriptions of the port adventures and onboard activities available during your sailing, including excursions, spa treatments, adult dining, child care, and more. After you've paid your cruise fee in full and as your travel date nears, this becomes the booking center for these items.

- **My Online Check-In** You may check in online up to three days before your sailing. This is where you'll give DCL specifics about your travel, authorize credit card payment for onboard purchases, and provide additional information about your party. While Online Check-In is optional, it can reduce your wait time at the port terminal. If you're using My Online Check-In, you'll be able to print a signature and payment-authorization form. Bring this with you to your embarkation port.

- **Fun Aboard the Ship** Information on amenities specific to your sailing vessel.

- **Character Calls** Arrange for a Disney character to place a recorded phone call to your home welcoming members of your party to their cruise (which is particularly fun if the cruise is a surprise for those with whom you're cruising.)

- **Packing List** General recommendations for what to pack, along with some specifics based on your cruise itinerary.

- **Air & Ground Transportation** This is where you'll enter your flight/port-transfer information or add port transfers and so on to your package.

- **Passport & Travel Documentation** Notifications about specific travel documents required for your itinerary.

- **Stay Connected** Allows you to register for e-mail or text reminders about your trip.

- **In-Room Gifts & Shopping** Lets you buy presents and floral arrangements for members of your party who may be celebrating birthdays, anniversaries, or other milestones during your voyage. Gifts will be delivered to your stateroom during your sailing.

- **Driving Directions** Detailed directions to your port. Also includes the correct address to make your GPS happy.

- **Custom Pre-Arrival Guide** You can download a PDF of most of the information provided at the Planning Center. The file will include your booking information as well as your general itinerary and any excursions, spa treatments, or adult dining you may have booked.

If you're like most guests, you'll visit the Planning Center more than a few times before your trip. One of our most recent DCL voyages was a four-day quickie, with just two guests. Even with this relatively simple profile, we stopped by the Planning Center nearly a dozen times before our trip—sometimes just to feel good knowing we were headed out on a cruise.

OTHER PREP WORK

PACKING

HAVING TRAVELED WITH LOTS OF PEOPLE over many years, we realize that asking "What do I need to pack?" is like asking "What is art?" Everyone will have their own answer based on their experience and preferences. Some people assume that they're going to do laundry on the ship and pack three days' worth of clothes for a seven-night cruise. Others would rather pay for an extra suitcase to carry more clean clothes. The amount you pack is up to you.

Knowing what to pack is equally important, and the range of opinions regarding packing essentials is huge. The DCL Planning Center has a pretty good page with suggestions on appropriate clothing for the ship's restaurants and ports of call, along with a

unofficial **TIP**
Check out *Unofficial Guide* blogger Scott Sanders's excellent DCL packing tips at **blog.touringplans.com.**

short, reasonable list of incidentals to pack (as well as stuff you can't bring aboard).

Beyond that, type "Disney Cruise Line packing list" into any search engine and you'll see thousands of lists with hundreds of items. Some of them read like an Amazon jungle-trek prep list (mosquito netting appears on more than one). It's useful to read through a couple of lists to see if they mention anything you can't live without. Our most important packing advice is this: Don't drive yourself crazy trying to pack for every scenario. You're going to lug those bags a lot farther than you might think. If you're not absolutely certain you're going to use something, *leave it at home.*

You can buy most everyday personal items on board the ship if needed. We generally don't make a special trip to the drugstore to buy motion-sickness pills, antibiotic/anti-itch creams, or over-the-counter pain relievers if we don't already have them on hand at home.

Besides appropriate clothing, our short packing list includes the following essentials:

- **Prescription medication** Pack these in carry-on luggage, in their original containers.

- **Tablet computer** Load enough books, music, movies, TV shows, games, and apps for the cruise, plus the trip to and from the port.

- **White-noise mobile app** Useful for drowning out noise from hallways, next-door cabins, and ship machinery. Try Sleepmaker Rain (available in free and paid versions on iTunes and Google Play).

- **Hats, sunglasses, and sunscreen** Sunscreen is reasonably priced on the ships, in case you don't want to pack it.

- **Water shoes or flip-flops** For the pool and beach.

ELECTRICAL OUTLETS

ALL OUTLETS ON THE SHIPS conform to the North American 110V/60Hz standard. If you live in the US or Canada, any device you have that operates normally at home should work on board. All staterooms have hair dryers, so if you're tight on space or not attached to your own model, you won't need to pack one.

If you're visiting from outside the US, you may need an adapter or converter for your electric gadgets. What's the difference? An adapter ensures that the plug on your device will fit into the electrical receptacle in the wall, but it doesn't change the electrical voltage. A converter does both (and costs more). Your local version of Amazon almost certainly has an excellent selection. Our advice is to have one converter per person, or two if you're traveling alone.

PASSPORTS AND TRAVEL DOCUMENTS

EVERYONE IN YOUR FAMILY, including children, will need to provide proof of citizenship before boarding the ship. If you're a US citizen and you have a valid passport or passport card, it's easiest if you bring that.

If you don't have a passport but (1) you're a US citizen traveling from an American port such as Port Canaveral, Miami, or San Juan; (2) you're traveling only within the Western Hemisphere (the US, Canada, Mexico, or the Caribbean); and (3) you're returning to the same port on the same ship, you may be able to present a valid government-issued photo ID (such as a driver's license) along with proof of citizenship (an original or copy of a birth certificate, a Consular Report of Birth Abroad, or a Certificate of Naturalization). Most Disney cruises to Canada, Alaska, the Caribbean, and the Bahamas qualify. See **getyouhome.gov** for details (click "USA" on the home page, then click the "Special Groups" link).

unofficial **TIP**
If you're a US citizen taking a cruise that begins or ends outside the States, you *must* have a passport.

Other valid forms of identification include a state-issued Enhanced Driver's License (currently available only in Michigan, New York State, Vermont, and Washington State) or a valid Trusted Traveler Card. For the latter, see

getyouhome.gov for details (click "USA" on the home page, then click "Trusted Traveler Programs"). Children under age 16 can present a birth certificate (original or copy), a Consular Report of Birth Abroad, or a Certificate of Naturalization.

If you're a divorced, separated, or single parent traveling abroad with your child and without your child's other parent, it's recommended that you obtain a signed, notarized letter from the child's other parent stating that you have his or her permission to take your child on the trip. This letter is in addition to the ID requirements listed above, and should include the following:

- The child's full name and birth date
- The other parent's full name, address, and phone number
- Your full name, address, and phone number
- A description of the entire trip, including dates, countries, and cruise information, plus transportation information if available
- The purpose of the trip
- The other parent's original signature, in ink, and the date of his or her signature

Depending on where you live, it may take a couple of days to find a notary public, so don't wait until the last minute to get this done. Banks and post offices usually have notaries on staff. Keep in mind that the notary will have to witness the other parent signing the form, so it's best to have the other parent present the form to the notary. The same advice holds for aunts, uncles, and grandparents traveling with someone else's child, and families who have invited their children's friends along for the cruise.

Requirements for Canadian citizens are almost identical: A Canadian passport, a Canadian Enhanced Driver's License, and a Trusted Traveler Card are all valid forms of ID.

Citizens of countries other than the US and Canada should remember that some countries may require that you present a visa or passport to enter, regardless of their rules for US citizens.

CREDIT CARDS AND PAYMENT METHODS

DCL SHIPS ACCEPT CASH, traveler's checks, Visa, MasterCard, American Express, Discover, Diners Club, JCB, and the Disney Visa card for payment. They also accept Disney gift cards, Disney Rewards Dollars (available to Disney Chase Visa–card holders), and Disney Dollars.

Cash is rarely used on board—your stateroom key serves as a credit card. (In fact, cash is not accepted as payment for beverages, spa or salon services, photography, laundry, or retail purchases.) It's still useful to have some cash available for luggage attendants and while you're in port, however. You can cash checks and obtain change from the Guest Services desk. You can also use other credit cards while on board.

US dollars are widely accepted throughout most of the Caribbean and in the Bahamas, and most prices are quoted in dollars. US-based credit cards are also accepted at many shops and stores, but don't expect smaller stores, bodegas, markets, and taxis to take them.

If you're traveling to Europe, Mexico, or Canada, you have a few options:

- **Ask your local bank to convert your US dollars before you leave home.** Many US banks will do this at a reasonable exchange rate; some charge a small exchange fee. Give your bank about a week to obtain the foreign currency because many branches don't keep euros, pesos, or Canadian dollars on hand. Your bank will likely convert any unspent foreign currency back to dollars when you return, too.

- **Use a local ATM that's part of your bank's network.** If you're traveling in Europe and you're not sure how much cash to bring, you can usually get a fair exchange rate by withdrawing money at a local cash machine. Visa's website has a handy worldwide ATM locator (**visa.com/atmlocator**), and in our experience there are usually many more ATMs available than the ones listed online. Keep in mind that your local bank will probably add a withdrawal fee and a foreign-transaction fee, so it's better to make a few large withdrawals than lots of small ones.

- **Exchange traveler's checks for local currency when you disembark.** Traveler's checks are safer than carrying cash because they can be replaced if lost or stolen. The downside: Converting them to local currency takes more time than using an ATM or obtaining local currency before you leave home.

unofficial **TIP**
To prevent any sudden stops on your accounts, let your bank and credit card companies know that you're traveling abroad before you leave home.

If you want to convert your traveler's checks to cash, try to find a local bank willing to do the exchange, and verify the exchange calculations by hand. We've heard from readers who were promised one exchange rate outside a local currency-exchange stand (not a bank) and got another, lower rate when the conversion was done inside.

Finally, note that the US dollar is unofficially accepted in many markets, bodegas, and taxis throughout Mexico, but you'll rarely get a good deal that way. You'll probably be offered a simple exchange rate of 10 pesos per dollar, whereas the current exchange rate is something like 12 pesos per dollar—almost 17% more than what you're likely to be offered.

HEALTH INSURANCE

US RESIDENTS TRAVELING OUTSIDE OF THE STATES should contact their health-insurance providers to check their coverage for emergencies outside the country. While Disney offers trip insurance for its cruises, it currently limits coverage to $10,000 per person for medical and dental emergencies. Ten grand at most hospitals these days is going to get you some ice, a Band-Aid, and a kiss from the doctor to make your boo-boo better . . . if you're lucky. If you're going to pay for additional insurance, make sure it's enough to be helpful in an emergency.

Residents of most European countries taking a Disney cruise in Europe should also investigate the use of the **European Health Insurance Card,** which covers travel through much of Europe (visit **ehic.org.uk** for details). If you need additional travel insurance, companies such as American Express offer it for around 3% of the total cost of your trip.

unofficial **TIP**
As you pack for your trip, plan to carry three copies of your health insurance information: one in a wallet or purse, one in carry-on luggage, and one in checked luggage.

Finally, some websites, such as **insuremytrip.com,** offer a handy feature for comparing travel-insurance policies from different companies. **MouseSavers** (**mousesavers.com**) also contains some good tips.

CELL PHONES

MOST US MOBILE CARRIERS, including AT&T, Sprint, T-Mobile, and Verizon, have international call plans at reasonable rates, while data plans tend to be very expensive. (The notable exception is T-Mobile, which includes free unlimited international data in its Simple Choice Plan.) In addition, many of these plans can be turned on and off from the carrier's website, so you only need to pay for coverage while you're traveling. Check your carrier's website for details on its international plans, including whether there's coverage in the countries you plan to visit.

You'll also need to check whether your phone's communications technology is compatible with the wireless infrastructure of the countries you plan to visit. Almost all cell phones throughout the world use either CDMA or GSM to transmit calls. (GSM phones have SIM cards; CDMA phones don't.) The two technologies don't work together, so a CDMA phone won't work on a GSM network, and vice versa.

unofficial **TIP**
Verizon's US versions of the iPhone 4s, 5, 5c, and 5s have both CDMA and GSM support, while the Verizon iPhone 4 is CDMA-only.

Most carriers in the US, including Verizon, Sprint, MetroPCS, and U.S. Cellular, use CDMA, while AT&T and T-Mobile in the US use GSM, which is also the standard for most phones in the rest of the world. If you have an AT&T or T-Mobile phone, it will likely work almost anywhere you're headed.

If you're using a CDMA carrier, check to see whether your phone supports GSM anyway. Some newer phones, including the iPhone as well as some BlackBerry, HTC, Motorola, and Samsung devices, support both protocols and will automatically detect when they're on a GSM network. A quick Web search or call to your carrier will provide the information you need.

Again, using mobile data outside the US can be obscenely expensive, with typical rates anywhere from 5 to 20 times as much as you're likely paying at home, and it's common to hear stories of unwitting travelers racking up thousands of dollars in charges without ever making a call, because they didn't know to do the following:

1. **Turn off your phone completely when you're not using it.** This prevents your phone from using a foreign carrier's data network to check e-mail and other messages.

2. **Disable data roaming unless you absolutely need it.** Look for an icon or button called "Settings" on your phone, and from there something called "Data," "Data Settings," or "Mobile Data." Make sure that's turned off. You can turn it back on if, say, you need to check Google Maps to see where you're at in town, but turn it off once you've downloaded enough of the map to navigate.

If the prospect of turning off your phone gives you the shakes, you have a third option, recommended by a reader:

Put your phone in airplane mode instead of turning it off. This way you can still use your camera and listen to music. You can also use Wi-Fi—some ports have free wireless, or you can pay for it on the ship.

PART THREE

STATEROOMS

DISNEY CRUISE LINE'S SHIPS BOAST some of the largest cabins in the cruise industry, which helps explain—a bit—why their fares are correspondingly high. An inside cabin, generally the least expensive on any ship, is 169–184 square feet on Disney's ships, compared with 114–165 square feet on Royal Caribbean and 160–185 on Carnival. Disney's ocean-view and verandah (balcony) cabins are larger than Royal Caribbean's and Carnival's, too.

In addition to space, Disney's bathroom layout is an improvement over those of other cruise lines. Disney staterooms in Categories 10–4 feature a split-bath design, in which the shower and toilet are in separate compartments, each with its own door and sink. The advantage of this design is that two people can get ready at the same time. (Category 11 staterooms have the shower and toilet in the same compartment.)

Disney's clever incorporation of storage space is one of the things we were most impressed with on our first few cruises. Most cabins have two sliding-door closets, each big enough for one large or two small suitcases; under-bed storage for carry-on or soft-sided luggage; and several drawers built in to the cabin's desk area. In addition, some cabins on the *Wonder* offer a steamer trunk for storage, while the *Magic* has dressers instead of trunks. (For a list of these cabins, see **tinyurl .com/steamertrunklist.**)

While Disney's staterooms are well designed and large for the cruise industry, most are smaller than the typical hotel room. A room at a Walt Disney World Value hotel, such as Pop Century Resort, is about 260 square feet—about 40% larger than a DCL inside cabin. Even a well-appointed Family Oceanview Stateroom with Verandah is 304 square feet, a little smaller than a room at a Disney Moderate hotel, such as Caribbean Beach Resort.

unofficial **TIP**
On the *Dream* and *Fantasy,* some inside cabins have "virtual portholes"—video screens that combine real-time views from outside the ship with animated snippets of various Disney characters. Many children strongly prefer these to actual verandah views, and inside cabins are usually much less expensive.

OUR STATEROOM RECOMMENDATIONS

AT 169–184 SQUARE FEET, an **Inside Stateroom** has enough room for two adults, or two adults and one small child. (Just remember: They give you 60 square feet per person in prison.) These are Category 10 and 11 cabins, so a family of this size shouldn't have much contention for bathrooms when getting ready.

If you're a family of three or four and you have two tweens or teens, you'll appreciate the extra space of a **Deluxe Oceanview with Verandah Stateroom** (246 or 268 square feet) or **Deluxe Family Oceanview with Verandah Stateroom** (about 300 square feet). Alternatively, you could book two cabins: two inside connecting rooms or an inside and outside cabin across the hall from each other. The advantage to two rooms, besides the extra space and extra bathroom, is that the kids can sleep late if they want.

CABIN APPOINTMENTS

EVERY DISNEY CRUISE LINE (DCL) stateroom is outfitted with the following:

- Private bath with sink and toilet
- Desk with chair and dedicated lighting—big enough to actually get work done
- Sleeper sofa
- Satellite television with remote
- Closet with two sliding doors (*Magic* and *Wonder*) or two hinged doors (*Dream* and *Fantasy*)
- Hooks (for towels) and hangers (for clothes)
- Electronic safe—just big enough for passports, wallets, and other small valuables
- Coffee table—the top opens for storage (only *Dream* and *Fantasy*).
- Privacy curtain—separating the sleeping area from the sofa
- Beverage cooler—keeps drinks cool, not necessarily cold. No freezer.
- In-room phone with voice mail
- Wave Phone—a mobile phone you can use aboard the ship
- Digital alarm clock—typically an iHome. (Bring a Lightning-to-30-pin converter if you have a newer iPhone.)
- Toiletries—H2O Plus soap, shampoo, conditioner, and body lotion
- Life jackets
- Room-service menus
- Bedside lamps
- Ice bucket and glasses

- In-room thermostat (digital on the *Dream* and *Fantasy;* older-style dial on the *Magic* and *Wonder*)
- Custom artwork—usually depicts Disney characters and themes relevant to the cruise line, ships, islands, or travel.

Cabins with exterior windows also include blackout curtains, which do an amazing job of blocking the sun. If you need light to wake up in the morning, don't shut them unless you want to sleep until noon.

WHAT YOU *WON'T* FIND Cabins don't have minibars, coffeemakers, microwaves, teakettles, steam irons, or ironing boards. An iron and ironing board are available in most of the ships' laundry rooms.

STATEROOM CATEGORIES

CATEGORIES 11A–11C: Standard Inside Stateroom
MAXIMUM OCCUPANCY 4 people
SIZE (square feet) *Magic/Wonder,* 184; *Dream/Fantasy,* 169

DESCRIPTION Has one queen-size bed or two twin beds (which can be pushed together), a sleeper sofa, and combined bath with tub and shower. Some rooms have a pull-down upper berth. These cabins are on Decks 2, 5, 6, and 7 on the *Magic* and *Wonder,* and on Decks 2, 5, 6, 7, 8, 9, and 10 on the *Dream* and *Fantasy.* They're generally available in the Forward (toward the bow/front), Midship (center), and Aft (toward the stern/rear) sections of the ships.

CATEGORY 10A (all ships), CATEGORIES 10B and 10C (*Magic* and *Wonder*): Deluxe Inside Stateroom
MAXIMUM OCCUPANCY 4 people

SIZE (square feet) *Magic/Wonder,* 214; *Dream/Fantasy,* 204

DESCRIPTION These cabins on the *Magic, Dream,* and *Fantasy* have one queen-size bed; cabins on the *Wonder* have one queen or two twin beds (which can be pushed together). Cabins on all ships have a one-person sleeper sofa and split bath; some rooms have a pull-down upper berth. Category 10C rooms, on the *Magic* and *Wonder,* are located entirely on Deck 1 Midship and Deck 2 Aft. Category 10B rooms, also found on the *Magic* and *Wonder,* are located entirely on Deck 2 Midship. Category 10A rooms are on Decks 5 and 7 on the *Magic* and *Wonder* and Decks 5, 6, 7, 8, and 9 on the *Dream* and *Fantasy,* anywhere along the ship.

CATEGORIES 9A–9D: Deluxe Oceanview Stateroom
MAXIMUM OCCUPANCY 4 people
SIZE (square feet) *Magic/Wonder,* 214; *Dream/Fantasy,* 204

DESCRIPTION Same size and features as a Category 10 Deluxe Inside, plus a window view of the ocean. These cabins on the *Magic, Dream,* and *Fantasy* have one queen-size bed; cabins on the *Wonder* have one queen or two twin beds (which can be pushed together). All cabins on all ships have a sleeper sofa and split bath; some rooms have a pull-down upper berth. Categories 9B–9D are found only on Decks 1 and 2 on the *Magic* and *Wonder* and only on Deck 2 Midship on the *Dream* and *Fantasy.* Category 9A cabins are found on the Forward section of Decks 5, 6, and 7 on the *Magic* and *Wonder,* and on Decks 5, 6, 7, and 8 of the *Dream* and *Fantasy.* The 9A cabins on Decks 6, 7, and 8 of the *Dream* and *Fantasy* are interesting because they're at the extreme Forward and Aft ends of the ships, affording them unique views at a relatively low cost.

CATEGORIES 8A–8D (exclusive to the *Dream* and *Fantasy*): Deluxe Family Oceanview Stateroom
MAXIMUM OCCUPANCY 5 people
SIZE (square feet) 241

DESCRIPTION These cabins have one queen-size bed. Most have a one-person pull-down bed in the wall; a few also have one-person pull-down beds in the ceiling. All cabins have a one-person sleeper sofa as well as a split bath; most have round tubs and showers.

Categories 8A–8D: Deluxe Family Oceanview Stateroom

CATEGORY 7A: Deluxe Oceanview Stateroom with Navigator's Verandah

MAXIMUM OCCUPANCY 3 people

SIZE (square feet) *Magic/Wonder,* 268 (including verandah); *Dream/Fantasy,* 246 (including verandah)

DESCRIPTION Found on Decks 5, 6, and 7 on all ships (Fore and Aft on the *Dream* and *Fantasy;* Aft only on the *Magic* and *Wonder*), these cabins have one queen or two twin beds (which can be pushed together). All cabins have a one-person sleeper sofa and split bath. The interesting feature about these cabins is the Navigator's Verandah: a small, semi-enclosed, teak-floored deck attached to the stateroom and featuring either a large exterior window or open railing. The window doesn't open, so in those rooms the extra space and teak deck are the difference between these cabins and the Category 9 staterooms on the *Magic* and *Wonder*. On the *Dream* and *Fantasy,* these cabins have an undersized or obstructed-view verandah.

CATEGORIES 6A (all ships) and 6B (*Dream* and *Fantasy* only): Deluxe Oceanview Stateroom with Verandah

MAXIMUM OCCUPANCY 4 people

SIZE (square feet) *Magic/Wonder,* 268 (including verandah); *Dream/Fantasy,* 246 (including verandah)

DESCRIPTION These cabins have a queen-size bed, a one-person sleeper sofa, and a one-person pull-down bed, typically above the sofa. All have a split bath, most with round tubs and showers. Category 6A cabins are found Aft on Decks 5, 6, and 7 of the *Magic* and *Wonder* and Aft on

CATEGORIES 6A and 6B Deluxe Oceanview Stateroom with Verandah

Decks 8, 9, and 10 on the *Dream* and *Fantasy.* Category 6B staterooms are found only on the *Dream* and *Fantasy,* Aft on Decks 5, 6, and 7. These staterooms differ from Category 5 staterooms because they have private verandahs with a short white wall instead of a railing with Plexiglas. In addition, some of the Category 5 cabins are found Midship, whereas all Category 6 cabins seem to be Aft.

CATEGORIES 5A–5C (all ships), 5D and 5E (*Dream* and *Fantasy* only): Deluxe Oceanview Stateroom with Verandah

MAXIMUM OCCUPANCY 4 people

SIZE (square feet) *Magic/Wonder,* 268 (including verandah); *Dream/Fantasy,* 246 (including verandah)

DESCRIPTION There seems to be little difference between these and the Category 6 cabins on the *Magic* and *Wonder.* All have the same square footage and amenities, and are on Decks 5, 6, and 7. Category 5E cabins have oversize verandahs, and some have a white wall instead of railing with Plexiglas. No other Category 5 cabins have a white wall on the verandah.

CATEGORIES 4A and 4B (all ships), 4C and 4D (*Dream* and *Fantasy* only), 4E (*Magic* and *Wonder* only): Deluxe Family Oceanview Stateroom with Verandah

MAXIMUM OCCUPANCY 5 people

SIZE (square feet) *Magic/Wonder,* 304 (including verandah); *Dream/Fantasy,* 299 (including verandah)

CATEGORIES 4A–4E Deluxe Family Oceanview Stateroom with Verandah

DESCRIPTION These cabins have a queen-size bed and sleeper sofa (fits one person); most have a pull-down wall bed (sleeps one). Some also have a pull-down upper-berth bed. All have a split bath, most with round tubs and showers. One issue with the pull-down wall bed in these cabins is that you'll have to move the desk chair in order to use the bed. The Category 4E cabins are found only Aft on Decks 7 and 8 of the *Magic* and *Wonder.* There are only two 4E cabins on Deck 7, and what makes them interesting is that they have an angled view directly off the ship's stern. They're also adjacent to Deck 7's "secret" sun deck. On the *Dream* and *Fantasy,* the A–D designations for this category represent the deck on which the stateroom is located: 4A staterooms are on Decks 9 and 10 Midship, 4B staterooms are on Deck 8 Midship, 4C staterooms are on Deck 7 Midship, and 4D staterooms are on Deck 6 Midship.

CATEGORY V (*Dream* and *Fantasy* only): Concierge Family Oceanview Stateroom with Verandah
MAXIMUM OCCUPANCY 5 people
SIZE (square feet) 306 (including verandah)

DESCRIPTION These cabins have a queen bed, a sleeper sofa for two, and an upper-berth pull-down bed that sleeps one. These rooms have an extra half-bath, giving the shower side of the split bath a sink and vanity. Category V staterooms are on Decks 11 and 12 Forward.

CATEGORY T: Concierge 1-Bedroom Suite with Verandah
MAXIMUM OCCUPANCY 5 people
SIZE (square feet) *Magic/Wonder,* 614 (including verandah); *Dream/ Fantasy,* 622 (including verandah)

CATEGORY T: Concierge 1-Bedroom Suite with Verandah

DESCRIPTION These cabins feature a separate bedroom with queen bed and a bathroom with whirlpool tub and separate shower. The living room has upholstered chairs and a sofa, plus a separate table and chairs. The living room also sleeps three: two on the convertible sofa and one in the pull-down bed. These staterooms are found all along Deck 8 on the *Magic* and *Wonder* and the Forward sections of Decks 11 and 12 on the *Dream* and *Fantasy*.

CATEGORY S (*Magic* and *Wonder* only): Concierge 2-Bedroom Suite with Verandah
MAXIMUM OCCUPANCY 7 people
SIZE (square feet) 954 (including verandah)

DESCRIPTION The master bedroom has a queen bed, a walk-in closet, a vanity, two sinks, and a walk-in shower. The other bedroom has twin beds, a bathroom with tub and sink, and a walk-in closet. Two others can sleep on the convertible sofa in the living room, and a pull-down bed sleeps one more. In addition, the 2-Bedroom Suite features a large living room with seating for 10 people, a huge private verandah suitable for entertaining a few guests, and another half-bath. Category S cabins are on Deck 8 Forward.

CATEGORY R: Concierge Royal Suite

MAXIMUM OCCUPANCY 7 people (*Magic/Wonder*); 5 people (*Dream/Fantasy*)

SIZE (square feet) *Magic/Wonder,* 1,029 (including verandah); *Dream/Fantasy,* 1,781 (including verandah)

DESCRIPTION On the *Magic* and *Wonder,* the master bedroom has a queen bed, a walk-in closet, a vanity, two sinks, and a walk-in shower. The other bedroom has twin beds, a bathroom with tub and sink, and a walk-in closet. Two others can sleep on the convertible sofa in the living room, and a pull-down bed sleeps one more. On the *Magic* and *Wonder,* the Royal Suite includes a separate dining room, living room, and media room, plus a private verandah that you should rent out to other families for birthdays (it'll fit an elephant) and another half-bath. Royal Suites on the *Dream* and *Fantasy* have one long room separated into dining and living areas. The master bedroom features a queen bed and bath with two sinks, a shower, and a tub. An in-wall pull-down double bed and a single pull-down bed in the living room complete the

**CATEGORY R: Concierge Royal Suite
on the *Magic* and *Wonder***

CATEGORY R: Concierge Royal Suite
on the *Dream* and *Fantasy*

sleeping arrangements. The most impressive feature of these suites on the *Dream* and *Fantasy* may be the verandah, which curves around the suite to follow the contour of the deck. Besides being large enough to land aircraft, it includes a whirlpool tub.

PART FOUR

ARRIVING, GETTING YOUR SEA LEGS, *and* DEPARTING

TRANSPORTATION *to* YOUR CRUISE

CHOOSING A DEPARTURE PORT BASED ON TIME AND MONEY

MOST DISNEY ITINERARIES depart from two or three different ports at various times of the year. While the differences in the ports' quality are relatively small, your departure port is more likely to affect your trip's transportation cost.

If you live within a few hours' drive of one of Disney's ports, your least expensive option is almost certainly going to be using that port. Otherwise, consider flying in the day before you depart to account for flight cancellations.

If you're taking a European cruise and flying in from North America, consider arriving two days before your cruise. This will protect you against most flight cancellations and also give you a bit more time to adjust to the time-zone difference.

As for quality, Disney's Port Canaveral terminal is the nicest in the United States, with easy, ample parking; good directional signage; and a comfortable waiting area. We wouldn't choose a cruise, however, based on the hour or so spent in the terminal. Instead, include the transportation cost to and from the port, plus lodging, in the total cost of the cruises you're considering to see how the overall cost shakes out.

GETTING TO AND FROM THE PORT

MOST NORTH AMERICAN DISNEY CRUISE LINE (DCL) GUESTS have three options when arranging transportation to the cruise terminal: book transportation through Disney, book through a third-party service, or drive themselves. This section covers all three options in detail, including driving directions, GPS settings, and terminal parking rates for those taking their own car.

Using Disney Transportation from the Airport

If you're flying in to Orlando, you can use Disney's shuttle service to get to Port Canaveral. The cost is $70 per person, free for kids under 3, and should be arranged ahead of time through your travel agent or Disney. Disney recommends that your flight into Orlando arrive by 1:45 p.m. and your flight out depart after 11:30 a.m.

Disney also provides shuttle service from other city airports to its cruise terminals. Round-trip prices in Barcelona, for instance, are $60–$120 per person, depending on whether you're staying at a hotel the night before and/or the night after your cruise. It's $40–$80 in Miami; $100 in San Diego; $40 in San Juan, Puerto Rico; $50–$66 in Vancouver, British Columbia (depending on the airport); and $60–$340 (not a typo) in Venice. See **tinyurl.com/dclgroundtransfers** for more details.

Using Disney Transportation from Walt Disney World

Disney provides round-trip transfer service among Walt Disney World hotels at a cost of $70 per person, round-trip.

LUGGAGE TRANSFER If you're taking a DCL cruise after staying at a Disney-owned resort at Walt Disney World and you've booked transportation from the resort to the ship through Disney, cruise representatives can transfer your luggage from your hotel room to your ship's stateroom.

Contact DCL at least three days before you leave home to take advantage of this service. They'll ask you for the number of bags and tell you when and where to meet for your drive to the ship. They'll also give you instructions on what to do with your bags; typically, you'll simply leave them in your hotel room, with your DCL luggage tags attached, and Disney will transfer them directly to your stateroom.

Surprisingly, you may not find this service as smooth as one might expect from Disney, as this reader reports:

> The staff at Pop Century Resort want nothing to do with helping you get ready for your cruise. When I stopped at the concierge desk to ask about luggage transfer, they simply gave me a card with the DCL phone number on it and told me to call it myself. When I called the number, I got an automated message telling me what time I would be picked up, but no indication of the meeting spot or what to do with our bags. We finally did get printed instructions about the port transfer at 9:30 p.m. We were told to leave our luggage in the room, by the door, with the DCL tags attached no later than 8:30 a.m. and that we should meet in the Pop Century lobby at 12:30 p.m. to check in with the cruise-line staff.
>
> You really do have to be ready on time—cast members were at our door at 8:31 to collect our luggage. Also, the DCL staff was in the Pop lobby at noon; we left as soon as everyone scheduled to be on the bus was there.

One thing to note: If you use Disney transportation to get to Port Canaveral, you don't have any control over what time you get to the port. They tell you where to be and when to be there. So if you want a few more minutes in the parks, you can't leave WDW a bit later, and if you want more time to explore the ship, you can't leave earlier.

Third-Party Shuttle Services

If you have more than four people, it's often less expensive to hire a third-party shuttle service to transport you to your cruise terminal.

PORT CANAVERAL Mears Transportation (☎ 407-423-5566; **mears transportation.com**) offers private-town-car, SUV, and van shuttles from Orlando to Port Canaveral. Round-trip costs are $270 for up to 3 people in a town car ($90 per person), $360 for up to 5 in an SUV ($72 per person), or $360 for up to 10 in a van ($36 per person). The big advantage to using a third-party service is that you can depart as soon as your group is ready. One-way rates are half of the round-trip figures listed; tips aren't included.

SAN DIEGO If you're flying in for a cruise out of San Diego, **SuperShuttle** (☎ 800-258-3826; **supershuttle.com**) offers one-way and round-trip transfers from virtually every airport in the region. Cost is about $12 per person between San Diego's airport and port. Check SuperShuttle's website for details; use "San Diego Cruise Ship Terminal" as your destination when you reserve online.

Driving Yourself

This section provides driving directions for Disney's ports in Florida, California, and Canada, plus information on on-site versus off-site parking rates at the various cruise terminals.

TO PORT CANAVERAL It takes about an hour to drive from Orlando to Port Canaveral under normal conditions. Traffic and road construction on the Beachline Expressway (FL 528), a toll road, can turn that 60-minute trip into a 3-hour ordeal. And because Port Canaveral and Orlando are linked by only three main roads—with limited connections between them—there are a couple of points along the Beachline where you have no way of taking an alternate route if

unofficial **TIP**
Text the location and a photo of your parking spot to other members of your group before you leave the parking facility. This will help you remember where you parked when you return from your cruise.

traffic is delayed. Our advice is to allow at least 2 hours for this trip or, better yet, 2½ hours. If you get to the port early, Disney's cruise terminal is air-conditioned and comfortable, with enough room for restless kids to run around in while you wait to board.

If you're using a GPS, enter this address as your destination: **Port Canaveral Terminal A, 9155 Charles M. Rowland Dr., Port Canaveral, FL 32920.** Use "Cape Canaveral" if your GPS doesn't recognize Port Canaveral as a city.

If you're not using a GPS, DCL's Planning Center (**disneycruiseline .com/plan**) has very clear driving directions for getting to Port Canaveral. If you're driving from Walt Disney World, the most direct route uses eastbound FL 536 to the Central Florida GreeneWay (FL 417) and then to the Beachline Expressway. The GreeneWay and Beachline are toll roads, so have $10 in cash available for the round-trip.

You're on the Beachline almost the entire way to Port Canaveral. Once you arrive, the port's terminals function almost exactly like an airport's. The same kinds of signs for airline terminals are posted for cruise-line terminals at Port Canaveral. DCL ships usually depart from Terminal A, so you'll be looking for road signs to that effect. If you want to see what the drive looks like, the Canaveral Port Authority has an excellent video (complete with catchy reggae soundtrack) that shows what the exits, terminal, and parking options look like from a car passenger's perspective: **portcanaveral.com/drive.**

Once you arrive at Terminal A, you'll park and walk to the security checkpoint. Parking rates at DCL's Port Canaveral terminal are $60 for three days, $75 for four days, $90 for five days, and $120 for seven days. You may also prepay for your parking at the terminal online at **portcanaveral.com/cruising/parking.php.** There is no price cut for booking ahead of time.

TO MIAMI Driving here is a challenge because of the traffic, one-way streets, and constant construction. We recommend using a GPS, preferably one with traffic information, to guide you to the port. Use this address: **Port of Miami, 1015 N. America Way, Miami, FL 33132.** DCL recommends turning off your GPS once you've reached the port's bridge, and then staying in the left lane and following the signs to the parking garage closest to your terminal.

Like Port Canaveral, Miami has both parking garages and open-air lots. Parking is $20 per day. If the lots closest to your ship are full, drop off some of your family and luggage near the cruise terminal, and then swing around and find a spot in one of the other garages—the nearest open garages can be half a mile from the terminal, and there's no reason to have everyone haul their luggage that far.

Miami's ports are supposed to have shuttles running between the parking garages and terminals, but we've never seen them operating. (We *have* seen giant iguanas running around, though, so keep your eyes open!)

Once inside the terminal, you'll be directed to a check-in line. Miami's terminals are older and smaller than Port Canaveral's, but DCL's section is well maintained and efficient. Once you're checked in, you'll go up a set of escalators and then through a long corridor to board the ship.

TO SAN DIEGO You will need to park in the Economy Lot on Pacific Highway (**3302 Pacific Hwy., San Diego, CA 92101**) at the San Diego International Airport, and take a shuttle from the lot to the Port of San Diego. Parking is $11 per day.

TO VANCOUVER The port is about a 30-minute drive from Vancouver's airport: **Cruise Terminal, 999 Canada Place, Vancouver, BC, Canada V6C 3C1.** The cruise terminal has 775 parking spaces, which cost $32 CDN (about $32 USD) or $184 CDN ($184 USD) per week. Reservations are recommended and can be made online at **vinciparkcanadaplace.ca /reserve-a-space.html.**

The **DAY** *Before* **YOUR CRUISE**

STAYING AT A LOCAL HOTEL THE NIGHT BEFORE

YOUR CRUISE WILL START ON TIME even if you're not on the ship. One way to minimize the chance of that happening is to arrive at the port the day before your cruise and spend the night at a local hotel. While it adds a night's lodging to your trip's cost and another day to your trip's length, we think the peace of mind you get from knowing you'll make your cruise is worth it.

If you're driving to your cruise, most hotels near cruise ports offer their guests inexpensive parking and taxi and shuttle transportation to the port; some offer these services to the general public too. The hotel's parking rates are often substantially less than what you'd pay at the cruise terminal. For example, parking at many Port Canaveral hotels costs around $6 per day, compared with $17–$20 per day at the terminal.

If You're Cruising out of Port Canaveral

You have the option of spending the night at a hotel in Port Canaveral or Orlando. We've done both, and there are advantages to each. The advantage to staying in Port Canaveral is that you're only a few minutes from the cruise terminal. You can have a relaxed breakfast on the morning of your cruise, take a swim in the pool, and pick up any last-minute items at one of Port Canaveral's grocery stores. The one downside to Port Canaveral is that it doesn't offer as many entertainment options as Orlando, and you may find yourself staying at your hotel for the evening, either watching TV or swimming. While many families find this relaxing, some would prefer to maximize their vacation activities.

Our favorite hotel in Port Canaveral is the **Residence Inn Cape Canaveral Cocoa Beach** (8959 Astronaut Blvd.; ☎ 321-323-1100; **tinyurl.com/residenceinncanaveral**). This hotel offers studio, one-bedroom, and two-bedroom suites that sleep up to six people, plus a free breakfast buffet and Internet access at reasonable prices. There's no restaurant on-site, but you have plenty of nearby options.

The advantage to staying in Orlando is that you can visit a Disney theme park, Downtown Disney, or Universal Orlando before your trip. You'll have a wide variety of entertainment options and dozens of restaurants from which to choose. Some hotels, including the **Hyatt Regency Orlando International Airport** (9300 Jeff

Fuqua Blvd.; ☎ 407-825-1234; **orlandoairport.hyatt.com**), offer transportation to Port Canaveral for cruise guests. The downside to staying in Orlando is that you'll still need to allow a couple of hours in the morning for the trip to the cruise terminal. See page 39 for more details.

If You're Cruising out of Miami

You'll have many hotel options. We've spent the night before our Miami departures as far away as Orlando. Because there are so many ways to get to the Port of Miami by car, traffic and construction aren't as much of a concern as for Port Canaveral, although driving in a city as large as Miami has its own challenges (see page 40). And unlike hotels in Port Canaveral, most in Miami charge about as much for parking—around $15 per day—as does the Port of Miami (around $20), so there's little benefit to parking off-site.

The **Holiday Inn Port of Miami–Downtown** (340 Biscayne Blvd.; ☎ 305-371-4400; **tinyurl.com/hiportofmiami**) sits within a mile of the port, with plenty of restaurants, shopping, and activities a short walk or drive away, plus an on-site fitness center and high-speed wireless Internet. Its one weakness is the small number of on-site parking spaces: If one isn't available, you'll have to find space at a nearby pay-parking lot and walk back. The **Courtyard by Marriott Miami Downtown** (200 SE 2nd Ave.; ☎ 305-374-3000; **miamicourtyard.com**) is another moderately priced hotel. Renovated at the end of 2012, the Courtyard is near restaurants, shopping, and other activities; has an on-site gym; and offers high-speed wireless Internet.

If You're Cruising out of San Diego

You're in luck—it's possible to stay at a Disneyland hotel before your trip! Disneyland is typically less than 3 hours (with traffic) away from the San Diego port terminal. The **Disneyland Hotel** (1150 Magic Way, Anaheim; ☎ 714-778-6600; **disneyland.disney.go.com/disneyland -hotel**) is our favorite Disney-run hotel on-property, while **Disney's Paradise Pier Hotel** (1717 S. Disneyland Drive; ☎ 714-999-0990; **disneyland.disney.go.com/paradise-pier-hotel** is usually the least expensive. **Disney's Grand Californian Hotel & Spa** (1600 S. Disneyland Dr.; ☎ 714-635-2300; **disneyland.disney.go.com/grand-californian-hotel**) has the advantage of being adjacent to Disney California Adventure, making it an easy walk if you'd like to enjoy DCA's Cars Land during the evening.

In addition to Disney's hotels, many good off-site hotels are situated around the park. One of the most popular is the **Howard Johnson Anaheim** (1380 S. Harbor Blvd.; ☎ 714-776-6120; **hojoanaheim .com**), across the street from Disneyland and a shorter walk to Disneyland's entrance than Disney's own Paradise Pier Hotel.

If You're Cruising out of Vancouver

The **Pan Pacific Vancouver** (999 Canada Place, Ste. 300; ☎ 604-662-8111; **panpacificvancouver.com**) is located at Vancouver's port. It's posh and pricey, with rates between $400 and $500 USD per night. Also pricey—and fabulous!—is the **Shangri-La Vancouver** (1128 W. Georgia St.; ☎ 604-689-1120; **shangri-la.com/vancouver**), with spectacular views of the ocean and mountains, huge marble bathrooms, and friendly staff. A more economical option is the **Metropolitan Hotel Vancouver** (645 Howe St.; ☎ 604-687-1122; **metropolitan.com/vanc**), with rates around $200 USD per night.

Vancouver is a worthwhile destination in its own right, combining global sophistication and Canadian charm. The city is easily accessible by foot, taxi, and transit. Cruisers in search of international cuisine should make a point to sample the city's Asian specialties, from sushi to Indian to dim sum. For upscale dining, stick close to the downtown core around Robson Street and the cruise terminal. For an authentic experience, head to Vancouver's **Chinatown** (**vancouver-chinatown .com**) one of the largest in North America. If you're looking for something unique, try a Japanese-style hot dog sold from a food cart. It's Tokyo meets New York meets your belly.

Fashionistas will love hitting the high-end designer shops (**Chanel, Hermès, Louis Vuitton,** and so on), while shoppers looking for a Canadian experience should head to **Roots** (1001 Robson St.; ☎ 604-683-4305; **canada.roots.com**) or **Hudson's Bay Company** (674 Granville St.; ☎ 604-681-6211; **thebay.com**), home of the eponymous blankets. Fans of food souvenirs can pick up maple treats, British sweets and biscuits, and ketchup-flavored crisps all over the city.

If you arrive in the afternoon, walk to **Stanley Park,** along the waterfront, to see the beautiful Canadian Rockies in the distance (**vancouver.ca/parks-recreation-culture/stanley-park.aspx**). Or check out **Gastown** (**gastown.org**) and its steam-powered clock. For nightlife, check ahead before your arrival for live theater, musical concerts, or any festivals that are happening during your stay. A few good websites to try are **tourismvancouver.com, hellobc.com/vancouver,** and **timeout.com/vancouver.**

GET *in the* BOAT, MEN
(and Women and Kids)!

CHOOSING A BOARDING TIME

YOU'LL BE ABLE TO CHECK IN at least 75 days in advance using DCL's online Planning Center (see page 19). This offers you a chance to verify information, ensure that you have the right credit card on file, and so on. You'll also be able to choose your boarding window—the time when you provide Disney your travel documents and board the ship.

The earliest boarding windows are usually around 10:30 a.m. We recommend choosing as early a board time as you can, or after 1:30 p.m. Here are the pros and cons to both approaches:

Early Boarding Time

PROS An uncrowded ship. You'll find smaller crowds at the pools and buffet, and you'll be among the first in line for last-minute spa, restaurant, or shore-excursion availability.

CONS Most staterooms don't open to guests until at least 1:30 p.m. This means you'll be carrying everything you brought on board with you until you're able to enter your room. Guests with lots of camera equipment or big laptops may find this inconvenient.

Later Boarding Time

PROS The ability to sleep later on your boarding day, and the ability to access your stateroom as soon as you board the ship. If you have children who require an afternoon nap, this may be your best option.

CONS The ship is already full of people, including lines for the pools and food. Moreover, the elevators off the atrium tend to be packed with folks and their luggage trying to get to their rooms.

CHECKING IN AT THE TERMINAL

HAVE YOUR CRUISE DOCUMENTS and government-issued ID ready as soon as you get out of the car. Many terminals, including Port Canaveral, have an initial security checkpoint outside the perimeter to ensure that only ticketed passengers enter.

Once you're past that checkpoint, you'll undergo another round of security screening just inside the terminal's entrance. You'll pass through a metal detector, and your luggage will undergo X-ray scanning. If you have bags too large to get through the security screening, use the porters at the terminal.

Disney's cruise terminals, especially those at Port Canaveral and Vancouver, are spacious, clean, and comfortable. (Miami's is a little smaller than the others, and Barcelona's offers the finest in Catalan folding chairs for seating while you wait.) If you have to wait a few minutes for your group to be called, you'll find enough seating for your family to sit down and relax. Vending machines and bathrooms are available, and Disney provides everything from character greetings to ship models to maps on the floor to keep your kids occupied.

Once in the terminal, look for cast members handing out a mandatory (but mercifully short) health questionnaire. This questionnaire asks if anyone in your travel party has suffered from fever or nausea within the last 24 hours. Answering "yes" means you may be denied boarding, so be sure everyone is in good health. You'll return the completed form at the check-in desk.

Head for the check-in desk and have your signed cruise documents, health questionnaire, and IDs ready. If this is the first Disney cruise for anyone in your group, they'll need to accompany you to check in. Concierge has a dedicated check-in desk, and returning DCL guests can use a separate line for its Castaway Club (though given the number of return cruisers DCL sees, it's not always as fast as you'd think).

The check-in desk is where you'll receive your cabin number (if you don't already have one) and get issued your magnetic-stripe Key to the World stateroom cards. If this is your first Disney cruise, Disney will also take your photo. You may also choose to replace your photo with a current one if it's been awhile since your last cruise. The photo is used to ensure the person who gets off and back on the ship is the same person who boarded at the beginning of the cruise. The computerized systems at Disney's boarding gates display your photo when you swipe your room key to get off and on the ship.

The check-in desk will also issue your party a boarding number, usually 1–30. Rather than have everyone try to board the ship at once, Disney organizes passengers into boarding groups of about 25–30 families at a time. Loudspeakers announce every few minutes which group numbers are currently allowed to board.

If you've not yet done so, you'll have an opportunity in the cruise terminal to sign up your children for the kids' clubs before boarding. A good time to do that is while you're waiting for your boarding group to be announced.

Your Key to the World Card Explained

This card contains helpful information about your cruise.

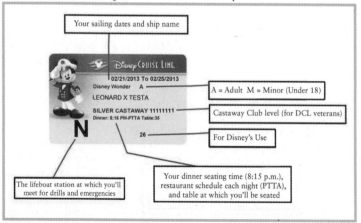

Your dining schedule will be printed on your card as a series of letters. One letter will be shown for each night of your cruise. In the example shown on the previous page, the four letters **PTTA** indicate that this is a four-night cruise. Each letter in the series also represents the first letter of the name of one of the ship's standard restaurants. In the example shown above, **P** is the *Wonder*'s Parrot Cay, **T** is for Triton's, and **A** signifies Animator's Palate. The two consecutive letter T's here mean that we'll be dining at Triton's back-to-back, on nights two and three of our cruise.

Finally, your Key to the World card also shows your transfer information, if you booked transportation through Disney to or from the port.

BOARDING THE SHIP

YOU CAN BOARD THE SHIP anytime after your boarding number is called. Have your room keys out, as they're scanned whenever you come on and off the ship.

Just before you enter the ship, photographers will offer to take a photo of your party. If this is important to you, a quick mirror check in the restroom and dressing in something you'd like recorded for posterity is a good idea. If you don't care to be photographed, breeze on past the people getting photos; they're certainly not mandatory, and lines can back up.

As you step on board, a cast member will ask your family name. Why they do this when so many parties traveling together don't necessarily have the same last name, we don't know. Either give your first names (Thurston and Lovey are our favorites) or make up a portmanteau combining your last names—no one is checking your ID—or just give a name. What doesn't work is saying you'd rather not, and it's easiest to just board as the Howells if you'd rather not announce your presence. (I mean, we all know how the paparazzi are.)

YOUR FIRST AFTERNOON ABOARD

IF YOU DIDN'T GET A *Personal Navigator* handout (see opposite page) in the terminal, pick one up at Guest Relations while you're still on Deck 3. This is also a good time to do any last-minute reservations or change your dining rotation or seating time. If this isn't your first Disney cruise and you're already familiar with the ship, you may choose to split up your group to do these tasks and meet up after you're done. It will save you time running around the ship.

Our first stop is usually Senses Spa, to book its Rainforest Room. It has even more limited availability than adult dining or a beach cabana, and you can't book it ahead of time.

Next, check for any last-minute openings at Palo or Remy if you wish to dine there and haven't booked yet. The location for this check-in desk will be noted in your *Personal Navigator*.

If it's after 1:30 p.m., you can head to your room and drop any bags you carried on. You may also see your room attendant already sprucing up your cabin for the evening.

In the afternoon, people will start to swarm the Cabanas buffet (Beach Blanket Buffet on the *Wonder*) as if they've never seen food before. We find it far more peaceful to hit the pool deck's quick-service options, Vista Café, or Cove Café (if you're all over 18) than to queue up to eat. We love Cabanas, but there's no shortage of food on the ship, and you've already spent enough of your day in lines.

The pool deck will be full of folks swimming and lounging. And when we say "full," we mean that it will be hectic to chaotic. If you want to relax, don't go there. But do pick up a drink at the beverage station to stay hydrated.

The chaos comes to a head with the **Sail-Away Celebration,** the kind you've seen memorialized in reruns of *The Love Boat,* with Champagne toasts, confetti, and Gavin MacLeod in shorts. It's kind of fun and a nice way to start your cruise, though this event isn't a must-do for us.

THE LIFEBOAT DRILL

THIS IS USUALLY HELD around 4 p.m. before the ship leaves port. Every member of your group will need to be present, and you'll need to bring your stateroom keys to the drill; attendance is tracked by computer, which reads your room key to validate your presence.

The lifeboat drill is the last must-do activity for the day. If you're down for an early dinner seating, it will soon be time to dress for dinner. If not, you may choose to attend the first evening show. And with that your afternoon is done, things calm down, and you can finally relax and start your vacation.

▌█ BARE NECESSITIES

THE *PERSONAL NAVIGATOR*

YOU'LL BE GIVEN THIS HANDOUT (shown on the next page) when you board the ship. The *Personal Navigator* is a daily guide to all of the ship's activities and events, including times, locations, shop and restaurant hours, and more. You'll receive a new one every night for the following day, and extra *Navigator*s are available at Guest Services and by asking your stateroom attendant.

The format is roughly the same each day. Page 1 usually shows the date, ship's location, and sunrise/sunset times. If the ship is in port, the *Navigator* will list the time you need to be back on the ship ("All Aboard") and the ship's departure time. Also listed are the times and locations for the evening's entertainment; important announcements; games, shows, and events, including times and locations; and the dinner-menu theme and "Drink of the Day."

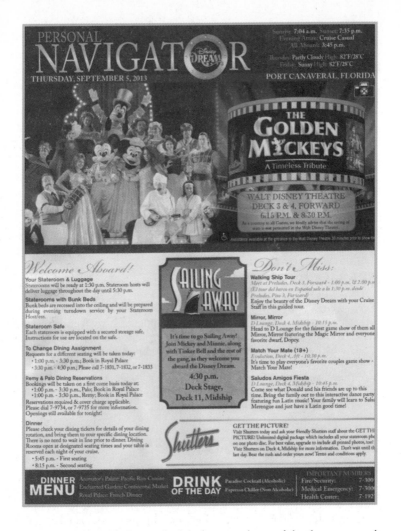

Page 2 holds the ship's schedule for every hour of the day, separated into three sections: The top section holds the morning's activities, usually running from 8:30 a.m. until 1:30 p.m.; the middle section contains afternoon activities, from 1:45 p.m. until around 6:45 p.m.; and the bottom section lists the evening's events, from about 7 p.m. to midnight.

Each section is separated into approximately 10 rows of activities, and each row generally corresponds to an age group, location, or event. For example, you'll see rows for special events at the pool, character greetings, movies, family activities, and stuff for adults, plus the schedule for the Vibe, Edge, and Oceaneer Club/Lab kids' activities.

Page 3 has in-depth information about the daily activities described on page 2. Page 4 lists the ship's restaurant, store, and service-desk hours, plus mealtimes. Other services, such as onboard airline check-in, are also listed here. Finally, any open space on this page is usually filled with shopping advertisements.

DISNEY CRUISE LINE NAVIGATOR APP If you're cruising on the *Magic, Dream,* or *Fantasy* (and we have to believe that the *Wonder* isn't far behind), and you prefer an electronic version of the *Personal Navigator,* there's an app for that! Available free at iTunes and Google Play, it works through the ships' onboard Wi-Fi, so you can keep your device in airplane mode while using it.

ONBOARD SERVICES

A 24-HOUR GUEST SERVICES DESK is just off the lobby on each ship to answer questions, make reservations, and provide other help. You can also contact Guest Services from your stateroom by touching the Guest Services button on your phone.

The best amenity that comes with your stateroom is likely to be your stateroom attendant, who will tidy up your cabin after you depart in the morning, deliver your *Personal Navigator,* and turn down your beds each night. You'll almost certainly see him or her more than any other crew member, and you'll be amazed at how little sleep these hardworking staff seem to need.

AIRLINE CHECK-IN

EVEN BEFORE YOU BOARD THE SHIP, you can request airline check-in for your flight home by making arrangements at your terminal's check-in desk. To do this, have the airline name, flight number(s), departure time and date, names of each passenger as printed on their ticket(s), and the flight confirmation number(s) for each flight segment.

While on board, you can ask Guest Services to check you in to your flight if you're flying home the day your cruise returns to port. Stop by the Guest Services desk before 10 p.m. on your second night to make this request. This service is available to anyone flying out of Orlando International Airport on domestic flights (including the US Virgin Islands and Puerto Rico) on AirTran Airways, Alaska Airlines, American Airlines, Delta Air Lines, JetBlue Airways, United Airlines, and US Airways.

No matter when you register, your first flight's departure must be after 11:25 a.m. on the day your cruise ends, to ensure the ship has enough time to make it back. There's a limit of two bags per person, and each bag must weigh less than 50 pounds. (According to Disney, a few randomly selected passengers may be required to undergo additional screening at the airport, and thus are ineligible for early check-in.)

The day before your cruise ends, you'll receive printed instructions in your stateroom, along with your boarding passes and temporary luggage tags. Affix the tags to your bags and leave them in the hallway outside your stateroom between 8:30 and 10:30 p.m. The next time you see your bags will be on the baggage carousel at your destination airport. This makes for easy maneuvering at Orlando International (the airport for most DCL guests) because you simply proceed directly to the security line and on to your gate. Your airline's baggage fee will be added to your DCL bill and will appear on your checkout statement.

LAUNDRY SERVICES

SELF-SERVICE LAUNDRY FACILITIES are available on several decks on each ship, furnished with washers, dryers, and detergent for purchase. It costs around $2 to wash a load of clothes and another $2 to dry them; detergent is another $1 per load.

Payment is made using your stateroom key card; card-swipe terminals are attached to the machines. In the setups we've seen, a clothes dryer is always stacked on top of a washing machine. The washer and dryer have separate swipe terminals, usually mounted between the washer and dryer. Labels on each terminal tell you whether it's for the washer or dryer. Be sure to read the label before you swipe your key card; otherwise you may end up paying for someone else's laundry cycle.

In addition to do-it-yourself laundry, each ship offers full-service laundry and dry cleaning on board, with pickup from and delivery to your stateroom. Simply drop your clothes in the plastic dry-cleaning bag hanging inside your closet, and complete the attached paper form with any cleaning instructions. The laundry service usually takes 24 hours, but we've had simple requests—laundering and ironing a couple of shirts—done on the same day.

PORT ADVENTURES

IN ADDITION TO GUEST SERVICES, a separate Port Adventures desk on Deck 3 (*Magic* and *Wonder*) or Deck 5 (*Dream* and *Fantasy*) handles booking for shore excursions. The staff are usually knowledgeable about the most popular excursions at each port. In addition to providing information about cost and time, they can typically answer questions regarding the appropriateness of a particular activity for the members of your family. They can also help you reschedule an activity if needed. See Part Eleven for details.

HEALTH SERVICES

EACH SHIP'S HEALTH CENTER employs a third-party doctor and nurse for medical issues. The most common reasons for visiting the Health Center are motion sickness, sunburn, and nausea, although the staff have seen their share of broken bones over the years. The Health Center (Deck 1 Forward; open 9:30–11 a.m. and 4:30–7 p.m.) can provide doses of basic over-the-counter and some prescription medicines; anything serious, such as surgery, will probably require an airlift to the nearest hospital. Also, note that use of the Health Services center isn't free, and rates are comparable to those of US hospitals—in other words, expensive—so check your insurance coverage before you leave home (see page 24 for more on that). However, just like the First Aid Centers in the Disney parks, Health Services will often provide you with a dose or two of over-the-counter medicine, such as aspirin or motion sickness tablets, for free.

TIPPING

YOU'LL ENCOUNTER CREW MEMBERS throughout your cruise, many of whom you'll see several times per day and who will have a direct impact on the quality of your trip. It's customary to give a small tip to these crew members in recognition of their service. The chart below indicates the suggested tip for these staff for each person in your cabin. Thus, if you have four people in your family and you're taking a seven-night cruise, budget $336 ($84 times four) for the personnel shown, plus any spa, bar, or other dining gratuities you'll need.

These suggested gratuity amounts are automatically added to your stateroom account based on the number of people in your cabin and your cruise length. Once on board, you can adjust these amounts or pay in cash by visiting the Guest Services desk (open 24 hours a day) on Deck 3. Lines at Guest Services get long on the last night of your cruise, so plan to make any adjustments sooner rather than later if you wish to avoid a wait.

STAFF MEMBER	SUGGESTED GRATUITY PER DAY	SUGGESTED GRATUITY 3 NIGHTS	SUGGESTED GRATUITY 4 NIGHTS	SUGGESTED GRATUITY 7 NIGHTS
Stateroom Attendant	$4	$12	$16	$28
Dining Room Server	$4	$12	$16	$28
Dining Room Assistant Server	$3	$9	$12	$21
Dining Room Head Server	$1	$3	$4	$7
TOTAL (Per Guest)	**$12**	**$36**	**$48**	**$84**

At Palo and Remy, a gratuity is automatically added only for alcohol; an additional gratuity for dining service is left to your discretion. It's also customary to add a gratuity for room service, again at your discretion. Finally, note that an automatic 15% gratuity is added to Cove Café and bar tabs, plus any alcohol ordered elsewhere on deck.

■ CHECKOUT *and* DEPARTURE

YOUR LAST NIGHT ON THE SHIP

YOU'LL RECEIVE DEBARKATION INFORMATION—including what to do with your luggage, where you'll be eating breakfast, and when you need to be off the ship—the night before your last night on board (for example night six of a seven-night cruise). This information is also available at Guest Services the last night of the cruise.

Packing

If you haven't already arranged onboard airline check-in, you'll receive luggage tags and gratuity envelopes in your stateroom on your last evening aboard, along with instructions for getting breakfast before departing in the morning. Use the luggage tags if you'd like Disney to transport your bags from the ship to the port terminal upon docking. (This enables you to walk off the ship without having to carry bags; you'll pick up your luggage before you go through Customs.) The luggage tags will be in colorful shapes of Disney characters: green Tinker Bell, orange Goofy,

blue Donald Duck, and so on. Write your stateroom number, name, home address, and number of bags on each tag, and attach one tag to each piece of luggage you want Disney to transport. Place your tagged bags outside your stateroom between 8:30 and 10:30 p.m.

A few packing tips:

- Don't forget to leave out clothes to wear to breakfast and off the ship the last morning.

- If you're flying home, note that any alcohol you purchased on the ship must be packed in your checked bags.

- Don't pack your passports, birth certificates, Key to the World card, or any other travel documents in your checked bags. You'll need them before you can pick up your luggage, so keep them in a bag you plan to carry by hand off the ship. Also keep out a change of clothes to wear off the ship.

- Remove any old airline or cruise tags from your luggage before placing on a new tag.

- Keep inside your stateroom any luggage you'll carry off the ship by hand. When you've gotten off the ship, you'll find a section of the terminal dedicated to checked baggage. Checked bags will be organized by color and character, with all of the green Tinker Bell–tagged luggage together, all of the orange Goofy luggage together, and so on. Overhead signs will direct you to each section.

*un*official **TIP**
You'll need your Key to the World cards to exit the ship, so keep them handy until you're back on land.

Luggage will be sorted by stateroom number within each section, so look for yours by finding your stateroom number within your section. If you can't find one of your bags, check a few feet up and down the row too—sometimes the stateroom order isn't exact. Ask a cast member for help if you still can't find your luggage after checking the nearby spaces.

EXPRESS WALK-OFF

FOR GUESTS WHO WISH TO BE among the very first off the ship (those who need to get straight to the airport or who have other time-dependent plans that day), DCL offers Express Walk-Off. As soon as the ship clears Customs, guests may depart the ship. You must carry all of your own luggage to take advantage of this service; you may not leave it out the night before. Be considerate and let your cabin attendant know if you're doing this, so he or she isn't waiting for your bags to appear in the hallway the last night of the cruise.

BREAKFAST ON THE MORNING OF YOUR DEPARTURE

YOU'LL HAVE THE CHANCE FOR ONE MORE SIT-DOWN MEAL. The table-service breakfast seatings are assigned based on your seating time for dinner. Guests with the early dinner seating are scheduled for their final breakfast on board at 6:30 a.m. Guests with the later dinner seating get a last-day breakfast assignment at 8 a.m. This effectively means that any guest with a late dinner seating and an early flight will be unable to eat a table-service breakfast on their last morning. For guests in this situation, the Cabanas buffet is open beginning at 6:30 a.m. This isn't quite the gargantuan spread offered on other mornings—expect pastries, fruit, bacon, eggs, cold cereal, and not much else. Cove Café is also open beginning at 6 a.m.

unofficial **TIP**
Concierge guests may order room service breakfast the last morning of the cruise.

US CUSTOMS ALLOWANCES

EACH FAMILY WILL NEED to fill out a Customs Declaration form (see next page). Besides the usual name and address, the form asks which countries you've visited, whether you're bringing in prohibited items such as fruits or vegetables, whether you've handled livestock, and whether you're carrying more than $10,000 in cash. (Answering "yes" to all three is probably the start of the next installment in the *Hangover* series.) See **tinyurl.com/customsdutyinfo** for more information.

unofficial **TIP**
Guests with flights out of Orlando International Airport before 1 p.m. are required to leave the ship by 8 a.m.

U.S. Customs and Border Protection

Customs Declaration

FORM APPROVED
OMB NO. 1651-0009

19 CFR 122.27, 148.12, 148.13, 148.110,148.111, 1498; 31 CFR 5316

Each arriving traveler or responsible family member must provide the following information (only ONE written declaration per family is required):

1. Family **Name**

   First *(Given)*   Middle

2. **Birth date**   Day   Month   Year

3. Number of **Family members** traveling with you

4. (a) U.S. Street **Address** (hotel name/destination)

   (b) City   (c) State

5. **Passport issued by** (country)

6. **Passport number**

7. Country of **Residence**

8. **Countries visited** on this
   trip prior to U.S. arrival

9. **Airline/Flight No.** or **Vessel Name**

10. The primary purpose of this trip is **business**:   Yes   No

11. I am (We are) bringing

    (a) fruits, vegetables, plants, seeds, food, insects: Yes   No

    (b) meats, animals, animal/wildlife products: Yes   No

    (c) disease agents, cell cultures, snails: Yes   No

    (d) soil or have been on a farm/ranch/pasture: Yes   No

12. I have (We have) been in close proximity of
    (such as touching or handling) **livestock**:   Yes   No

13. I am (We are) carrying **currency or monetary
    instruments** over $10,000 U.S. or foreign equivalent: Yes   No
    (see definition of monetary instruments on reverse)

14. I have (We have) **commercial merchandise:**   Yes   No
    (articles for sale, samples used for soliciting orders,
    or goods that are not considered personal effects)

15. **Residents** — the **total value of all goods,** including commercial
    merchandise I/we have purchased or acquired abroad, (including
    gifts for someone else, but not items mailed to the U.S.) and am/are
    bringing to the U.S. is: $

    Visitors — the **total value of all articles** that will remain in the U.S.,
    including commercial merchandise is: $

Read the instructions on the back of this form. Space is provided to list all the items you must declare.

I HAVE READ THE IMPORTANT INFORMATION ON THE REVERSE SIDE OF THIS FORM AND HAVE MADE A TRUTHFUL DECLARATION.

X _____
   (Signature)   Date (day/month/year)

For Official Use Only

CBP Form 6059B (10/07)

U.S. Customs and Border Protection Welcomes You to the United States

U.S. Customs and Border Protection is responsible for protecting the United States against the illegal importation of prohibited items. CBP officers have the authority to question you and to examine you and your personal property. If you are one of the travelers selected for an examination, you will be treated in a courteous, professional, and dignified manner. CBP Supervisors and Passenger Service Representatives are available to answer your questions. Comment cards are available to compliment or provide feedback.

Important Information

U.S. Residents — Declare all articles that you have acquired abroad and are bringing into the United States.

Visitors (Non-Residents) — Declare the value of all articles that will remain in the United States.

Declare all articles on this declaration form and show the value in U.S. dollars. For gifts, please indicate the retail value.

Duty — CBP officers will determine duty. U.S. residents are normally entitled to a duty-free exemption of $800 on items accompanying them. Visitors (non-residents) are normally entitled to an exemption of $100. Duty will be assessed at the current rate on the first $1,000 above the exemption.

Agricultural and Wildlife Products — To prevent the entry of dangerous agricultural pests and prohibited wildlife, the following are restricted: Fruits, vegetables, plants, plant products, soil, meat, meat products, birds, snails, and other live animals or animal products. Failure to declare such items to a Customs and Border Protection Officer/Customs and Border Protection Agriculture Specialist/Fish and Wildlife Inspector can result in penalties and the items may be subject to seizure.

Controlled substances, obscene articles, and toxic substances are generally prohibited entry.

Thank You, and Welcome to the United States.

The transportation of currency or **monetary instruments,** regardless of the amount, is legal. However, if you bring in to or take out of the United States more than $10,000 (U.S. or foreign equivalent, or a combination of both), you are required by law to file a report on FinCEN 105 (formerly Customs Form 4790) with U.S. Customs and Border Protection. Monetary instruments include coin, currency, travelers checks and bearer instruments such as personal or cashiers checks and stocks and bonds. If you have someone else carry the currency or monetary instrument for you, you must also file a report on FinCEN 105. Failure to file the required report or failure to report the *total* amount that you are carrying may lead to the seizure of *all* the currency or monetary instruments, and may subject you to civil penalties and/or criminal prosecution. SIGN ON THE OPPOSITE SIDE OF THIS FORM AFTER YOU HAVE READ THE IMPORTANT INFORMATION ABOVE AND MADE A TRUTHFUL DECLARATION.

Description of Articles (List may continue on another CBP Form 6059B)	Value	CBP Use Only
Total		

PART FIVE

SPECIAL TIPS
for
SPECIAL PEOPLE

■ DCL *for* SINGLES

BECAUSE DISNEY CRUISE LINE (DCL) IS TARGETED TO FAMILIES, roughly 90% of its guests are couples or parents and kids. That's about 10 points higher than the cruise industry's average, and it means that there are around 200 solo travelers per cruise on the *Magic* and *Wonder,* and around 400 on the *Dream* and *Fantasy.*

Like the Disney parks, DCL is great for singles. It's safe, clean, and low-pressure. Safety and comfort are excellent, especially for women. If you're looking for places to relax without being hit on, Disney's ships are perfect. The bars, lounges, and nightclubs are clean, friendly, and interesting; the restaurants are welcoming; and the spas are excellent places for grabbing some solo time in public. One aspect that you have to be vigilant about when traveling alone is shore excursions in foreign countries; more on that a bit later.

If you're interested in meeting other singles, Disney usually runs a **Singles Mingle** session on one of the first couple of days of each cruise. These are informal get-togethers, usually held at the Cove Café in the adults-only part of the ship, and last about an hour. Similarly, single and not-single guests ages 18–21 are welcome to attend a **Club 18*21 Social** during one night of their cruise. It's a meet-up attended by guests and crew, generally during the evening after the second dinner seating, also usually at the Cove Café.

DINING Single travelers will likely be paired with other groups for dinner at the standard restaurants. When we've cruised solo, our dinner companions are usually one or two couples, which means we're sitting at a table for four or six. If the cruise is especially popular, Disney may try to squeeze in another single person to your group, too, so that everyone has a table. Our dinners with these new friends

unofficial **TIP**
Unlike some other cruise lines, DCL doesn't yet host dedicated events for LGBT passengers; nonetheless, Disney gets enthusiastic reviews from gay cruisers for its inclusive and welcoming atmosphere.

couldn't have gone better, and we say that as pretty strong introverts. We've met interesting people from many different places, never run out of things to talk about, and even kept in touch with a few folks when we got back home.

Solo travelers are also welcome at Palo and Remy, and we've had many fine dinners and brunches there. If you're having difficulty making a reservation for one using the DCL website before your trip, try stopping by the restaurant on the afternoon you board. We've found the staff to be exceptionally accommodating for these requests, especially if you're willing to arrive either early or late.

> *unofficial* **TIP**
> US law requires Disney to disclose most claims of crimes alleged to have taken place on board. DCL voluntarily discloses all such incidents on its website.

CRUISE FARES While some cruise lines are adding stateroom cabins designed especially for solo travelers, cabins on Disney's ships are all designed to hold at least two people. To make up for the room, bar, and shore excursion revenue lost when one person books a cabin that could hold two paying passengers, Disney adds a 100% surcharge (a single supplement, in cruise-industry lingo) to most solo-traveler fares, making the cost equivalent to two people taking the same trip. There's a small chance that you can find last-minute deals on unsold cabins without paying the full 100% supplement. Your best bet is to check the DCL website or have a travel agent research for you.

PORT ADVENTURES As with dining, there's a good chance you'll be paired with other couples for shore excursions. But unlike dinner, it's possible for a solo traveler to simply be a quiet observer during many excursions, especially those designed for groups.

> *unofficial* **TIP**
> If your port adventure involves boating, snorkeling, or any other water-based activity, you'll almost certainly be assigned another traveler or couple as a buddy for safety reasons.

We've been single travelers on everything from cooking demonstrations to snorkeling to city tours, and they've all gone well. All of the programs we've tried can accommodate single guests, and the port adventures staff make everyone feel welcome. That said, some excursions run by third-party companies will use private taxi or shuttle services to transport guests from the ship to their activity, and it's possible for a solo traveler to be the odd man out if the vehicle doesn't have enough seats to accommodate the entire group, as Len recounts:

> *I was once the only solo traveler in a group of nine for an excursion in Mexico that involved a 30-minute bus ride. When we got to the departure point, we saw that not all of us were going to fit on the eight-person bus that the excursion company brought. The couples were placed together, and the Port Adventures staff hurriedly brought around an unmarked, nondescript "taxi" for me.*

> As I got in this random car on a random street in a random Mex-
> ican town, my last words to the others were, "Take a good look.
> This is what I was wearing the last time you saw me." Of course,
> I made it to and from the shore excursion just fine, and we all had
> a laugh once we were reunited. But I wouldn't recommend that oth-
> ers do this, especially women traveling alone.

In the (unlikely) event that you're asked to travel alone to a shore
excursion, decline politely. Ask to be accompanied by a staff member
or to be escorted back to the ship. Along the same lines, if you're not
comfortable walking back to your stateroom at night, ask a member
of the crew to escort you. And use extra caution walking to and from
the parking lot at the cruise terminal.

DCL *"At Large"*

AS WITH ITS THEME PARK GUESTS, Disney realizes that its cruise
guests come in all shapes and sizes and makes many accommodations
to ensure that they're treated well.

Your stateroom's personal flotation devices (PFDs, also known as
life jackets) are designed to fit most bodies. With PFDs, chest size, not
weight, is the measurement that determines proper fit. Disney's PFDs
include a nylon strap that wraps around your body to keep the PFD
snug against your chest. Try on your PFD when you first get to your
stateroom to ensure that the strap fits around your body. If it doesn't,
mention it to your group's leader during the lifeboat drill.

The AquaDuck waterslide on the *Dream* and *Fantasy* seem able to
accommodate virtually all body shapes and sizes. We've heard success
stories from individuals weighing more than 300 pounds and couples
weighing more than 400. The AquaDunk slide on the *Magic* has a
weight limit of 300 pounds.

If an activity or port adventure has a weight limit, it will be printed
in the details describing the activity; look for phrases such as "Guests
must weigh" or "Weight must be" in the activity's listing. Some shore
excursions, including kayaking and some scuba and snorkeling trips,
have weight limits of 240 or 300 pounds per person. Segway tours
generally accommodate persons of up to 250 pounds. Other activities
have weight limits of up to 350 pounds per person. Again, check the
activity's details for more information, or check with the Port Adventures desk on board.

Ask for bench seating or chairs without arms at restaurants and
lounges. If you don't see them, the staff should be able to provide one.

Wear comfortable shoes. You'll be surprised at the amount of
walking you do on board the ship, not to mention the walking you'll
do from the cruise terminal to the ship.

DCL *for* EXPECTANT MOMS

DISNEY PROHIBITS MOTHERS-TO-BE FROM SAILING if they will reach their 24th week of pregnancy at any time during the cruise. For example, a woman who is 23 weeks pregnant would not be allowed by Disney to take a 12-night transatlantic cruise. In addition, note that if you're flying to or from your cruise, airlines may have their own, different policies regarding pregnant travelers.

On board, the AquaDuck and AquaDunk waterslides are off-limits to expectant mothers, as is the waterslide at Castaway Cay. Other shore excursions, such as scuba activities, off-road driving, and parasailing, also prohibit expectant mothers from participating. In addition, some tour operators have restrictions on snorkeling and dolphin encounters.

Talk to your doctor about any shore excursions you plan to take. Also note that some excursions require lengthy drives on pothole-strewn roads, some of them dirt, gravel, or sand, in vehicles that have seen years of use. Even if all you're planning to do is relax on a beach, the drive to get there may be bumpy enough to make you reconsider going.

DCL *for* SENIORS

MOST SENIORS FIND A DISNEY CRUISE less tiring than a Walt Disney World vacation. First, most seniors find considerably less walking required on the ship versus the parks. Second, the ships' adults-only areas provide a break from children (and their families) when needed. And even the most energetic onboard attraction, the AquaDuck, isn't as intense as a ride on Space Mountain or Big Thunder Mountain Railroad.

Because of their flexible schedules, retirees can often take advantage of off-peak cruise fares, especially during fall or spring, when the weather is nicest and crowds are lower because school is in session. If you're cruising to the Caribbean, the Bahamas, or Mexico, be sure to bring a jacket and sweater along with your warm-weather clothing—while temperature averages hover around 70°F in most of those locations, a cold front can drop temps into the upper 40s with little notice, and it's not uncommon to have morning temperatures in the lower 50s.

GUESTS *with* DISABILITIES

DCL STRIVES TO MAKE ITS SHIPS ACCESSIBLE TO ALL. Virtually the entire ship, from staterooms to restaurants to nightclubs and pools, is wheelchair- and ECV-friendly. More accommodations are available for other special needs too. This section describes each of those in more detail. Call DCL's Accessibility Desk at ☎ 407-566-3500 (voice) or 407-566-7455 (TTY) for specific questions.

Stateroom Furnishings

In addition to the standard amenities offered in each stateroom, Disney offers the following special equipment for guests with disabilities:

• Close-captioned TV (most stations)	• Raised toilet seat	• Shower stool
• Bed boards and rails	• Refrigerator	• Transfer benches
• Portable toilet	• Rubber bed pads	
• A Stateroom Communication Kit, including an alarm clock, door knock and phone alerts, phone amplifier, bed-shaker notification, strobe-light smoke detector, and text typewriter (TTY)		

WHEELCHAIR AND ECV USERS DCL suggests that guests using a wheelchair or ECV request a wheelchair-accessible stateroom or suite. Found on every Disney ship, wheelchair-accessible staterooms include the following features:

• Doorways at least 32 inches wide	• Fold-down shower seating and hand-held showerheads	• Open bed frame for easier entry and exit
• Bathroom and shower handrails	• Lowered towel and closet bars	• Ramped bathroom thresholds
• Emergency call buttons and additional phones in the bath and stateroom		

One advantage to having an accessible stateroom is that its wider door lets you store your wheelchair or ECV inside your cabin when it's not in use. This also makes it easier to recharge the equipment when needed. If you find yourself in a standard stateroom whose door won't fit your vehicle, you may be asked to park the vehicle in a designated area elsewhere on the ship, even at night. In practice, we've seen many ECVs parked in a corner of each deck's elevator-landing areas. Chances are that your vehicle will be stored within a short walk of your cabin.

Outside of your stateroom, special areas are set aside at most ship activities for guests in wheelchairs. At the Walt Disney Theatre, for example, Disney cast members direct guests in wheelchairs to a reserved seating area. Shops, restaurants, bars, and nightclubs are all accessible, and accessible restrooms are available throughout the ship's public areas. A limited number of sand wheelchairs are available on Castaway Cay too, on a first-come, first-served basis.

Note that DCL's pools require a transfer from wheelchair to use. For this reason, Disney recommends that guests in wheelchairs travel with someone who can help transfer them to and from the wheelchair.

Another area to be aware of is tendering from ship to shore. Some ports, such as the one at Grand Cayman, aren't deep enough to accommodate large cruise ships such as Disney's. When DCL ships anchor at

Grand Cayman, smaller boats, or tenders, pull up next to the ship, and guests board them for travel to and from Grand Cayman.

Some tenders use steps instead of ramps to get guests on board. In those cases, wheelchair passengers must use the steps. Also keep in mind that the Disney ship and tender craft both float freely in the ocean. It's not uncommon for the stairs to move 2 or 3 feet up and down during the course of a transfer. If the seas are too rough, wheelchair guests may be denied transfer.

SIGHT- AND HEARING-IMPAIRED GUESTS In addition to closed-captioning TVs, assistive listening devices and printed scripts are available for shows at the ships' main theaters and show stages. Stop by the Guest Services desk to pick those up. In addition, American Sign Language interpreters are available for live performances on some cruise dates.

CHILDREN WITH DISABILITIES Disney's youth programs are open to special-needs children ages 3–17. All children must be toilet-trained and able to play well with kids who are about their same age and size.

The number of children who can participate is limited and is based on the number of available counselors, the number of other children in the programs, the number of special-needs children already enrolled, and the specific needs of the child wishing to enroll. Check with the Youth Activities team when you get on board for more details. Disney is unable to provide youth counselors for medical attention, one-on-one care, or training for a specific need.

PORT ADVENTURES Many Port Adventures have requirements concerning mobility. These are noted in the Port Adventure descriptions. You may also inquire about which activities are available to you at the Port Adventures desk while on board.

Other amenities, such as disabled parking at the cruise terminal, are also available. See DCL's Guests with Disabilities FAQ (**tinyurl .com/dclguestswithdisabilities**) for more information.

DIETARY RESTRICTIONS

WITH ENOUGH ADVANCE NOTICE, DCL's sit-down restaurants can accommodate a wide variety of special dietary needs, including low-sodium, kosher, and allergen-free requests, at no additional cost. The best way to communicate these needs to Disney is through the Special Services Information Form, available when you check in online (see page 19). Disney asks that the form be submitted by e-mail, fax, or snail mail at least 30 days before your cruise. Note that counter-service restaurants and room service usually can't accommodate special requests, although some allergies, such as gluten, are more easily accommodated. If you book through a travel agent, he or she can make a note of this on your reservation. You should also let your serving team (including the head server) know your requirements on the first night of your cruise.

SMOKING *on* BOARD

SMOKING, INCLUDING CIGARETTES, CIGARS, PIPES, and electronic cigarettes, is prohibited in your stateroom, on your stateroom's outdoor verandah (if it has one), and any indoor space on the ship. On the *Magic* and *Wonder,* outdoor smoking areas are available on Deck 4 starboard (right side of the ship) between 6 p.m. and 6 a.m., and on Decks 9 and 10 starboard, excluding the Mickey Pool area.

Smoking areas on the *Dream* and *Fantasy* are on the port (left) side of Deck 4 Aft, also from 6 p.m. to 6 a.m.; the port side of Deck 12 Aft, accessed by walking through the Meridian Lounge; and near the Currents Bar on Deck 13 Forward, port side.

TRAVELING *with* MEDICATION

IF YOU'RE BRINGING PRESCRIPTION MEDICINE on your cruise, your best bet is to transport it in its original containers. The problem you're trying to avoid isn't one with Disney's security staff, but the customs staffs of the countries you're visiting and US border control when you return. While it's unlikely, those folks may ask to see either the original containers (with your name on them) or a copy of a valid prescription, to ensure that you're not importing illegal or prohibited substances. We also recommend that you keep these medicines in your carry-on bag instead of checked luggage. Finally, note that Disney's onboard Health Center may not to be able to refill prescriptions (especially for controlled substances) that run out during your cruise, so get them refilled before you leave home.

FRIENDS *of* BILL W.

BEER, WINE, AND SPIRITS flow freely on cruise ships, even those run by Disney. Daily **Alcoholics Anonymous** meetings are available on each cruise. While the time and location may vary, they're generally found here:

- 8:30 a.m. at Animator's Palate on the *Magic*
- 8:30 a.m. at the Cadillac Lounge on the *Wonder*
- 8:30 a.m. at the Outlook Lounge on the *Dream* and *Fantasy*

PART SIX

THE SHIPS
at a GLANCE

OVERVIEW *and*
OUR RECOMMENDATIONS

LAUNCHED IN 1998, the *Magic* holds roughly 2,700 passengers and 950 crew members. The *Wonder* has the same capacity and was launched in 1999. The *Dream* and *Fantasy*, which took their maiden voyages in 2011 and 2012, respectively, hold up to 4,000 passengers and 1,450 crew. The *Magic* and *Wonder* are the workhorses of the fleet: The *Magic* covers everything from Mexico to the Mediterranean, while the *Wonder* plies the seas from Alaska to the Caribbean.

All four ships share sleek lines, twin smokestacks, and nautical styling that calls to mind classic ocean liners, but with instantly recognizable Disney signatures. The colors—black, white, red, and yellow—and the famous face-and-ears silhouette on the stacks are clearly those of Mickey Mouse. Look closely at the *Magic*'s stern ornamentation, for example, and you'll see a 15-foot Goofy hanging by his overalls. (It's Donald on the *Wonder*'s stern, Mickey on the *Dream*'s, and Dumbo on the *Fantasy*'s.)

Interiors combine nautical themes with Art Nouveau and Art Deco inspiration. (Art Nouveau incorporates natural shapes, such as from plants and animals, into its geometric designs; Art Deco has the geometry without the nature.) Disney images are everywhere, from Mickey's profile in the wrought-iron balustrades to the bronze statue of Helmsman Mickey featured prominently in the *Magic*'s atrium, Ariel in the *Wonder*, Admiral Donald on the *Dream*, and Mademoiselle Minnie in full flapper style on the *Fantasy*. Disney art is on every

> *unofficial* **TIP**
> When it comes to choosing a ship, you'll do well with either the *Dream* or the *Fantasy*. We recommend going with whichever has the price or itinerary to meet your needs.

Continued on page 72

Disney Magic / Wonder *Deck Plans*

DECK 1   DECK 2   DECK 3   DECK 4

DECK 5   DECK 6   DECK 7   DECK 8

Continued on next page

Disney Magic / Wonder *Deck Plans (cont'd.)*

DECK 11

DECK 9

DECK 10

Disney Dream/Fantasy *Deck Plans*

DECK 1   **DECK 2**   **DECK 3**   **DECK 4**

Continued on next page

Disney Dream / Fantasy *Deck Plans (cont'd.)*

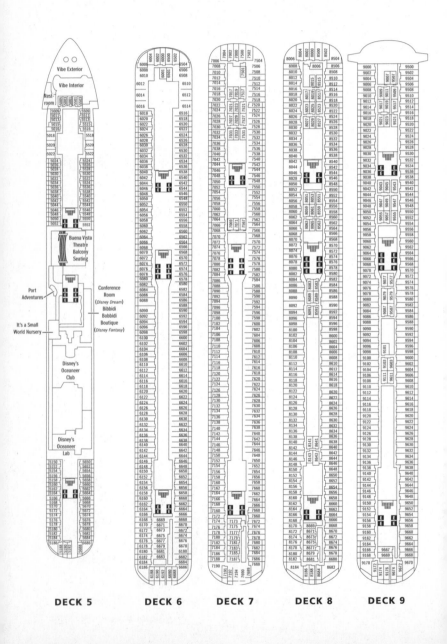

DECK 5   DECK 6   DECK 7   DECK 8   DECK 9

DECK 14

DECK 10

DECK 11

DECK 12

DECK 13

Continued from page 65

wall and in every stairwell and corridor. A grand staircase on each ship sweeps from the atrium lobby to shops peddling Disney Cruise Line–themed clothing, collectibles, jewelry, sundries, and more.

Ships have two lower decks with cabins, three decks with dining rooms and showrooms, and then three or five upper decks of cabins. Two sports and sun decks offer separate pools and facilities for families and for adults without children. Signs point toward lounges and facilities, and all elevators are clearly marked as Forward, Aft, or Midship.

Our main complaint concerning the ships' design is that outdoor public areas focus inward toward the pools instead of seaward, as if Disney wants you to forget that you're on a cruise liner. On the *Magic* and the *Wonder,* there's no public place where you can curl up in the shade and watch the ocean—at least not without a Plexiglas wall between you and it. On Deck 4 of the *Dream* and the *Fantasy,* however, an open promenade, complete with comfy deck chairs, circles the ship. It's shady and fairly well protected from wind, and it offers the opportunity to sit back and enjoy the sea without your having to look through Plexiglas barriers.

Speaking of Plexiglas, a predictable but nonetheless irritating design characteristic is the extensive childproofing. There's enough Plexiglas on all four ships to build a subdivision of see-through homes. On the pool decks especially, it feels as if the ships are hermetically sealed. Plus, verandah doors have a two-part locking mechanism, with one of the two parts 6 feet off the floor—causing even adults occasional consternation in trying to operate them.

unofficial **TIP**
Disney ships have no casinos or libraries.

FEATURES FOUND ON EVERY DCL SHIP

EVERY DISNEY SHIP INCLUDES a common set of amenities, including the following:

• Adult pool and deck areas	• Movie theater
• Bars, lounges, and cafés	• Outdoor basketball court, shuffleboard, and other sports areas
• Buffet restaurant	• Outdoor LED screen for movies, concerts, and videos
• Family pools and water-play areas	• **Palo,** an upscale Italian restaurant
• Fitness center	• Photo gallery for purchasing onboard photos
• Full-service spa and salon, with sauna	• Retail shopping, including duty-free alcohol
• Guest Services desk	• Theater for live performances
• Health Center	• Video-game arcade
• Infant, child, tween, and teen clubs	

Some ships offer amenities not found on others. The *Dream* and *Fantasy,* for example, have the following features not found on the *Magic* or *Wonder:*

- **AquaDuck** waterslide (the *Magic* has an **AquaDunk** slide, but it's significantly different)
- **Chill Spa** for teens (the *Magic* has a couple of treatment rooms branded as Chill Spa, but the two versions are vastly different)
- Dedicated Champagne bar (**Pink** on the *Dream,* **Ooh La La** on the *Fantasy*)
- **Remy,** an upscale French restaurant
- **Meridian,** a martini bar
- **Midship Detective Agency,** an interactive attraction for kids
- Miniature-golf course
- Separate decks for concierge rooms
- **Skyline** bar

Each ship has a few unique features too. The *Fantasy* has **Satellite Falls,** an adults-only splash pool and sun deck on Deck 13, and **Bibbidi Bobbidi Boutique** on Deck 5, providing makeovers for small children. The *Wonder* is the only ship with **Outlook Café,** a windowed indoor coffee bar–lounge on Deck 10 that's perfect for keeping warm while enjoying the views on Alaskan cruises.

RANKING THE SHIPS

IF YOUR CRUISE DESTINATION is the Bahamas or the Caribbean, one choice you'll have is whether to sail on either the *Magic* and *Wonder* or on the *Dream* and *Fantasy.* Ignoring the different itineraries each ship serves, here's how we rank the Disney ships:

1. *Fantasy*   **2.** *Dream*   **3.** *Magic*   **4.** *Wonder*

The *Fantasy* and *Dream* have better restaurants, bars, and pools than the older ships, plus more on-deck activities, more space for children's activities, more deck space for tanning, better spas, and more interactive games. These advantages make up for the slightly smaller cabin sizes on the *Dream* and *Fantasy,* whose nonconcierge staterooms are 2–9% (5–22 square feet) smaller than corresponding cabins on the *Magic* and *Wonder.* Another, minor downside: Because the newer ships carry more passengers, Castaway Cay is more crowded when they're in port.

We rank the *Fantasy* highest because of its **Skyline** bar, **The Tube** lounge, and the onboard interactive games. The *Magic*'s new **After Hours** lounge area replaces Beat Street, which in theme and execution was one of the ship's weak spots; in particular, the transformation of Rockin' Bar D into **Fathoms** improved both the theming and the bar menu. Minor changes to **Keys,** the piano bar formerly known as Sessions, and to **O'Gills Pub,** formerly Diversions, are welcome, albeit more cosmetic.

The *Wonder,* though ranked last, does have the **Outlook Café** on Deck 10, which the *Magic* does not. It's wonderful for reading, lounging, or sightseeing in cold weather.

The DISNEY MAGIC

THE FIRST DCL SHIP, the *Magic* was launched in 1998 and underwent an extensive renovation (or reimagining, in Disney-speak) during a two-month dry dock in Cadiz, Spain, during the summer of 2013. Major changes included the following:

- **After Hours,** a rethreming of the *Magic's* nightlife area, formerly known as Beat Street and one of the ship's weakest areas
- The new **AquaDunk** vertical-start waterslide. You begin by standing on top of a trapdoor, and then plunge down almost vertically before spinning through a couple of turns and sliding to a stop on the main deck.
- A rethemed buffet, **Cabanas,** on Deck 9
- **Carioca's,** a new Brazilian-themed restaurant—a big improvement over the dismal Parrot Cay
- A rethemed **Nephews' Pool,** the **Twist 'n' Spout** waterslide, the **AquaLab** water-play area for older kids, and the **Nephews' Splash Zone** water-play area for toddlers
- Newly rethemed **Oceaneer Club** and **Oceaneer Lab** kids' clubs, including the new Marvel Avengers Academy in the Oceaneer Lab
- A new Irish-themed sports bar, **O'Gills,** replacing the generic Diversions sports bar
- Newly refurbished retail shops
- A new stage show, *Walt Disney: The Dream Goes On*

The makeover also includes cosmetic updates to the *Magic's* lobby atrium; Keys (formerly Sessions), the piano bar; Palo, an adults-only, fine-dining Italian restaurant; and Fathoms (formerly Rockin' Bar D), the dance club. In addition, Vista Spa was changed to Senses Spa.

The DISNEY WONDER

LAUNCHED IN 1999, the second of Disney's four ships is in a bad situation for 2014 and beyond. With the *Magic* out of dry dock and with the *Dream* and *Fantasy* having launched in 2011 and 2012, respectively, the *Wonder* is now the "oldest" ship in the fleet, and it shows. By no means is the ship falling apart, but the wear and tear is especially evident compared with the condition of the other three ships. That said, there are deals to be found on the *Wonder,* and it's the only Disney ship serving Alaska and the California coast.

The *Wonder* went into a 10-day dry dock in January 2014, and we look forward to reviewing its improvements. We also expect the ship to undergo a more extended refurbishment at some point in the future to bring it in line with the *Dream, Fantasy,* and *Magic.* The timing of this is more dependent on work being done on the Panama Canal than on Disney's schedules—increasing the size of the ship would not allow it to fit the locks as they currently stand, making it impossible for the ship to return to Alaska.

The *Wonder* is nearly identical to the pre-2013 version of the *Magic,* with slightly different theming for the restaurants and lounges. When you board the ship at Deck 3, you're greeted by Ariel instead of Mickey and an Art Nouveau–style atrium rather than Art Deco. Following the *Little Mermaid* theme, one of the standard rotational-dining restaurants on the *Wonder* is **Triton's** (on the *Magic,* its counterpart is the *Beauty and the Beast*–themed **Lumiere's**).

From a technological standpoint, the *Wonder* is missing many of the features of the newer ships. There's no waterslide like the **AquaDuck** (*Dream* and *Fantasy*) or **AquaDunk** (*Magic*) on the pool deck. Though each ship has a restaurant called Animator's Palate, the version on the *Wonder* doesn't have the interactive show as do the restaurants on the other ships. Inside staterooms are missing the virtual portholes found on the *Dream* and *Fantasy,* and there is no interactive artwork or Midship Detective Agency in the corridors.

There is little to differentiate the restaurants on the *Wonder* from those on the *Magic,* though it does still have our two least favorite dining venues on any Disney ship: **Beach Blanket Buffet** and **Parrot Cay.** **Palo** remains a great choice for adults. We would choose (and have chosen) to dine there every night if there's availability.

Like all the ships in the fleet, the *Wonder* has impeccably themed kids' areas. We know your brood will have a great time no matter what their age.

The *Wonder* splits its time among Alaska, the California coast, and the Caribbean; repositioning cruises also take it through the Panama Canal. It sets sail from Miami, San Diego, and Vancouver.

Our favorite spot on the Wonder is the **Outlook Café,** just up the stairs from the Cove Café.

The **DISNEY DREAM**

FOLLOWING THE SUCCESS OF THE *MAGIC* AND *WONDER,* DCL ordered two new ships that would more than double the number of guests they could serve, allow them to expand the number of itineraries offered, and bring several first-evers to a cruise ship. The new

Dream-class vessels were built by Meyer Werft in Germany rather than Italy's Fincantieri, which created the *Magic* and *Wonder*.

The *Disney Dream*, the first of these new ships, set sail in 2011. It's 151 feet longer, 35 feet taller, and 15 feet wider than the *Magic* or *Wonder*. With three additional passenger decks, the ship can hold 50% more passengers and crew than its predecessors, yet it still has the classic lines of the smaller ships.

Disney Imagineering had a lot of fun designing the second-generation ships. Inside cabins were given virtual portholes, which show the view from the bridge on a round screen. This feature proved so popular with kids that on many cruises, interior cabins had fares higher than those of ocean-view cabins. On the top deck, the **AquaDuck**, a waterslide that circles the ship, was added to the usual pools. Between the pool deck and your cabin, you'll find interactive art that reacts when you pass by it, along with the **Midship Detective Agency**, a scavenger hunt–type game that sends families all over the ship collecting clues.

Restaurants were given a huge makeover. The dreadful Topsiders (formerly on the *Magic*) and Beach Blanket Buffet (on the *Wonder*) were replaced with **Cabanas**, a new buffet that improved on both traffic flow and food quality. **Animator's Palate** remained on board but was plussed up with new technology as part of the dinner show. The mediocre Parrot Cay became **Enchanted Garden,** the prettiest of the main dining rooms on board. Finally, Lumiere's (*Magic*) and Triton's (*Wonder*) were reimagined as **Royal Palace,** a tribute to all things Disney princess, but mostly Cinderella.

Both adults and kids scored big with improvements to the new ship. In addition to the adults-only Palo, **Remy** was added as another upscale-dining option for the 18-and-up crowd. With a subtle *Ratatouille* theme, and not one, but two celebrated chefs creating the menus, Remy initially shocked cruisers with its surcharge—$75 plus wine per diner, the highest in the industry—but diners were pleased nonetheless. The adult lounges, in the area called **The District** on Deck 4, provide more-intimate, better-themed spaces to take the edge off than the old Beat Street on the *Magic* and Route 66 on the *Wonder*. **Skyline,** one of The District's bars, showcases a great use of technology, with a cityscape behind the bar that changes every 15 minutes. It's mesmerizing.

unofficial **TIP**
We recommend the *Dream* or *Fantasy* over the *Magic* and *Wonder* to travelers who are more concerned with the ships and dining than the itineraries of their cruises.

Senses Spa replaced the Vista Spa and outdid it in every way.

Kids got greatly expanded club areas with a Pixar theme. The teen area got a makeover that left it one of the most stylish spaces on board and gave it its own pool (the cast-member pool area from the older ships). Teens also got their own pampering spot, **Chill Spa.**

Some categories of cabins are a few square feet larger or smaller than their equivalents on the *Magic* and *Wonder,* but all (as does the *Magic* after its refurbishment) have nicer furnishings and linens than the *Wonder.*

In spite of all this, the *Dream* feels different yet very familiar to people coming to it from the *Magic* or *Wonder*—kind of like seeing Walt Disney World after going to Disneyland. The theme is still Art Deco. The Cove Café still serves great coffee. Most of the shows are still not worth your time.

The **DISNEY FANTASY**

THE *FANTASY* SAILED ITS MAIDEN VOYAGE in 2012, one year after the *Dream* came into service. The ship is nearly identical to its sister but has some tweaks as a result of guest and cast-member feedback. Both the *Dream* and the *Fantasy* are based out of Port Canaveral and sail the Caribbean. While the *Dream* has mostly three- and four-night itineraries, the *Fantasy* is almost exclusively seven-night sailings.

Walking into the atrium of the *Fantasy,* you see a bronze statue of Minnie Mouse and a striking peacock-inspired carpet—an indication of the Art Nouveau style of the *Fantasy* as opposed to the *Dream*'s Deco look. A glance up to Deck 5 reveals one of the Fantasy's "improvements" over the *Dream*—the **Bibbidi Bobbidi Boutique**—that came in response to parents' desires to spend more money on board.

The *Dream*'s technology package got some enhancements on the *Fantasy.* The **Midship Detective Agency** has three different story lines (including the Muppets) for folks to experience, and the show at **Animator's Palate** got a very cool audience-interaction element that we won't spoil here. Other than this addition, the restaurants are identical to the *Dream*'s, with one subtle name change: Royal Palace is **Royal Court** and includes even more princess-y goodness. **Cabanas, Enchanted Garden, Palo,** and **Remy** are the same.

On the pool deck, the **AquaDuck** adds the **AquaLab** splash area, and adults get **Satellite Falls**, a quiet water feature on Deck 13 Forward.

The *Fantasy*'s nightlife area is **Europa. Skyline** is the one constant between the two bar-nightclub areas on the ships, though it displays different cityscapes in this rendition. **The Tube**'s *Austin Powers*–style decor makes it a very fun place to hang out, but **Ooh La La** is either too high-concept or low-concept for our tastes; we prefer the whimsical look of the *Dream*'s **Pink** for our Champagne needs. **O'Gills** doesn't feel particularly Irish, though it has the same big-screen TVs as **687,** the sports bar on the *Dream.*

PART SEVEN

DINING

NOSHES, NOSHES EVERYWHERE

THE FIRST THING MANY FOLKS DISCOVER when exploring the ships on embarkation day is the buffet. In the way that some people remember the birth of their first child, we remember our first look at the spread at Cabanas. (Sorry, Hannah. Love, Dad.) On one table sat crab legs in a pile that almost reached eye level. Next to it sat a trawler's worth of peel-and-eat shrimp. Surrounding these were tubs of melted butter and enough cocktail sauce to float the ship itself. On the other side of the aisle, a chef was flash-cooking a steak, the spices, sizzle, and flame making the air smell savory. It was glorious.

You'll never go hungry on a Disney cruise. The variety of dining options is staggering, including everything from coffee shops and pizza stands to Vegas-size buffets to ritzy French and Italian restaurants. That said, we've learned a few ways to increase your chances of enjoying memorable meals on board. This section describes your dining options in detail and includes our advice on how to make the most of them.

ROTATIONAL DINING

ONE OF THE INNOVATIONS that Disney Cruise Line (DCL) brought to the cruise industry is the concept of rotational dining, in which you visit one of three standard restaurants on a different night of your cruise. As you change from restaurant to restaurant, your server team—your waiter, beverage person, head waiter, and maître d'—all move with you. Your team will quickly learn your dining proclivities, including preferred drinks and favorite desserts, and make menu suggestions. Along with your stateroom attendant, you'll almost certainly rely on your dining team more than any other member of the crew during your trip.

The rotational restaurants have two dinner seatings, typically 5:45 p.m. and 8:15 p.m. Because Disney sets the schedule, there's no need to make reservations each night. You can request either the earlier or later seating when booking your trip or once aboard the ship. You can also request changes to your rotation, specifying which restaurants you visit each night.

You'll repeat at least one of the three standard restaurants on cruises of four nights and longer. Rather than visit the same restaurant twice on a four-night cruise, we recommend using one of those nights to visit Palo (on any ship) or Remy (on the *Dream* and *Fantasy*). You must pay an additional charge to dine at these restaurants, but the food is stellar, the crowds are small, and the service is impeccable.

Another, less formal (and less expensive) option to rotational dining is the dinner buffet on each ship. Finally, at least one of the rotational restaurants is open for breakfast and lunch each day. Check your *Personal Navigator* for details.

DCL RESTAURANT CATEGORIES

IN GENERAL, FOOD OFFERINGS on Disney Cruise Line are differentiated by freshness, quality, and service:

unofficial **TIP**
DCL restaurants (except Palo and Remy, naturally) have kids' menus for breakfast, lunch, and dinner. Kids (except for infants in the nursery) may also dine in their club areas free of charge.

COUNTER SERVICE Available on each ship's pool deck, fast food includes staples such as burgers, chicken strips, pizza, and sandwiches. In *The Unofficial Guide to Walt Disney World*, we equate the quality of the counter-service restaurants in the theme parks with that of McDonald's and Taco Bell. With a few exceptions, the food quality at DCL's counter-service restaurants is more like what you'd find in your local supermarket's frozen-food aisle: edible but not as good as something made from scratch (or even at McDonald's). The best items on board are the fresh sandwiches and wraps and, if your timing is right, pizza straight from the oven. A complete list of counter-service restaurants by ship begins on page 83.

CAFÉS AND LOUNGES Each ship has a dedicated coffee bar called **Cove Café** that serves espresso, cappuccino, teas, and smoothies, plus wine, mixed drinks, and spirits. A good alternative to a big dinner is Cove Café's small selection of complimentary cold appetizers, available each evening.

Besides Cove Café, a few of the ships' bars and lounges serve appetizers too. These are described in detail in Part Eight, Entertainment and Nightlife.

BUFFETS Each ship has at least one large buffet, usually open for breakfast and lunch. Buffets tend to serve a bit of everything at each meal and are the easiest way to satisfy disparate appetites. The buffets at **Cabanas** on the *Magic, Dream,* and *Fantasy* are as large and diverse as those at many Las Vegas hotels. Besides offering variety, buffets let picky kids see exactly what food they're getting. They also offer plenty of seating with ocean views, indoors and out.

FULL-SERVICE RESTAURANTS Each Disney ship has four or five full-service restaurants. Three of these are part of the standard rotational-dinner schedule available to every guest on the ship.

ADULT DINING The upscale Italian restaurant **Palo,** found on each ship and for which Disney charges an additional fee of $25, serves dinner to cruisers 18 and older. The *Dream* and *Fantasy* have a fifth restaurant, **Remy,** which serves high-end French cuisine and levies a $75 surcharge. Both Palo and Remy serve brunch on selected sea days (still adults-only). Both are also difficult to get into, so book a table at **disneycruise.com** at least 75 days before you sail. See the next page for more information.

Along with dinner, one sit-down restaurant is usually open for breakfast and lunch each day, even when the ship is in port. Breakfast and lunch may include both a buffet and the option to order from a menu.

Virtually all of the food served at the rotational restaurants will be familiar to American palates. Most dishes, especially at dinner, feature cuts of steak, chicken, and fish no different from those you'd find at a chain eatery. DCL's chefs will add some sort of flavor twist to these, such as soy and sesame if it's an Asian-themed restaurant, but the basic ingredients will be recognizable to almost everyone.

Although fresher and of higher quality than the counter-service restaurants, most of the food served at the full-service restaurants is prepared well ahead of time. You get your order faster this way, but it's also well-nigh impossible to customize that order. We've been told, for instance, that we couldn't order a roast-beef-and-mayo sandwich without the mayo. If you're a moderately finicky eater, you can do the customizing yourself, provided your dish consists of discrete ingredients that you can subtract easily. A BLT without lettuce is probably doable; tomato-and-basil soup sans the basil probably isn't.

THEME NIGHTS

ON CRUISES OF LONGER THAN THREE NIGHTS, DCL adds themed dinners. These include a Pirates' menu (somewhat Caribbean-influenced, on Pirate Night), Till We Meet Again (the last night of your cruise), the Captain's Gala, and Prince and Princess menus. The menus available on your cruise will depend on your itinerary. On these nights, each main dining area serves the same menu.

DRESS CODE

SHORTS AND T-SHIRTS are acceptable at all meals at the standard restaurants, even for adults. We think most adults will feel more appropriately dressed in pants or dresses at dinner; Bermuda shorts paired with a nice button-down shirt and shoes would probably also work.

A mother of four from Midland, Texas, is happy for this shorts-tolerant policy:

unofficial **TIP**
Remy's dress code requires a tuxedo or jacket for men, along with dress pants. Ties are optional. Acceptable women's attire includes evening gowns, cocktail dresses, blouses and skirts, and pantsuits.

unofficial **TIP**
If you don't have any fancy duds handy, you can rent them before you leave home by visiting **Cruise-line Formalwear** (**cruiselineformalwear .com**). Your garments will be delivered directly to your stateroom, and you'll return them to your stateroom attendant at the end of your cruise.

There was no way I was going to pack 8–10 pairs of pants—minimum!—for my kids and my husband for our seven-night cruise. Shorts take up less luggage space and can be worn all day. It's less laundry for me to do when we get home too.

Swimwear and tank tops are prohibited at any time, and frankly you'd be freezing for most of your meal.

The dress code at Palo is more upscale: dress pants and long-sleeved shirt or jacket for men; dress, blouse and skirt, or pantsuit for women. Athletic shoes, flip-flops, blue jeans, shorts, and capris aren't permitted, though we've seen women in black jeans paired with a smashing jacket and fabulous shoes.

MAKING RESERVATIONS

NO RESERVATIONS ARE REQUIRED for any night at any of the three standard rotational-dining restaurants. Reservations are required for Palo and Remy and can be made up to 120 days in advance in some circumstances. Reserve online at the DCL Planning Center (see page 19).

CATEGORY	DAYS IN ADVANCE RESERVATIONS CAN BE MADE
Guests in suites or concierge staterooms	**120 DAYS**
Platinum Castaway Club members	**120 DAYS**
Gold Castaway Club members	**105 DAYS**
Silver Castaway Club members	**90 DAYS**
All other guests	**75 DAYS**

FULL-SERVICE RESTAURANTS: RATED AND RANKED

TO HELP YOU MAKE YOUR DINING CHOICES, we've developed profiles of DCL's sit-down restaurants, listed alphabetically by restaurant following each ship's counter-service-dining coverage. The profiles allow you to quickly check a given restaurant's cuisine, star rating, quality rating, and specialties.

STAR RATING The star rating represents the entire dining experience: style, service, and ambiance, in addition to the taste, presentation, and quality of the food. Five stars is the highest rating and indicates that the restaurant offers the best of everything. Four-star restaurants are above average; three-star restaurants offer good, though not necessarily memorable, meals. Two-star restaurants serve mediocre fare. (No DCL restaurants merit one star.) Our star ratings don't correspond to ratings awarded by AAA, Mobil, Zagat, or other restaurant reviewers.

QUALITY RATING The food quality is rated on a scale of one to five stars, five being the best rating attainable. The quality rating is based on the taste, freshness of ingredients, preparation, presentation, and creativity of the food served. Price is not a consideration. If you want the best food available and cost is not an issue, you need look no further than the quality ratings.

DCL Rotational Restaurants by Cuisine

RESTAURANT	SHIP	OVERALL RATING	QUALITY RATING
AMERICAN/ASIAN			
Animator's Palate	All	★★★	★★★
AMERICAN/BRAZILIAN			
Carioca's	Magic	★★★	★★★
AMERICAN/CARIBBEAN			
Parrot Cay	Wonder	★★	★★
AMERICAN/CONTINENTAL			
Enchanted Garden	Dream, Fantasy	★★★	★★★
AMERICAN/FRENCH			
Lumiere's	Magic	★★★	★★★
Royal Court	Fantasy	★★★	★★★
Royal Palace	Dream	★★★	★★★
Triton's	Wonder	★★★	★★★
BUFFET			
Cabanas	Dream, Fantasy, Magic	★★★	★★★
Beach Blanket Buffet	Wonder	★★½	★★½

DCL Adult-Only Restaurants by Cuisine

CUISINE	SHIP	OVERALL RATING	QUALITY RATING	VALUE RATING
FRENCH				
Remy	Dream, Fantasy	★★★★½	★★★★½	★★★★½
ITALIAN				
Palo	All	★★★½* / ★★★★★**	★★★½* / ★★★★★**	★★★½* / ★★★★★**

*Magic, Wonder   **Dream, Fantasy

DISNEY MAGIC DINING

COUNTER-SERVICE RESTAURANTS
Daisy's De-Lites

QUALITY B   **PORTION Small–Medium**   **LOCATION Deck 9 Aft**

WHEN TO GO Typical hours: breakfast, 6:30 a.m.–9 a.m.; lunch, 11 a.m.–6:30 p.m. Check your *Personal Navigator* for exact schedule.

SELECTIONS Breakfast includes pastries, croissants, muffins, and yogurt; lunch offerings include sandwiches, wraps, salads, fruit, and cookies.

COMMENTS A good alternative to the breakfast buffet if all you're looking for is a few croissants and some coffee. The wraps are small and tasty and make an excellent snack between lunch and dinner. *Note:* Daisy's De-Lites was named Goofy's Galley before the *Magic*'s 2013 dry dock.

Pete's Boiler Bites

QUALITY B   PORTION Medium   LOCATION Deck 9 Aft

WHEN TO GO Typical hours: 11 a.m.–6 p.m. Check your *Personal Navigator* for exact schedule.

SELECTIONS Grilled hot dogs and sausages; hamburgers and veggie burgers; chicken strips; chicken sandwiches; tacos; fries.

COMMENTS The tacos are a surprise find here. A nearby fixin's bar provides toppings for your order.

Pinocchio's Pizzeria

QUALITY C   PORTION Medium   LOCATION Deck 9 Aft

WHEN TO GO Typical hours: 11 a.m.–6 p.m. Check your *Personal Navigator* for exact schedule.

SELECTIONS Cheese, pepperoni, barbecue-chicken, and veggie pizza slices, plus a specialty pizza every day.

COMMENTS About the same quality as frozen pizza . . . but there are plenty of times when that's exactly what you want.

FULL-SERVICE RESTAURANTS

Animator's Palate ★ ★ ★   Deck 4 Aft

AMERICAN/ASIAN   QUALITY ★ ★ ★   SERVICE ★ ★ ★ ★   FRIENDLINESS ★ ★ ★ ★

Reservations Not accepted. **When to go** Dinner. **Bar** Yes. **Alcohol** Red, white, and sparkling wines, plus mixed drinks and spirits. All alcohol costs extra. **Dress** Casual; no tank tops or swimwear. **Hours** Nightly dinner seatings usually at 5:45 and 8:15 p.m.; check your *Personal Navigator* for the exact schedule.

SETTING AND ATMOSPHERE The idea behind Animator's Palate is that you begin dining inside an old-fashioned black-and-white animated film that is slowly colorized as dinner goes along. The entrance's walls are decorated with black charcoal sketches of various Disney characters. Inside, the entire color scheme starts out in black, white, and gray from floor to ceiling, including checkerboard-tile floor, black chairs, white tablecloths with black napkins, and black-and-white uniforms for the waitstaff. Even the ship's support columns are dressed up, in this case as white artist's brushes pointed to the ceiling.

Along the outside wall are video monitors that display images and "how to draw" sketches from Disney films. As the evening progresses, you'll notice bits of color being added to the walls and artwork, eventually becoming fully saturated by the end of your meal.

Animator's Palate on the *Magic* will receive an upgrade during summer 2014, adding the *Animation Magic* dinner show that debuted on the

Fantasy. At the beginning of your second night's dinner at Animator's Palate, you're given a sheet of paper and crayon and told to draw a self-portrait. At the end of the evening, all of the diners' self-portraits are shown in an animated cartoon similar to Disney's 1929 short cartoon *The Skeleton Dance.*

HOUSE SPECIALTIES Vegetable stir-fry; roasted-garlic or red-pepper dip with bread.

COMMENTS Disney characterizes the cuisine at Animator's Palate as Pacific Rim/American, but it's really just standard chain-restaurant fare. There are probably as many Italian selections—pasta, risotto, focaccia—as Asian. A handful of dishes, such as the vegetable stir-fry, have origins in the East; others are American dishes enrobed in a culinary kimono of sesame, ginger, or teriyaki sauce to make them "Pacific Rim." The food isn't *bad* . . . but neither is it Asian.

Cabanas ★★★ Deck 9 Aft

AMERICAN/BUFFET QUALITY ★★★ SERVICE ★★★★ FRIENDLINESS ★★★★

Reservations Not accepted. **When to go** Breakfast, lunch, and dinner. **Bar** Yes. **Alcohol** Red, white, and sparkling wines, plus mixed drinks and spirits. All alcohol costs extra. **Dress** Casual; no tank tops or swimwear at dinner. **Hours** Daily breakfast buffet, 7–10:45 a.m.; daily lunch buffet, noon–1:30 p.m.; nightly sit-down dinner, 6:30–8:30 p.m. Hours are subject to change, so check your *Personal Navigator* for the exact schedule.

SETTING AND ATMOSPHERE Recently renovated and rethemed, Cabanas is entered from either side of Deck 9 Aft. On either side is a line of buffet tables that run the length of the restaurant. Indoor and outdoor seating are arranged around the buffet. The indoor seating is air-conditioned and features floor-to-ceiling windows, affording excellent ocean views. Outdoor seating is great on mornings when the ship is docking, since you're sometimes able to watch the port come into view. Large murals lining the walls display pirate and fish imagery. Coffee, soft drinks, juices, and water are served from dispensers placed at regular intervals throughout the restaurant.

HOUSE SPECIALTIES Made-to-order omelets for breakfast; lunch seafood bar including oysters, clams, crab legs, and peel-and-eat shrimp.

COMMENTS The breakfast and lunch buffets would be competitive with those at many Las Vegas resorts and serve about as wide a variety of items as you'll find anywhere. Breakfast includes everything from fruit, yogurt, and oatmeal to doughnuts, lox, and custom-made omelets. Even cold cereal has options: Besides the usual cornflakes and granola, there's a "build your own" muesli bar where you can add ingredients ranging from brown sugar to exotic dried fruits. Don't worry if you skipped dessert last night—you can get several at breakfast here. We haven't asked, but we'd bet hard cash that the staff would make you filet mignon if you requested nicely.

Lunch is a similarly lavish spread, with everything from chicken tenders, sandwiches, and burgers to salmon steaks and pasta. A big draw at lunch is the peel-and-eat shrimp, usually complemented by clams, oysters, and crab legs.

Cabanas switches from buffet to sit-down service for dinner. The menu changes frequently, usually along with the menus at the other main restaurants. Appetizers typically include soups and salads, along with meat- and fish-based dishes. Entrées usually include chicken, fish, steak, and vegetarian options. We recommend Cabanas for dinner at sunset on longer cruises, as an alternative to dining a second time at one of the main restaurants, especially Lumiere's.

Carioca's ★ ★ ★   Deck 3 Aft

AMERICAN/BRAZILIAN QUALITY ★ ★ ★ SERVICE ★ ★ ★ ★ FRIENDLINESS ★ ★ ★ ★

Reservations Not accepted. **When to go** Dinner. **Bar** Yes. **Alcohol** A decent selection of reds, whites, and sparkling wines. If you're in the mood for a cocktail, try the berry-flavored Caipirosa. All alcohol costs extra. **Dress** Casual; no tank tops or swimwear at dinner. **Hours** Breakfast buffet on select days, 8:30–10:45 a.m.; lunch buffet on select days (hours vary); nightly dinner seatings usually at 5:30 and 8 p.m. Hours are subject to change, so check your *Personal Navigator* for the exact schedule.

SETTING AND ATMOSPHERE The *Magic*'s newest restaurant, Carioca's is named for José Carioca, one of the three birds in Disney's animated 1944 film *The Three Caballeros.* The word *carioca* is slang for a native of Rio de Janeiro, and so Carioca's theme is Brazilian festival. The restaurant uses lighting effects to transform the setting: When the lighting effects are off at breakfast and lunch, Carioca's interior has a cool white-and-gray floor, white walls, and white tablecloths. Round white lanterns hang from the ceiling, accented by a handful of colorful red, orange, and yellow lights. For dinner, rich yellow and brown lighting transforms the restaurant into a cinnamon-and-gold nightspot. It's a little darker than you'd expect at night, but still way nicer than when it was Parrot Cay.

HOUSE SPECIALTIES The menu also got an overhaul, and it's much improved. Lunch and breakfast are unremarkable American fare—dinner is when Carioca's really shines. The signature dish is the José Carioca's: three grilled skewers of Brazilian sausage, chili-crusted lamb, and beef tenderloin, with a side of tomato-flavored rice and a delicious *chimichurri* sauce (think a South American pesto). The tenderloin and lamb can be a bit dry, but the chimichurri sauce balances it out. At least one person at your table should try this.

The other entrée we really liked—in small bites—was the slow-roasted pork belly, with sides of mashed sweet potato, grits, and collard greens. The pork's skin was incredibly crispy, almost to the point where you'd think it was fried, yet the meat underneath was tender and juicy. Combined with the grits and sweet potatoes, it's almost *too* rich, which is why we suggest ordering this as an entrée for the table to share, with each person also ordering another entrée.

Vegetarian options include corn tortillas with Veracruzan refried-bean dip and a relish of green tomatillo, chile, and shredded white cabbage and carrot. It's not as spicy as the black-bean soup appetizer, which has a touch of habanero pepper, but the tortillas are a filling dish.

Beyond the vegetarian black-bean soup, the other appetizers we like are salads: the tiger shrimp ceviche, with cucumber, cilantro, and tomato-citrus dressing; and the Cuban salad, with avocado, pineapple, toasted Cuban bread, and a tangy cider-vinegar dressing. We'd avoid the ahi-tuna-and-avocado tower—the tuna at Palo is much better.

OTHER RECOMMENDATIONS If you subscribe to the "everything tastes better on a stick" philosophy and you're also in the mood for seafood, try the lobster, shrimp, and mahimahi skewers. These are served on a salad of quinoa (the grain of the moment, judging from how many recipes in which Disney uses it) with dried-mango, pineapple, and toasted-coconut salsa.

COMMENTS We're glad to see the menu improve, and we'd be happy to dine at Carioca's twice on longer sailings.

Lumiere's ★ ★ ★   Deck 3 Midship

AMERICAN/FRENCH   QUALITY ★ ★ ★   SERVICE ★ ★ ★ ★   FRIENDLINESS ★ ★ ★ ★

Reservations Not accepted. **When to go** Breakfast. **Bar** Yes. **Alcohol** Limited selection of red, white, and sparkling wines, plus mixed drinks and spirits. All alcohol costs extra. **Dress** Casual; no tank tops or swimwear at dinner. **Hours** À la carte breakfast on select days, 8–9:30 a.m.; à la carte lunch on select days, 11:45 a.m.–1:30 p.m.; nightly dinner seatings usually at 5:45 and 8:15 p.m. Hours are subject to change, so check your *Personal Navigator* for the exact schedule.

SETTING AND ATMOSPHERE Despite the name, there are only a few references to *Beauty and the Beast* inside the restaurant. The most notable are the light fixtures, which contain a single red rose. There's also a mural on the back wall that depicts characters from the movie. Besides these, most of Lumiere's decor is Art Deco, which makes sense given the restaurant's location, just off the ship's atrium.

HOUSE SPECIALTIES Lobster mac and cheese; crispy roasted duck breast.

COMMENTS Disney puts escargot and French onion soup on the menu of each French-themed standard dining room in the cruise line. Besides these, however, most of the rest of the menu is decidedly un-French, and would be equally at home at your neighborhood TGI Friday's: grilled meats and chicken, a vegetarian tofu selection, and pasta. A couple of entrées, such as the lamb shank and crispy duck breast, stand out. The Grand Marnier soufflé is the most popular dessert, but the brioche bread pudding with toffee sauce is better.

Palo   ★ ★ ★ ½   Deck 10 Aft

ITALIAN   QUALITY ★ ★ ★ ½ VALUE ★ ★ ★ ½ SERVICE ★ ★ ★ ★ ½ FRIENDLINESS ★ ★ ★ ★

Reservations Required. **When to go** Brunch on sea days; dinner nightly. **Bar** Yes. **Alcohol** Large list of Italian wines, listed by region, plus select wines from around the world; mixed drinks and spirits; *limoncello*; grappa; ice wine. All alcohol costs extra. **Dress** Pants and dress shirt or jacket for men; dress, skirt and blouse, or pantsuit for women. No blue jeans, shorts, capris, flip-flops, or athletic shoes. **Hours** Brunch on sea days on cruises of 4 nights or longer, 10 a.m.–12:30 p.m.; nightly dinner, 6 p.m.–8:30 p.m. Hours are subject to change, so check your *Personal Navigator* for the exact schedule.

Special comments An additional $25/person charge will be added to your cruise bill for each meal at Palo. If you need to cancel a reservation, you must do so by 2 p.m. on the day of your reservation, or the full per-person charge will be applied to your bill. Guests must be age 18 and up to dine.

SETTING AND ATMOSPHERE Palo sits across the entire Aft section of Deck 10, which means that almost every seat has a spectacular view of the ocean sunset during dinner. On the *Magic,* Palo has a contemporary decor, with tan-wood panels, round leather benches, and deep-purple fabric on the wood chairs. A small bar is available for guests waiting for their table to become available; part of the kitchen is open to the view of guests sitting in the middle of the restaurant. Red-and-white-striped poles near the bar, evocative of those used to steer gondolas, call to mind Palo's roots in Venice (*palo* means "pole").

Because Palo has an adults-only policy, the restaurant is much quieter than DCL's main dining rooms. The quietest tables are those on the port side, aft (left and forward), tucked away behind the curve of the restaurant. If you're looking to do some people-watching with dinner, request a table on the starboard (left) side of the ship, near Palo's entrance. Brunch offers open seating, so sit wherever the view is best. Background music is mostly Italian and ranges from Vivaldi to Sinatra, as God intended.

HOUSE SPECIALTIES For a first course at dinner, try the fish-and-seafood soup, laden with mussels, clams, and lobster. The *antipasto freddo,* which comprises a selection of familiar cheeses and cured meats, could be a little more adventurous. Our favorite entrées are the lobster ravioli in truffle-butter sauce; the spicy penne *arrabbiata;* and the rack of lamb, roasted with garlic and shallots. The chocolate soufflé, by far the most popular dessert, is served with both dark- and white-chocolate sauces.

Palo's brunch menu is the best on board. One large table is dedicated to breads, muffins, and pastries, along with sliced fruits and fresh vegetables (the roasted asparagus is tasty). An entire aquarium's worth of fish is available in another section, including shrimp cocktail, cured salmon, smoked-trout mousse, seared tuna, scallops, crab legs, crawfish, and mussels. Eggs cooked in every conceivable way, including Benedict, Florentine, Julia, and customized omelets, are on the menu too. Not enough? Try the selection of made-to-order pizzas.

COMMENTS Palo, the *Magic's* one upscale restaurant, is its own little island of adult serenity and food. Service is very good, and don't be surprised if the maître 'd and your server are from Italy.

Dinners at Palo are tasty and relaxing, especially with a glass or two of wine. That being said, we think Palo is better for brunch—besides the best selection of midday food anywhere on the ship, the view out of Palo's windows is much better during the day; once the sun sets at dinner, Palo's spectacular windows just reflect the inside of the restaurant. If we could improve one thing at Palo, it would be the coffee served, which is Illy. A restaurant this good should offer better.

Finally, note that we rate Palo on the *Dream* and *Fantasy* higher overall, as well as for quality and value. It's undeniably very good on both the *Magic* and the *Wonder,* but the decor on the *Dream*-class ships is more sophisticated, and the kitchens are larger, allowing for better food preparation.

 # *DISNEY WONDER* DINING

COUNTER-SERVICE RESTAURANTS
Goofy's Galley

QUALITY B   PORTION Small–Medium   LOCATION Deck 9 Aft

COMMENTS Menu selections and hours are the same as for Daisy's De-Lites on the *Magic;* see page 83 for details.

Pinocchio's Pizzeria

QUALITY C   PORTION Medium   LOCATION Deck 9 Aft

COMMENTS See profile of Pinocchio's Pizzeria on the *Magic* (page 84) for details.

Pluto's Dog House

QUALITY B   PORTION Medium   LOCATION Deck 9 Aft

COMMENTS Menu selections and hours are the same as for Pete's Boiler Bites on the *Magic;* see page 84 for details.

FULL-SERVICE RESTAURANTS
Animator's Palate ★ ★ ★   Deck 4 Aft

AMERICAN/ASIAN   QUALITY ★ ★ ★   SERVICE ★ ★ ★ ★   FRIENDLINESS ★ ★ ★ ★

COMMENTS See profile of Animator's Palate on the *Magic* (page 84) for details.

Beach Blanket Buffet ★ ★ ½   Deck 9 Aft

AMERICAN/BUFFET   QUALITY ★ ★½ SERVICE ★ ★ ★ ★   FRIENDLINESS ★ ★ ★ ★

Reservations Not accepted. **When to go** Lunch. **Bar** Yes. **Alcohol** Limited selection of red, white, and sparkling wines, plus mixed drinks and spirits. All alcohol costs extra. **Dress** Casual; no tank tops or swimwear at dinner. **Hours** Daily breakfast, as early as 6:45 a.m. on port days and 7:45 a.m. on sea days, until 10:45 a.m.; daily lunch, noon–2 p.m.; nightly dinner, 6:30–8:30 p.m. Hours are subject to change, so check your *Personal Navigator* for exact times.

SETTING AND ATMOSPHERE A beach-themed cafeteria on Deck 9 Aft, with both indoor and outdoor seating. The inside area gets busy and noisy starting around 8:30 a.m., with lines developing even for coffee refills. We prefer having breakfast at the outdoor tables on the starboard side, with less-trafficked walkways, better views, and fresh air.

HOUSE SPECIALTIES Breakfast features the usual buffet staples: fruit, cereal, eggs, waffles, bacon, sausage, and pastries. Lunch includes soups, salads, sandwiches, and burgers, plus a couple of alternative offerings such as pasta or fish. Beach Blanket Buffet's lunches are loosely themed each day, with Italian, Asian, and seafood as examples of the offerings. The fact that you can make it through a meal and not realize the cuisine until well into it—"Hey, this seems to be Italian!"—gives you an example of how loosey-goosey the theming is. The dinner menu features selections from the main dining rooms, so there will be something to everyone's liking available.

COMMENTS Beach Blanket Buffet has two separate and identical buffet setups, on either side of the main entrance. There's not enough space, however, to pop back to one station just to grab another croissant—you've got to either excuse your way up the line or start at the beginning. The coffee situation is similar, with the only dispensers placed at the end of the buffet.

Because you're issued a tray and flatware as soon as you enter BBB, it gives off a distinct cafeteria vibe, but if you're feeling a little overfed after your dinners (and maybe late-night buffets), Beach Blanket Buffet is a good option for those who wish to control portions and load up on fruit and vegetables for breakfast and lunch.

Palo ★ ★ ★ ½   Deck 10 Aft

ITALIAN QUALITY ★★★½ VALUE ★★★½ SERVICE ★★★★½ FRIENDLINESS ★★★★

COMMENTS See profile of Palo on the *Magic* (page 87) for details. A slight difference is the coffee, which is Nescafé instead of Illy—again, though, a restaurant this good should serve better.

Parrot Cay ★ ★   Deck 3 Aft

AMERICAN/CARIBBEAN   QUALITY ★★ SERVICE ★★★★ FRIENDLINESS ★★★★

Reservations Not accepted. **When to go** Breakfast; avoid otherwise if you can. **Bar** Yes. **Alcohol** Limited selection of red, white, and sparkling wines, plus mixed drinks and spirits. All alcohol costs extra. **Dress** Casual; no tank tops or swimwear at dinner. **Hours** Breakfast buffet on select days, 7:30–10:45 a.m.; lunch buffet on select days, noon–1:30 p.m.; nightly dinner seatings at 5:45 p.m. and 8:15 p.m. Hours are subject to change, so check your *Personal Navigator* for exact times.

SETTING AND ATMOSPHERE This is possibly the least attractive restaurant on the entire ship, if not the entire cruise line. Parrot Cay is supposed to evoke images of Caribbean-island architecture, with shades of blue, green, and teal. Unfortunately, the low ceiling and poor lighting make it feel more like a "Jamaica Me Crazy" party at a fraternity house.

HOUSE SPECIALTIES None worth recommending.

COMMENTS Parrot Cay tries to Caribbean-ize standard-issue DCL dishes by adding jerk seasoning, plantains, and tropical fruits as garnishes, but it's essentially the same food you can get anywhere on the ship. Need to turn an Italian mozzarella-and-tomato plate into an island-themed appetizer? Add a bit of grilled gourd and it becomes the St. Maarten Stack! You'll be much happier if you can swing reservations at Palo on the night you're supposed to eat at Parrot Cay. If that doesn't work, try the Cove Café's antipasto sampler or room service.

Triton's ★ ★ ★   Deck 3 Midship

AMERICAN/FRENCH   QUALITY ★ ★ ★   SERVICE ★ ★ ★ ★   FRIENDLINESS ★ ★ ★ ★

Reservations Not accepted. **When to go** Lunch. **Bar** Yes. **Alcohol** Limited selection of red, white, and sparkling wines, plus mixed drinks and spirits. All alcohol costs extra. **Dress** Casual; no tank tops or swimwear at dinner. **Hours** Daily breakfast, 8–9:30 a.m.; daily lunch, noon–1:30 p.m.; nightly dinner seatings at 5:45 and 8:15 p.m. Hours are subject to change, so check your *Personal Navigator* for details.

SETTING AND ATMOSPHERE In case you've forgotten that King Triton is Ariel's father in *The Little Mermaid,* a large tile mosaic of Triton and Ariel sits at the back of this restaurant as a reminder. Besides the art, Triton's blue, beige, and gray colors lend a vague sea theme to the inside, but if you've visited any of the other restaurants, you'll be inclined to think that any of them could be switched out just by changing the paint and light fixtures.

HOUSE SPECIALTIES Breakfast features the usual suspects: fruit, cereal, eggs, waffles, bacon, sausage, and pastries. Lunch includes soups, salads, sandwiches, and burgers, plus a couple of alternative offerings such as pasta or fish. Dinner appetizers include escargots and French onion soup; order one of the crispy duck breast for the table if no one is adventurous enough to try it themselves. The Grand Marnier soufflé is probably the most popular dessert.

COMMENTS You know Disney is serious about the French theme when they put snails on the appetizer menu. *C'est si bon!* There are other Gallic influences on the menu—many of the entrées have sauces made with butter, wine, or spirits—plus enough standard vegetarian, chicken, beef, and pork dishes to make anyone happy.

DISNEY DREAM DINING

COUNTER-SERVICE RESTAURANTS
Fillmore's Favorites

QUALITY C   PORTION Small–Medium   LOCATION Deck 11 Midship

WHEN TO GO Typical hours: 10:30 a.m.–6 p.m. Check your *Personal Navigator* for the exact schedule.

SELECTIONS Sandwiches, wraps, salads, fruit, cookies.

COMMENTS While the lineup can change, it usually includes a roast-beef-and-Cheddar sandwich, a "Greek salad" veggie wrap, and a chicken Caesar wrap. Fresh fruit, such as whole bananas, grapes, and oranges, is also available.

Luigi's Pizza

QUALITY C   PORTION Medium   LOCATION Deck 11 Midship

WHEN TO GO Typical hours: 10:30 a.m.–6:30 p.m. Check your *Personal Navigator* for the exact schedule.

SELECTIONS Cheese, pepperoni, barbecue-chicken, and veggie pizza slices.

COMMENTS As with the pizza joints on the *Magic* and *Wonder,* no one will mistake Luigi's for authentic pizza, but it's fine in a pinch. Occasionally open after dinner, when ordering a whole pie is a convenient alternative to room service or restaurant dining.

Tow Mater's Grill

QUALITY C   PORTION Large   LOCATION Deck 11 Midship

WHEN TO GO Typical hours: 10:30 a.m.–11 p.m. most days. Check your *Personal Navigator* for the exact schedule.

SELECTIONS Grilled hot dogs, sausages, burgers, and chicken sandwiches; fried-chicken strips; fries.

COMMENTS The fries and burgers aren't anything special—they serve primarily as sustenance for chlorine-addled kids (that is, if they can be pried out of the nearby pool long enough to eat). The chicken strips and hot dogs are the best things on the menu. A nearby fixin's bar provides toppings for burgers and sandwiches.

FULL-SERVICE RESTAURANTS
Animator's Palate   ★ ★ ★   Deck 3 Aft

AMERICAN/ASIAN   QUALITY ★ ★ ★   SERVICE ★ ★ ★ ★   FRIENDLINESS ★ ★ ★ ★

Reservations Not accepted. **When to go** Dinner. **Bar** Yes. **Alcohol** Red, white, and sparkling wines, plus mixed drinks and spirits. All alcohol costs extra. **Dress** Casual; no tank tops or swimwear. **Hours** Nightly dinner seatings usually at 5:45 and 8:15 p.m.; check your *Personal Navigator* for the exact schedule.

SETTING AND ATMOSPHERE Each DCL ship has a restaurant called Animator's Palate, and all four pay tribute to Disney's (and Pixar's) animation processes. And although all Disney ships have a restaurant called Animator's Palate, there are three different implementations. Unlike the black-and-white decor on the *Magic* and *Wonder,* that of Animator's Palate on the *Fantasy* (and the *Dream*) features vivid colors: The floor has red carpet with stars of silver, gold, and blue, and the walls are the color of caramel. The backs of the dining-room chairs are patterned after Mickey Mouse's pants, with red backs, yellow buttons, and a black "belt" at the top.

Shelves along the walls hold small toy versions of Disney and Pixar icons, in between video screens displaying animation sketches from popular Disney movies. The more interesting ones will show on one screen how one complete animated cel is drawn, starting from sketches of the main characters to how key background elements are drawn, color samples for walls and floors, and the finished art. The art changes throughout the evening, keeping the view fresh for everyone.

At certain points during your dinner, some of the screens will switch from sketches to an interactive video featuring the surfer-dude turtle

Crush from *Finding Nemo.* When we say "interactive," we mean it—Crush will ask you questions and react to your responses, allowing you to have an actual conversation with the animated turtle. Based on the same real-time computer graphics found in Epcot's *Turtle Talk with Crush* attraction (also found at other Disney parks), the technology behind this minishow allows Crush's mouth to move in the appropriate way as his words are spoken. Parents may be more amazed than children.

HOUSE SPECIALTIES Vegetable stir-fry; roasted-garlic or red-pepper dip with bread.

COMMENTS The "wow" factor doesn't extend to the food—as is the case at the other Animator's Palates, the cuisine isn't much different from what you might get at Applebee's or Chili's, despite the Pacific Rim/American designation.

Cabanas ★★★   Deck 11 Aft

AMERICAN/BUFFET   QUALITY ★★★   SERVICE ★★★★   FRIENDLINESS ★★★★

COMMENTS See profile of Cabanas on the *Magic* (page 85) for details.

Enchanted Garden ★★★   Deck 2 Midship

AMERICAN/CONTINENTAL QUALITY ★★★ SERVICE ★★★★ FRIENDLINESS ★★★★

Reservations Not accepted. **When to go** Lunch, especially on your embarkation day, when the crowds are headed to Cabanas. **Bar** Yes. **Alcohol** Limited selection of red, white, and sparkling wines, plus mixed drinks and spirits. All alcohol costs extra. **Hours** Breakfast buffet on select days, 8–10 a.m.; lunch on select days, noon–1:30 p.m.; nightly dinner seatings at 5:45 and 8:15 p.m. Hours are subject to change, so check your *Personal Navigator* for the exact schedule.

SETTING AND ATMOSPHERE Designed to evoke a 19th-century French greenhouse, with patinaed cast-iron arches supporting a spectacular ceiling display of plants, sun, and sky, Enchanted Garden is surely the prettiest of the *Dream*'s three main rotational restaurants.

During lunch, lights in the ceiling simulate the midday sun, and diners see what appears to be ivy climbing up the side of the ironworks; as the sun sets, the "sky" turns to dusk and eventually to dark. Lights, in the shape of flowers and hung from the ceiling, open their "petals" as night falls.

The centerpiece of Enchanted Garden is a burbling concrete fountain, 7 feet tall, topped by Mickey Mouse. The best seats are the round, raised, high-backed booths along the center walk, which allow you to see all the action in one half of the restaurant. Look for framed Hermès scarves outside the restaurant—a nice (and expensive) touch of France. Disney says Enchanted Garden is inspired by the gardens at Versailles, but we think it looks more like the hothouse at Paris's Les Jardin des Plantes. We could be wrong.

HOUSE SPECIALTIES Roast pork tenderloin seasoned with smoked salt; scallops with roasted asparagus; seared-tuna salad on field greens and seaweed with squid.

COMMENTS The menu is more American bistro than Paris brasserie, despite the French setting. Besides substituting brioche for bread, the most French thing on the menu is usually the use of the words *julienne* to describe how the vegetables are cut and *consommé* to describe the soup.

There's usually at least one pork dish, such as roast pork tenderloin, one chicken dish (baked or roasted), and a steak or prime rib available, along with several seafood and vegetarian options. Honestly, you could serve these dishes at Animator's Palate or Royal Court without anyone noticing, but maybe the scenery here makes the food taste a little bit better.

Palo ★★★★ Deck 12 Aft and Starboard

ITALIAN QUALITY ★★★★ VALUE ★★★★ SERVICE ★★★★½ FRIENDLINESS ★★★★

Reservations Required. **When to go** Brunch on sea days; dinner nightly. **Bar** Yes. **Alcohol** Large list of Italian wines, listed by region, plus select wines from around the world; mixed drinks and spirits; *limoncello*; grappa; ice wine. All alcohol costs extra. **Dress** Pants and dress shirt or jacket for men; dress, skirt and blouse, or pantsuit for women. No jeans, shorts, capris, flip-flops, or athletic shoes. **Hours** Brunch, 10 a.m.– 12:30 p.m. on sea days on cruises of 4 nights or longer; nightly dinner, 6 p.m.–8:30 p.m. Hours are subject to change, so check your *Personal Navigator* for the exact schedule. **Special comments** An additional $25/person charge will be added to your cruise bill for each meal at Palo. If you need to cancel a reservation, you must do so by 2 p.m. on the day of your reservation, or the full per-person charge will be applied to your bill. Guests must be age 18 and up to dine.

SETTING AND ATMOSPHERE Palo is on the starboard side at the back of Deck 12, opposite the adults-only French restaurant Remy (see next profile) and adjacent to the Meridian bar. Although all four Disney ships have a restaurant named Palo, the restaurants on the *Dream* and *Fantasy* have the nicest furnishings.

The entrance to Palo on the *Dream* has a pretty gold-and-ruby-colored glass chandelier, surely one of the most photographed parts of the restaurant. Guests entering Palo walk past a glass-enclosed wine closet and see the main dining room, decorated with deep mahogany wood–paneled walls and columns, and rich burgundy carpet. One half of the room features deep-green patterned fabric on the booths and chairs, with paintings of the Italian countryside and seashore along the walls. The other half of Palo uses a saturated red fabric for its seating; illustrations of Italian villas hang on the walls. Also within the *Dream*'s Palo, and unique to Disney's larger ships, are small private dining rooms with custom fabrics, wallpaper, and lighting. Stick your head inside if one is empty, and you'll see how the wealthy merchants of Venice might have lived.

Naturally, tables next to Palo's floor-to-ceiling windows afford the best views, but tables near the back wall sit on an elevated platform, allowing diners there to see over the tables nearest the windows. Our favorite table is to the left of the entrance, tucked by itself in a rounded corner along the inside wall and surrounded by a mural depicting Venice from the water. It's a bit high profile, though; quieter seats are available at the far ends of either side of the restaurant. Brunch offers open seating, so sit wherever the view is best.

HOUSE SPECIALTIES Start your dinner with the cioppino, a tomato-based fish stew with squid, clams, and shrimp, or the white-bean soup, with prosciutto and perfectly al dente beans. A complete selection of pasta is available, either as a separate course or as an entrée. One of these, the vegetarian mushroom risotto, is so rich you'd swear it had beef in it. Our favorite meat entrée is the rack of lamb, which comes in a crispy crust of Parmesan cheese and oregano. For seafood, we like the grilled tuna with potato risotto a bit more than the grilled scallops. The chocolate soufflé, by far the most popular dessert, comes with both dark- and white-chocolate sauces.

As on the other ships, Palo's brunch menu is very good. One large table is dedicated to breads, muffins, and pastries, along with sliced fruits and fresh vegetables (the roasted asparagus is tasty). An entire aquarium's worth of fish is available in another section, including shrimp cocktail, cured salmon, smoked-trout mousse, seared tuna, scallops, crab legs, crawfish, and mussels. Eggs cooked in every conceivable way, including Benedict, Florentine, Julia, and customized omelets, are on the menu too. Not enough? Try the selection of made-to-order pizzas. If there's any room left for dessert, small cups of tiramisu will take care of your sweet tooth.

COMMENTS Given what you've already spent on the cruise, dropping another $25 to dine at Palo requires no thought whatsoever. Because the food is cooked to order, it tastes substantially better than anything coming from the main dining rooms. The menu offers a wide selection, and many dishes—especially the soups—are done very well. It's no wonder that DCL allows guests to make only one reservation before boarding.

Remy ★ ★ ★ ★ ½ Deck 12 Aft

FRENCH QUALITY ★★★★½ VALUE ★★★★½ SERVICE ★★★★½ FRIENDLINESS ★★★★

Reservations Required. **When to go** Dinner. **Bar** Yes. **Alcohol** An extensive selection of French wines and Champagnes. **Dress** Jackets and dress shirts for men; dresses, blouses and skirts, or pantsuits for women. **Hours** Brunch on sea days on cruises of 4 nights or longer, 10 a.m.–12:30 p.m.; nightly dinner, 6 p.m.–9 p.m. Hours are subject to change, so check your *Personal Navigator* for the exact schedule. **Special comments** An additional $50/person charge will be added to your cruise bill for each brunch at Remy, $75/person for each dinner. The wine pairing for dinner is $99/person. If you need to cancel a reservation, you must do so by 2 p.m. on the day of your reservation, or the full per-person charge will be applied to your bill. Guests must be age 18 and up to dine.

SETTING AND ATMOSPHERE Remarkably understated for a Disney restaurant, and one named after a cartoon rat at that. The most prominent features at Remy are the floor-to-ceiling windows, which look out over the ocean on the port side of the ship from high on Deck 12; and the Art Nouveau lights, which seem to spring from the floor as thick vines, branching out into yellow lights as they reach the ceiling. Besides those touches, and perhaps the oval mirrors along the wall opposite the windows, the rest is simple and elegant: oval, round, and square tables, all with white-linen tablecloths, and round-backed wood chairs with white upholstery. The olive-green carpet pattern matches the Art Nouveau decor without being distracting. A small teak deck wraps around Remy, allowing you to walk out for a quick breath of fresh air between courses.

HOUSE SPECIALTIES The tasting menu may be one of the best 3-hour dining experiences you'll ever have. Splurge on the wine pairing. If the tasting menu sounds like too much food, Remy's meat entrées usually include Australian Wagyu beef and pork from central France.

Remy also offers an extensive brunch on days when the ship is at sea. Like the brunch at Palo, Remy's has an extensive selection, including fruit, pastries, seafood, beef, pork, pasta, and fish. A Champagne pairing is available for an additional $25 per person. We prefer the dinner experience, but spending the morning at Remy is a lovely way to start a day at sea.

COMMENTS What makes a great restaurant such as Remy different from restaurants that are simply very good is that, while the latter usually have a few signature dishes that they do very well, virtually *everything* at Remy is nothing short of exceptional. An appetizer of carrots—yes, the root vegetable—will be the most extraordinary carrots you've ever had, probably in varieties and colors you didn't know existed, and with a flavor that is the pure essence of carrot-ness. Now imagine a meal of three to eight courses, all equally as good, ranging from soups, seafood, and beef, to sides, cheese courses, and desserts. That's an average evening at Remy.

Remy offers both a standard dinner menu and a chef's tasting menu. If you have the time or the inclination, order the latter—it allows you to savor every bit of creativity and technical mastery the kitchen can muster.

A couple of examples from our meals: One course early in the tasting menu was billed as the chef's interpretation of a grilled-cheese sandwich with tomato soup. The entire serving consisted of one small, golden-brown cube, about the size of a postage stamp on each side, designed to be eaten in one bite. The outside of the cube was a Cheddar cheese, coated with seasoned bread crumbs and fried lightly. Inside was a tomato sauce, barely seasoned and reduced to concentrate the flavor. The first bite—it took maybe two to finish the entire thing—tasted of crispy, butter-fried bread and melted cheese. The second was all tomato: bright, slightly acidic, and sweet at the same time, balancing out the butter and cheese from the outside coating. Remy's chefs had both amplified the flavors to their essence and reduced the size of the dish to its bare minimum.

Another appetizer was the chef's take on cheese pizza. Its base was a small, crispy wafer of baked bread, barely thicker than a sheet of paper. On top of that was a half-inch layer of white foam, about the consistency of whipped cream but made from Parmesan cheese. And on top of that were three small basil leaves.

The pizza's tomato "sauce" was presented in a Champagne flute as a clear, intensely flavored liquid. The kitchen had achieved this transparency by repeatedly filtering juice from ripe tomatoes through layers of fine cheesecloth, trapping the red bits and letting the clear juice through. We were instructed to follow a bit of the crust and cheese foam with a sip from the flute, and the flavors combined beautifully.

One last tip on the tasting menu: Remy offers a wine pairing for most courses. The selections are very good, but it's a *lot* of wine that could easily be split between two people. Len's first evening at Remy began with a martini at Meridian and continued with the wine pairing for dinner. The first few courses were memorable, but by the time he realized how much alcohol was involved, it was too late. The last quarter of the meal is a hazy memory that apparently involved Len applauding someone else's cheese cart as it rolled by for dessert. That called for another, alcohol-free, dinner at Remy. Pity his suffering.

Royal Palace ★★★ Deck 3 Midship

AMERICAN/FRENCH   QUALITY ★★★   SERVICE ★★★★   FRIENDLINESS ★★★★

Reservations Not accepted. **When to go** Lunch. **Bar** Yes. **Alcohol** Limited selection of red, white, and sparkling wines, plus mixed drinks and spirits. **Dress** Casual; no tank tops or swimwear at dinner. **Hours** Daily breakfast, 8–9:30 a.m.; daily lunch, noon–1:30 p.m.; nightly dinner seatings at 5:45 p.m. and 8:15 p.m. Hours are subject to change, so check your *Personal Navigator* for the exact schedule.

SETTING AND ATMOSPHERE The most attractive part of Royal Palace may be its entrance, done in gold-and-white-marble tile below a pretty flower-shaped chandelier accented with blue-glass "diamonds" and red "rubies." Inside the doors, gold-and-white faux-marble columns form a circle just inside one ring of tables; royal-blue carpet with gold trim lines the inner part of the restaurant. Drapes cover the windows lining one side of the room, and mosaic-tile pictures of Disney princesses line another.

HOUSE SPECIALTIES Breakfast is standard buffet fare: fruit, cereal, eggs, waffles, bacon, sausage, and pastries. Lunch includes soups, salads, sandwiches, and burgers, plus a couple of alternative offerings such as pasta or fish. Dinner appetizers include escargots and French onion soup; the wild-boar tenderloin entrée is tasty. The Grand Marnier soufflé is probably the most popular dessert.

COMMENTS You know Disney is serious about the French theme when they put snails on the appetizer menu. There are other Gallic influences on the menu—many of the entrées have sauces made with butter, wine, or spirits—plus enough standard vegetarian, chicken, beef, and pork dishes to make anyone happy.

▌*DISNEY FANTASY* DINING

COUNTER-SERVICE RESTAURANTS
Fillmore's Favorites

QUALITY C   PORTION Small–Medium   LOCATION Deck 11 Midship

COMMENTS See profile of Fillmore's Favorites on the *Dream* (page 91) for details.

Luigi's Pizza

QUALITY C   PORTION Medium   LOCATION Deck 11 Midship

COMMENTS See profile of Luigi's Pizza on the *Dream* (page 92) for details.

Tow Mater's Grill

QUALITY C   PORTION Large   LOCATION Deck 11 Midship

COMMENTS See profile of Tow Mater's Grill on the *Dream* (page 92) for details.

FULL-SERVICE RESTAURANTS

Animator's Palate ★★★   Deck 3 Aft

AMERICAN/ASIAN   QUALITY ★★★   SERVICE ★★★★   FRIENDLINESS ★★★★

Reservations Not accepted. **When to go** Dinner. **Bar** Yes. **Alcohol** Red, white, and sparkling wines, plus mixed drinks and spirits. All alcohol costs extra. **Dress** Casual; no tank tops or swimwear. **Hours** Nightly dinner seatings usually at 5:45 and 8:15 p.m.; check your *Personal Navigator* for the exact schedule.

SETTING AND ATMOSPHERE Each DCL ship has a restaurant called Animator's Palate, and all four pay tribute to Disney's (and Pixar's) animation processes. And although all Disney ships have a restaurant called Animator's Palate, there are three different implementations. Unlike the black-and-white decor on the *Magic* and *Wonder*, that of Animator's Palate on the *Fantasy* (and the *Dream*) features vivid colors: The floor has red carpet with stars of silver, gold, and blue, and the walls are the color of caramel. The backs of the dining-room chairs are patterned after Mickey Mouse's pants, with red backs, yellow buttons, and a black "belt" at the top.

Shelves along the walls hold small toy versions of Disney and Pixar icons, in between video screens displaying animation sketches from popular Disney movies. The more interesting ones will show on one screen how one complete animated cel is drawn, starting from sketches of the main characters to how key background elements are drawn, color samples for walls and floors, and the finished art. The art changes throughout the evening, keeping the view fresh for everyone.

The version of Animator's Palate on the *Fantasy* includes *Animation Magic,* an impressive special effect. At the beginning of the second night you dine there, you're given a sheet of paper and crayon and told to draw a self-portrait. At the end of the evening, all of the diners' self-portraits are shown in an animated cartoon similar to Disney's 1929 short cartoon *The Skeleton Dance.*

At your first scheduled dinner at Animator's Palate, you get a different show. At certain points during your second dinner, some of the screens will switch from sketches to an interactive video featuring the surfer-dude turtle Crush from *Finding Nemo.* When we say *interactive,* we mean it—Crush will ask you questions and react to your responses, allowing you to have an actual conversation with the animated turtle. Based on the same real-time computer graphics found in Epcot's *Turtle Talk with Crush* attraction (also at other Disney parks), the technology behind this minishow allows Crush's mouth to move in the appropriate way as his words are spoken. Parents may be more amazed than children.

HOUSE SPECIALTIES Vegetable stir-fry; roasted-garlic or red-pepper dip with bread.

ROYAL COURT ROYAL TEA   Royal Court, Deck 3 Midship

EXCLUSIVE TO THE *Fantasy,* this event combines afternoon tea with Disney-princess meet-and-greet opportunities, including music, singing, and dancing. It's very expensive—prices start at $279 and can reach $500 pretty quickly—but the prices hold down the crowds, so you're likely to get lots of personal princess attention.

You'll be served a selection of teas, plus small sandwiches, cookies, cakes, and other finger food. Children also receive a few souvenirs: Girls get a tiara, necklace, jewelry box, friendship bracelet, necklace, and Cinderella doll; boys receive a Duffy teddy bear doll, autograph book, sword and shield, and Disney pins.

The Royal Court Royal Tea is for guests ages 3 and up. Prices start at $279 for one adult and one child; each additional child is $210 and each additional adult is $69. Space is very limited. Reservations can't yet be made online, so stop by Guest Services to make arrangements.

COMMENTS When it comes to the food, it's the same old story—as is the case at the other three Animator's Palates, the dishes are pedestrian chain-restaurant fare, despite the Pacific Rim/American designation. On the *Fantasy,* anyway, the entertainment makes up for whatever the food lacks.

Cabanas ★★★   Deck 11 Aft

AMERICAN/BUFFET   QUALITY ★★★★ SERVICE ★★★★ FRIENDLINESS ★★★★
COMMENTS See profile of Cabanas on the *Magic* (page 85) for details.

Enchanted Garden ★★★   Deck 2 Midship

AMERICAN/CONTINENTAL QUALITY ★★★ SERVICE ★★★★ FRIENDLINESS ★★★★
COMMENTS See profile of Enchanted Garden on the *Dream* (page 93) for details.

Palo ★★★★   Deck 12 Aft and Starboard

ITALIAN QUALITY ★★★★ VALUE ★★★★ SERVICE ★★★★½ FRIENDLINESS ★★★★
COMMENTS See profile of Palo on the *Dream* (page 94) for details.

Remy ★★★★½   Deck 12 Aft

FRENCH   QUALITY ★★★★½ VALUE ★★★★½ SERVICE ★★★★½ FRIENDLINESS ★★★★
COMMENTS See profile of Remy on the *Dream* (page 95) for details.

Royal Court ★★★   Deck 3 Midship

AMERICAN/FRENCH   QUALITY ★★★   SERVICE ★★★★   FRIENDLINESS ★★★★

Reservations Not accepted. **When to go** Lunch. **Bar** Yes. **Alcohol** Limited selection of red, white, and sparkling wines, plus mixed drinks and spirits. **Dress** Casual; no tank tops or swimwear at dinner. **Hours** Breakfast, 8–9:30 a.m.; lunch, noon–1:30 p.m.; nightly dinner seatings at 5:45 p.m. and 8:15 p.m. Hours are subject to change, so check your *Personal Navigator* for the exact schedule.

SETTING AND ATMOSPHERE The most distinctive design elements of Royal Court are the gold-colored wood columns on the floor, which rise to attach to the ceiling through flared white glass decorated with plant stems and shaped like flower petals. Along with these, white-marble columns and carpet patterned to look like fancy rugs give Royal Court a formal feel, even when it's half-full of kids. Small, round lamps placed around the room are designed to look like Cinderella's pumpkin coach, and some of the walls feature tile murals depicting scenes from *Cinderella* and other Disney princess films. Tables near the starboard wall sit under portholes that offer ocean views, although these are partially blocked by a privacy wall running along the inside perimeter of the restaurant.

HOUSE SPECIALTIES Breakfast is standard buffet fare: fruit, cereal, eggs, waffles, bacon, sausage, and pastries. Lunch includes soups, salads, sandwiches, and burgers, plus a couple of alternative offerings such as pasta or fish. Dinner appetizers include escargots and French onion soup; the wild-boar tenderloin entrée is tasty. The Grand Marnier soufflé is probably the most popular dessert.

COMMENTS Only differences in decor distinguish Royal Court from Royal Palace on the *Dream* (see page 97). There are Gallic influences on the menu—many of the entrées have sauces made with butter, wine, or spirits—plus enough standard vegetarian, chicken, beef, and pork dishes to make anyone happy.

PART EIGHT

ENTERTAINMENT *and* NIGHTLIFE

◼▮ LIVE THEATER *on the* SHIPS

LIVE ENTERTAINMENT IS PRESENTED at the **Walt Disney Theatre** most nights, on most itineraries. Shows are typically either Disney-themed theatrical productions (typically musicals) or variety acts such as comedians, magicians, or ventriloquists. The theatrical shows are usually of two types: retellings of familiar stories and "jukebox" musicals.

Disney's Aladdin: A Musical Spectacular, on the *Fantasy,* is an example of the retelling genre. The cruise version features live actors and multiple Arabian-themed sets reprising key scenes from the animated film, including the most popular songs, in about half the time of the original movie. The *Magic's* ***Twice Charmed: A Twist on the Original Cinderella Story,*** is probably the best show in this category; the *Fantasy's Aladdin* is a distant second; and the *Wonder's* ***Toy Story: The Musical*** is third.

Examples of jukebox musicals include ***Disney Dreams, Disney Wishes, Disney's Believe, The Golden Mickeys,*** and ***Villains Tonight!*** Each features songs and characters from many different Disney films, the numbers linked by an original story. We're generally not fans of these shows, especially *Villains Tonight!* The story lines are threadbare, serving to string together the musical numbers rather than provide interesting narrative. Lack of plot, however, isn't our primary objection to these shows—we realize it's a Disney cruise. Rather, they recycle the same handful of characters and songs played in every entertainment venue throughout the ship. If you haven't heard "Be Our Guest" from *Beauty and the Beast* performed a dozen times on board, have your hearing checked when you get home.

Finally, the *Magic* puts on a welcome-aboard show on the first night of its seven-nights-and-up itineraries and a farewell show on the last night. The welcome show commingles a few musical numbers with a review of the ship's major features and schedule. The farewell show is a recap of the same, with guest photos from throughout the cruise thrown in. These are good times to go to the spa.

A BIT OF ADVICE You'll probably see at least one musical if you're taking small children on your cruise. Along with reading the show profiles that follow, we recommend watching a few minutes of each show on YouTube before you leave for the cruise. This will not only help you decide which show is worth your time, but it will also let you know what you're missing in case another entertainment option is available.

THE *MAGIC'S* SHOWS

All Aboard: Let the Magic Begin ★ ★
Walt Disney Theatre, Deck 4 Forward

Welcome-aboard show with a few songs and a lot of talk about the cruise

When to go Typical showtimes are 6:15 and 8:30 p.m. on your embarkation day. Presented on cruises of 7 nights and longer. **Duration** 50 minutes. **Our rating** Skip it and tour the ship instead; ★ ★.

DESCRIPTION AND COMMENTS More than half of *All Aboard*'s 50-minute showtime consists of the *Magic*'s cruise director explaining the ship's dining, entertainment, and shopping options, plus port logistics. The rest is a handful of song-and-dance numbers featuring Disney characters and involving a young boy who dreams of becoming the ship's captain. Featuring a couple of original songs, the show serves as an introduction to the Walt Disney Theatre. It's a shame they can't put all the songs at the beginning of the show, because we'd skip the rest of it.

Disney Dreams: An Enchanted Classic ★ ★ ★ ½
Walt Disney Theatre, Deck 4 Forward

Peter Pan saves the day

When to go Typical showtimes are 6:15 and 8:30 p.m. Check your *Personal Navigator* for specific dates. **Duration** 55 minutes. **Our rating** Not to be missed; ★ ★ ★ ½.

DESCRIPTION AND COMMENTS *Disney Dreams* is one of the better stage shows on any Disney ship. Peter Pan must help a young girl named Anne Marie "find her own magic" before sunrise. Peter does this by whisking her through scenes from *Aladdin, Beauty and the Beast, Cinderella, The Little Mermaid,* and *The Lion King,* with each story's main characters appearing in key scenes from their respective movie and singing their signature songs. The sets are attractive, the special effects are good, and the script is fast-paced and entertaining. The cast seems to enjoy it too, and it shows. We rate *Disney Dreams* as not to be missed.

Remember the Magic: A Final Farewell ★ ★
Walt Disney Theatre, Deck 4 Forward

Recap of your *Magic* cruise

When to go Typical showtimes are 6:15 and 8:30 p.m. on the night before your cruise concludes. Presented on cruises of 7 nights and longer. **Duration** 25 minutes. **Our rating** Not worth seeing; ★ ★.

DESCRIPTION AND COMMENTS *Remember the Magic* uses sets and characters from the ship's other shows, including *All Aboard* and *Disney Dreams,* to recap the cruise's highlights. Photographs and video clips of families at play, taken by Disney photographers during the itinerary, are shown on video screens during the songs. Expect songs and dances by Disney princesses and jokes about eating too much at the buffet. We recommend skipping this show and spending your last night revisiting your favorite activities on board.

Twice Charmed: An Original Twist on the Cinderella Story
★★★½   Walt Disney Theatre, Deck 4 Forward

A fresh take on a classic tale

When to go Typical showtimes are 6:15 and 8:30 p.m. Check your *Personal Navigator* for specific days. **Duration** 55 minutes. **Our rating** A new narrative for a familiar story; ★★★½.

DESCRIPTION AND COMMENTS If you recall from the original *Cinderella* movie, the stepmother breaks the first glass slipper just as it's about to be fit on Cinderella's foot. Cinderella, however, produces the second glass slipper, shows that it fits, and goes on to marry the prince.

  Twice Charmed begins where that story ends. As the show opens, Cinderella's evil stepmother and stepsisters are lamenting the fact that they didn't know Cinderella had the second slipper. A wicked fairy godfather appears to send the evil stepfamily back in time and destroy Cindy's slipper before the prince's foot-fitting team ever arrives. Cinderella must then find a new way to convince the prince that they're meant to be together. As is the case with any Disney film, you can guess in the first 5 minutes how it's all going to end, but *Twice Charmed* is interesting anyway because it has a new narrative. The sets are pretty, the songs aren't bad, and it's an enjoyable way to spend an evening.

Villains Tonight!   ★★   Walt Disney Theatre, Deck 4 Forward

Disney heels do comedy

When to go Typical showtimes are 6:15 and 8:30 p.m. Check your *Personal Navigator* for specific days. **Duration** 55 minutes. **Our rating** The villain here is the show itself; ★★.

DESCRIPTION AND COMMENTS In *Villains Tonight!,* Hades, ruler of the underworld, has lost his edge after being defeated by Hercules. He's visited by the Fates, who tell Hades he must prove he's still truly evil or give up his throne. Hades dispatches his two sidekicks, Pain and Panic, to bring every Disney villain they can find back to the underworld. Musical numbers pop up every time Pain and Panic make contact with a villain, including *The Little Mermaid*'s Ursula the Sea Witch in a burlesque number, the evil queen from *Snow White,* Malificent from *Sleeping Beauty,* and *The Lion King*'s Scar, in what, judging by the costumes, is a *Mad Max Beyond Africa* musical number.

  Disney villains *should* be comedy gold. They don't have to follow the same rules as Disney's good guys—they can hurl insults and petty criticisms and express self-centered opinions. There's some of that in this script, but it's done at such a glacial pace that you wonder whether the long pauses are intended solely to extend the show's run time. A tighter, more up-tempo script would make better use of the performer's talents.

Every *Villains* show includes a painful effort to make the show hip and contemporary. On one recent sailing there were three separate references to the Kardashians, including making fun of Kim's baby. And on each occasion the joke fell flat and the character responded with "Too soon?" We were embarrassed for the performers.

Walt Disney: The Dream Goes On ★ ★ ★   Walt Disney Theatre, Deck 4 Forward

Retrospective of Walt's life and art

When to go Typical showtimes are 6:15 and 8:30 p.m. Check your *Personal Navigator* for specific days. **Duration** 45 minutes. **Our rating** An improvement over *All Aboard,* it has potential; ★ ★ ★.

DESCRIPTION AND COMMENTS A new show for the *Magic,* the show uses film clips, audio, and stage reenactments to trace Walt's life from the creation of Mickey Mouse through the theme parks. The show's highlights include songs from Disney-theme-park attractions such as Main Street, U.S.A.; The Haunted Mansion; and *Country Bear Jamboree.* The show also benefits from not drawing heavily from *Beauty and the Beast, The Little Mermaid,* or *The Lion King.* The pacing is a little uneven—it could be improved with better dialogue to link the segments—but overall the show is a nice tribute to the guy who started it all.

THE *WONDER*'S SHOWS

Disney Dreams: An Enchanted Classic ★ ★ ★ ½
Walt Disney Theatre, Deck 4 Forward

Peter Pan saves the day

COMMENTS See profile of this show on the *Magic* (page 102) for details.

The Golden Mickeys ★ ★   Walt Disney Theatre, Deck 4 Forward

Disney spin on an awards show

When to go Typical showtimes are 6:15 and 8:30 p.m. Check your *Personal Navigator* for specific days. **Duration** 45 minutes. **Our rating** There are better uses of your time; ★ ★.

DESCRIPTION AND COMMENTS One of the least coherent live shows on any Disney cruise ship, *The Golden Mickeys* starts out as an Oscar-style awards show, except it's the Disney gang giving themselves awards for their own movies in different, made-up categories. As each award winner is announced, live performers reenact the movie's key scenes on stage, including songs, as clips from the movies play on the stage's screen backdrop.

There are many problems with the show. For one, the "awards" stop making sense almost as soon as they're presented: The "Best Heroes" award is simply a montage of main characters from Disney films, and one of the last awards, "A Salute to Friendship," is apparently the only way the show's writers could think of getting Woody, Buzz, and Jesse together on stage. Unless you have a pressing need to see another rendition of songs from *The Lion King* and *Beauty and the Beast,* this show isn't worth your time.

Toy Story: The Musical ★ ★ ★ ½ Walt Disney Theatre, Deck 4

Retelling of the original film

When to go Typical showtimes are 6:15 and 8:30 p.m. Check your *Personal Navigator* for specific days. **Duration** 55 minutes. **Our rating** Worth seeing; ★ ★ ★ ½.

DESCRIPTION AND COMMENTS This is a stage adaptation of the first *Toy Story* movie, with a new soundtrack not heard in the original film. Besides Buzz and Woody, all of the film's major characters make appearances in the show, including Rex, Hamm, and Mr. Potato Head. The show's sets are complemented by video projections displayed on the stage's back screen.

Virtually everyone taking a Disney cruise will already have seen the movie, so the stage version won't hold any surprises. Still, the songs and lyrics are interesting enough to make the show worth watching.

THE *DREAM'S* SHOWS

Disney's Believe ★ ★ ★ Walt Disney Theatre, Deck 3 Forward

Magic triumphs over cynicism

When to go Typical showtimes are 6:15 and 8:30 p.m. Check your *Personal Navigator* for specific days. **Duration** 50 minutes. **Our rating** Nice change of pace; ★ ★ ★.

DESCRIPTION AND COMMENTS A botanist father who doesn't believe in magic must learn to believe in order to reconnect with his daughter on her birthday. The father's guide is *Aladdin*'s wisecracking Genie, who takes Dad through time, space, and Disney music on his journey to acceptance.

Believe has one of the most sophisticated sets of any Disney stage show at sea, and there are enough visual elements to entertain almost any kid. Although it's not a holiday show, the plot seems like a loose adaptation of Charles Dickens's *A Christmas Carol,* with a committee of ghosts including Mary Poppins, Peter Pan, Baloo from *The Jungle Book,* Rafiki from *The Lion King,* and Pocahontas from Scarsdale, judging by her accent. (Erin begs to differ: "No princess from Scarsdale would be caught dead in that *shmata.*")

Many other Disney stars appear throughout the show, but thankfully, *Believe* includes some less familiar characters and songs. The final stretch has a hit parade of other princesses and ends with performances by Mickey and Minnie.

The Golden Mickeys ★ ★ Walt Disney Theatre, Deck 3 Forward

Disney spin on an awards show

COMMENTS See profile of this show on the *Wonder* (opposite) for details.

Villains Tonight! ★ ★   Walt Disney Theatre, Deck 3 Forward

Disney heels do comedy

COMMENTS See profile of this show on the *Magic* (page 103) for details.

THE *FANTASY'S* SHOWS

Disney's Aladdin: A Musical Spectacular ★ ★ ★
Walt Disney Theatre, Deck 3 Forward

Song-filled extravaganza

When to go Typical showtimes are 6:15 and 8:30 p.m. Check your *Personal Navigator* for specific days. **Duration** 45 minutes. **Our rating** Needs more Genie; ★ ★ ★.

DESCRIPTION AND COMMENTS A song-filled retelling of Disney's *Aladdin,* this live show features stage sets of Agrabah, the Cave of Wonders, and the Sultan's palace, along with the film's main characters: Aladdin, Princess Jasmine, Jafar, Iago, and the Genie. All of the major numbers are performed, including "Friend Like Me" and "A Whole New World." Because it's an adaptation of an existing film, *Aladdin* has less saccharine Disney sweetness than, say, *Believe.*

Having seen the film in theaters and the live stage show at Disney California Adventure, we were disappointed in the *Fantasy*'s production of *Aladdin.* The actors' performances and singing were fine, but the set design and script aren't quite as good as we'd expected. For example, in the movie and the theme park show, Genie has the most important role in the production: Besides providing narrative and background, he tells jokes to keep the script moving. In live performances at DCA, Genie often ad-libs topical humor into the act, and so many one-liners come so fast that he's virtually guaranteed the biggest ovation at the end.

For some reason, though, Genie's onboard humor has been diluted so much that it doesn't provide the spark the rest of the script needs. He tells fewer jokes, and with less bite, than in either the DCA show or the film. (Perhaps the ship's flaky onboard Internet keeps the Genie from regular access to TMZ.com.) Also, we're surprised that the stage sets on a $900 million cruise ship aren't as detailed as those made for a theme park more than 10 years ago.

Disney's Believe ★ ★ ★   Walt Disney Theatre, Deck 3 Forward

Magic triumphs over cynicism

COMMENTS See profile of this show on the *Dream* (on the previous page) for details.

Disney Wishes ★ ★ ★ ½   Walt Disney Theatre, Deck 3 Forward

Teen-focused song and dance

When to go Typical showtimes are 6:15 and 8:30 p.m. Check your *Personal Navigator* for specific days. **Duration** 50 minutes. **Our rating** Entertaining; ★ ★ ★ ½.

DESCRIPTION AND COMMENTS In *Disney Wishes,* graduating high-schoolers Kayla, Nicole, and Brandon are visiting Disneyland Park in search of the ride of their lives. This search is complicated by the trio's imminent split for college, as well as Brandon's hush-hush crush on Kayla. Nicole, Brandon's sister, has her own dark secret: She wants to be an artist.

Wishes has young actors, fast-moving dance numbers, and lots of visual razzle-dazzle, so it's entertaining for tweens and teens. It's not bad for parents, either, especially if they can recognize the bits of Magic Kingdom park trivia interspersed in the dialogue. According to maritime law, which requires that Disney stage shows must include at least one song from *Aladdin, Beauty and the Beast, The Lion King,* or *The Little Mermaid,* there's also a rendition of "Under the Sea." But most of the show's songs come from less-familiar Disney films such as *Hercules, The Jungle Book, Mulan, Pinocchio,* and *Tangled,* making it easier to sit through than most other shows of this type.

OTHER LIVE PERFORMANCES

BESIDES LIVE STAGE SHOWS, the Walt Disney Theatre hosts variety acts including everything from magicians and comedians to ventriloquists, jugglers, and musicians. Many of these acts will do preview shows or short sets at various venues throughout the ship before their engagement at the theater. If there are previews, we suggest catching a few minutes (or asking other guests who've seen them) to decide whether the act is worth your time.

In our experience, the best live acts tend to be the magicians and comedians, who can adapt their material to the audience as the show is happening, and revamp parts of their act between shows.

▮ MOVIES

RECENT DISNEY MOVIES, including films released during the cruise, are shown at the **Buena Vista Theatre** on each Disney ship. Each theater is equipped with digital film projectors, state-of-the-art sound systems, and the capability to show 3-D films (complete with 3-D glasses for guests). Padded, upholstered seats are arranged stairlike behind the screen, allowing good views from almost anywhere in the theater. About half a dozen films are shown on any cruise, typically two or three per day beginning around 9:30 a.m. and running through midnight. Admission is free. Popcorn and drinks are sold outside the theater before and during each presentation; you can also bring your own snacks and drinks.

Classic Disney films are also shown on a giant 24-by-14-foot LED screen perched high above each ship's family pool (**Goofy's Pool** on Deck 9 of the *Magic* and *Wonder;* **Donald's Pool** on Deck 11 of the *Dream* and *Fantasy*).

LIVE SPORTS

ON THE *Wonder,* the main sports bar is **Diversions;** it's **687** on the *Dream* and **O'Gills** on the *Magic* and *Fantasy.* These are your primary venues for viewing baseball, basketball, and soccer. NFL football games are usually shown here too, and some games are also shown on the ships' **Funnel Vision** big screen on the pool deck. Keep in mind that the ship gets its TV broadcasts from satellite transmissions, which can be affected by weather. If you want to watch a specific game, show up at least 30 minutes beforehand and ask a crew member to find the right station—there are hundreds of channels, and it sometimes takes a while to find your game.

THEME NIGHTS *and* HOLIDAY ENTERTAINMENT

PIRATE NIGHT

THIS IS HELD ON ONE NIGHT on virtually every cruise. The crew, restaurants, and entertainment take on a pirate theme. The ship's transformation begins early in the day, when the usual background music is replaced by songs and audio from the theme parks' Pirates of the Caribbean ride and the spinoff film series. Afternoon craft sessions and family activities are pirate-themed as well. Sometime in the afternoon, your stateroom attendant will drop off in your cabin a pirate bandana for each member of your group to wear, as well as booty such as chocolate "coins" covered in gold foil.

unofficial **TIP**
Even cruises that go nowhere near the Caribbean will include the Pirates IN the Caribbean theme night. We don't get it either. If your cruise is only three nights long, you will miss out on the special menu on Pirate Night and be served your main dining room's standard menu.

On cruises of four-plus nights, each ship's main restaurant will have a special menu for the evening, designed to look like a treasure map. Virtually all of the crew, as well as the ship's officers, will wear special pirate outfits, and families have an opportunity to pose for photos with them before dinner. Many guests pack special outfits just for Pirate Night, including black knee-length boots, capri pants, white puffy shirts, and eyeliner. (The women dress up too.)

Pirate Night concludes with a stage show and video on the family pool's Funnel Vision screen, accompanied by a short fireworks display. The fireworks are usually shot from the starboard side, so you'll have a better view from there. The best viewing spots are as follows:

- *Magic* and *Wonder:* Deck 10 Starboard, looking over the Goofy Pool
- *Dream* and *Fantasy:* Deck 12 Forward, near Currents bar

FORMAL NIGHT

THIS IS A CHANCE FOR FAMILIES to put on the ritz. The crew and officers also get into the act by wearing their dress whites. While there are no special meals or activities, you'll see many families getting their photos taken in the ship's atrium before or after dinner.

As for what *formal* or *dress-up* means, you'll see a wide range of interpretations. Many men, if not most, will wear a long-sleeved dress shirt, usually with a jacket; ties are optional. Most women will wear dresses or skirts, or pants with dressy tops. A nice shirt and pants are appropriate for teen boys, and teen girls usually dress as if they're going to a high school dance. Small children are not expected to dress up, but young girls frequently take this opportunity to don the outfit of their favorite princess. Frequently, you'll see a family decked to the nines, with the gentlemen in tuxes and the ladies in gowns.

*un*official **TIP**
Formal Night is very popular for reservations at Palo and Remy.

If you don't have any fancy duds handy, you can rent them before you leave home by visiting **Cruiseline Formalwear** (**cruiselineformal wear.com**). Your garments will be delivered directly to your stateroom, and you'll return them to your stateroom attendant at the end of your cruise.

HALLOWEEN

ONE OF THE BEST PLACES TO CELEBRATE HALLOWEEN is on a Disney cruise. The crew and officers dress up, and many families bring special costumes to wear for this one night on board. Even the Disney characters dress up—one of our favorite memories is being "attacked" by Zombie Goofy one Halloween on board the *Magic*, while his guide murmured "Brains!" as they shuffled along.

Most of the family activities have a Halloween theme: Animation classes feature scary characters, the crafts sessions may be villain-themed, and even the karaoke is spooky. As darkness falls, photographers are stationed in each ship's atrium before and after dinner, so families can get photos of themselves dressed up. Kids can visit various areas of the ship to trick or treat.

DCL ships begin celebrating Halloween in September, just as at the theme parks. Expect to see pumpkins, black cats, and other decor starting around the last week of September and running through October 31. Every ship offers Halloween-themed movies, deck parties, craft-making, and more.

Introduce your kids to the audience-participation legacy of *The Rocky Horror Picture Show* at the **Nightmare Before Christmas Sing and Scream.** Sing along with the movie, and then meet Jack and Sally after the show. There's also a new deck Halloween-themed deck party, *Mickey's Calling All the Monsters Mouse-Querade,* along with story-telling sessions for kids. For the grown-ups, the ship's dance club hosts a costume party.

THANKSGIVING

IF YOUR CRUISE DATES INCLUDE THE FOURTH THURSDAY in November, you'll be celebrating Thanksgiving aboard your ship. Expect to see Mickey, Minnie, Goofy, and Donald in their Pilgrim costumes, plus many other Disney characters in seasonal outfits. However, don't be surprised to see the rest of the ship already decked out for Christmas. The main dining rooms on each ship will serve a traditional Thanksgiving menu. And it wouldn't be Turkey Day without (American) football, even on DCL. Games are broadcast on each ship's big Funnel Vision LED screen near the family pool, as well as at the sports bars.

CHRISTMAS, HANUKKAH, AND KWANZAA

DISNEY BEGINS DECORATING ITS SHIPS FOR THE WINTER holidays around the middle of November. Holiday-themed activities, events, and entertainment usually start around December 1 each year, including a Christmas tree, Hanukkah menorah, and Kwanzaa kinara placed in each ship's atrium. A tree-lighting ceremony typically takes place on the first night of each cruise in December.

Family activities include making holiday greeting cards, drawing Disney characters in holiday outfits, building gingerbread houses, and so on. As at Epcot theme park, each ship will have storytellers scheduled throughout the day, along with special holiday-themed merchandise. Expect to see Mickey, Minnie, Goofy, and other characters dressed in winter finery, and lots of holiday movies on your stateroom television.

The most interesting decorations, however, are on **Castaway Cay,** where palm trees are decorated with garland, lights, and bulbs, and plastic snowmen sit on the sand. Disney characters wear holiday-themed island outfits, and even the shuttle bus from the dock is decorated with reindeer antlers.

Religious services are typically offered during each night of Hanukkah. A Catholic Mass is held at midnight on December 24, and a Mass and interdenominational service are held on December 25. Santa Claus distributes small gifts to children in the atrium on Christmas morning, along with milk and cookies. Should you need a little gift-wrapping help, that service is available on board at no extra charge. Check your *Personal Navigator* for the location, or ask at Guest Services.

Finally, the ship's onboard music, piped into the hallways and public areas, switches from standard Disney tunes to Christmas-themed tracks. Some people enjoy it; others prefer the standard Disney music.

NEW YEAR'S EVE

DURING THE DAY, video screens on each ship's pool deck display a clock counting down the hours, minutes, and seconds until midnight. The pool deck is also the site for a big family-themed party in the evening, with DJs and live entertainment continuing through midnight. Each ship's dance club also hosts a party, complete with DJ, hats, noise-makers, confetti, and bubbly drinks at midnight. Families will want to see the special fireworks display and the atrium's balloon drop at midnight. The ships' kids' clubs host parties early in the evening, allowing the little ones to get to bed at a reasonable hour.

NIGHTCLUBS, BARS, CAFÉS, *and* LOUNGES

DISNEY CRUISE LINE'S SHIPS and entertainment are targeted primarily to families, but each ship has a collection of adult-oriented nightclubs and lounges to visit. All serve alcohol. Nightclubs typically offer dancing and live acts, such as magicians; lounges are oriented to conversation, with smaller spaces and comfortable seating.

> *unofficial* **TIP**
> The drinking age on all DCL itineraries is 21. The exception is round-trip sailings from a European port, in which case guests ages 18–20 may drink with a parent or guardian's written consent.

This section lists the nightclubs and lounges found across all four ships; we've included the **Cove Café** coffee bar as well, since it also serves alcoholic drinks. Club hours vary, so check your *Personal Navigator* for exact schedules.

ON THE *MAGIC*

Cove Café   LOCATION: Deck 9 Midship

SETTING AND ATMOSPHERE Cove Café is the *Magic*'s adults-only coffee bar and one of our favorite places on the ship. The walls are covered in a combination of light-cherry-colored wood paneling and upholstered fabric, while the floor is a mixture of honey-tinted hardwoods. What we like best is the way Disney has arranged seating along the curved, L-shaped bar: At one end is a private rounded corner cutout with a couple of comfortable stuffed chairs. At the opposite end is an open area with satellite TV, couches, and armchairs. Depending on how social you're feeling, you can sit by yourself at one end or be among a group at the other.

SELECTIONS Cove serves just about every java you can think of: espresso, cappuccino, latte, Americano, and flavored variations. The Cove serves Illy espresso and has excellent service. Cove also serves hot teas and has a good selection of wines, Champagnes, spirits, and mixed drinks. Prices for these are the same as throughout the rest of the ship.

> *unofficial* **TIP**
> If you're one of those people who need a coffee or six every day, ask your server for a **Café Fanatic** rewards card; you'll get every sixth specialty coffee free.

Besides beverages, the Cove Café has a self-serve refrigerated case stocked with small bites to eat throughout the day. Breakfast items usually include plain and chocolate croissants, Danish, and fruit. Afternoon and evening service usually consists of cookies, brownies, cakes, crackers, and fruit. Dinner, though, is our favorite, because for a couple of hours Cove Café brings out a selection of prosciutto, dried sausages, marinated olives, cheeses, and bread. You can make a light supper out of these and a drink, and because most families are either at dinner or preparing for it, there's a chance you'll have the café all to yourself.

COMMENTS The Wi-Fi signal here is fairly strong, making it a good spot to catch up on e-mail or the latest news. You'll also find here a small selection of current magazines and periodicals, and this is part of the real attraction at the Cove: the ability to sit in a comfy chair, surrounded by $350 million of luxury cruise ship, sip coffee, and flip through the pages of *The New Yorker* in blessed silence.

ACROSS THE SHIPS All four DCL ships have a Cove Café. Those on the *Magic* and *Wonder* are more or less identical, and a little larger than the Cove Cafés on the *Dream* and *Fantasy*. The Cove on the *Wonder*, however, connects to the **Outlook Café** (see page 115), which is unique to that ship. The Coves on the *Dream* and *Fantasy* are likewise almost identical twins, but they don't have the televisions found in the cafés on the *Magic* and *Wonder*. Guests at all Cove Cafés must be at least age 18 to enter, at least 21 to drink.

Promenade Lounge LOCATION: Deck 3 Aft

SETTING AND ATMOSPHERE The Promenade Lounge hosts family activities during the day and live music at night. It's done in the same Art Deco style as the rest of the *Magic*, with cherrywood finishes, creamy lighting, and brass accents. Sixteen computers line one wall, providing 24-hour Internet access . . . because nothing goes together like alcohol and the Web.

SELECTIONS Beer and wine by the glass, spirits, mixed drinks, and coffee. Free snacks are served starting in the afternoon—mostly chips, salsa, and the like.

COMMENTS Though one of the most attractive nightspots on the ship, the Promenade Lounge sits adjacent and open to pedestrian traffic from one of the *Magic*'s main inside walkways, making it louder and less relaxing than it could be. Nighttime entertainment is usually provided by a singing duo, such as a pianist and vocalist, making for an enjoyable way to spend half an hour after a meal. (For the performers, though, it's got to be like singing in a bus station due to the outside noise. Some glass and wood partitions would work wonders here.) We recommend using the Promenade as a meeting place for groups to get a drink before dinner at Carioca's or Lumiere's (see Part Seven, Dining) or to listen to the live music with a nightcap.

ACROSS THE SHIPS There's also a Promenade Lounge on the *Wonder*. Like the Promenade on the *Magic*, it's a nice place to have a before- or after-dinner cocktail, as long as you can deal with all the people promenading past on their way to other parts of the ship. The comparable bar on the *Dream* and *Fantasy* is **Bon Voyage** (see page 118).

Signals LOCATION: Deck 9 Midship

SETTING AND ATMOSPHERE Signals is an adults-only outdoor bar next to the adult pool. It has a few seats for those looking to get some shade, but most patrons take their drinks back to their deck chairs to sip in the sun.

SELECTIONS Much of Signals' menu is devoted to popular beers and frozen drinks, but they can whip up almost anything you can think of. Signals also serves coffee, juices, and bottled water. Soda machines are nearby.

COMMENTS It doesn't have much atmosphere to speak of, but due to its location near the Quiet Cove Pool, it is a little quieter than most bars.

ACROSS THE SHIPS Only the *Magic* and *Wonder* have Signals bars. The *Dream* and *Fantasy* have a total of four outdoor bars: one on each ship called **Currents** and another on each ship called **Waves** (see pages 119 and 120, respectively). Drinks and service are comparable at all of these, but we think Currents has the best views and the nicest decor. Also, Signals serves guests age 21 and older only, while Currents and Waves welcome kids.

After Hours

This is Disney's name for the collection of bars on the *Magic*'s Deck 3 Forward. It includes **Fathoms,** a venue for live entertainment and dancing; **Keys,** a piano bar; and **O'Gills Pub,** a sports bar. Newly rethemed after the ship's fall 2013 dry dock, After Hours has a contemporary urban nightclub theme, pulled together by a new white-and-silver color scheme, accented by chrome light fixtures. It's a welcome improvement over the former club space, Beat Street, which consisted of painted two-dimensional plywood shapes painted to look like a cityscape at night.

Some After Hours lounges, such as Fathoms, are home to family-oriented entertainment during the day, but all usually have an adults-only policy (age 18 and up to enter, 21 and up to drink) after 9 p.m.

After Hours' bars generally carry the same selection of wine and beer, although each serves its own unique line of cocktails. O'Gills Pub, the sports bar, also has a collection of Irish beers not found elsewhere.

Fathoms LOCATION: Deck 3 Forward

SETTING AND ATMOSPHERE Formerly Rockin' Bar D, Fathoms has an undersea theme: fiber-optic light fixtures shaped like jellyfish, sand-art murals along the bar, and silver-and-black bench seating that undulates like ocean waves. Six sets of couches are built into Fathoms' back wall, providing an excellent semiprivate view of the entertainment stage.

The middle of the club holds a dance floor and a raised stage with a professional sound system and lighting. Armchairs upholstered in silver fabric are arranged in groups of two or three around circular cocktail tables. These help control the echo in Fathoms' large, open floor plan.

SELECTIONS Sea-themed cocktails make up most of Fathoms' bar menu, although beer, wine, and spirits are also available. Drinks range in price from $8.75 for a **Black Pearl** (Crown Royal, Drambuie, and Coke) to $10.75 for a **Blue Tang** (Grey Goose citrus vodka, peach schnapps, blue curaçao, pineapple juice, and sugared rum). Our favorite is the $9.75

Anemone, with gin, mango puree, and muddled lemon, orange, and lime, topped with Champagne.

COMMENTS Like other DCL nightclubs, Fathoms does double-duty during the day by hosting family-oriented activities such as scavenger hunts, bingo, and talent shows. At night the stage hosts everything from game shows to live music, dancing, DJs, karaoke, comedians, magicians, and other performers. The game shows' setups follow well-known television models: There's one similar to *The Newlywed Game,* for example, where contestants try to guess how their partner will answer some random set of questions. This being Disney, though, you probably won't hear any questions about "making whoopee."

ACROSS THE SHIPS Fathoms doesn't have an identical sibling on the other ships, but it's most similar to **WaveBands** on the *Wonder* (see page 118), **Evolution** on the *Dream* (see page 122), and **The Tube** on the *Fantasy* (see page 130).

Keys **LOCATION:** Deck 3 Forward

SETTING AND ATMOSPHERE Keys features live piano music nightly. Six large porthole windows run along one of the rectangular room's long walls. The bar is in the middle of the opposite wall, and the piano player is between the two, at the far end of the room from the entrance doors.

Keys' theming got an overhaul during the *Magic*'s 2013 dry dock, and it's now supposed to evoke a Chicago-style lounge from the 1960s. The new furnishings include modern sofas and chairs whose curved, radius-style arms and backs are in marked contrast to the formless oversize chairs of the previous decor. Gone also is the pastel carpet, in favor of a crisp silver with geometric sunbursts. The live entertainment's audio levels tend to be a bit loud for such a small space, but it's a pleasant enough experience.

SELECTIONS The bar menu includes specialty drinks with music-themed names, such as the **Moji-Do,** a mojito; **Bloody Mi-Re,** a Bloody Mary with vodka, yellow-tomato juice, lime, and whiskey-flavored Worcestershire sauce; and **Rob Roy,** made the typical way (Scotch, vermouth, and bitters), only *Rob* is spelled with the musical symbol for a flat note. Most of these cocktails are about $10.75, about $5 more per drink that at O'Gills Pub (see next profile). The most expensive drink is a $15 Manhattan, made with Jack Daniel's Sinatra Select whiskey, Antica Formula vermouth, and Cointreau. Coffee, cappuccino, and espresso are available too, but we recommend the Cove Café if you're looking for those.

COMMENTS Live entertainment usually begins with a show around 7:30 p.m.; a typical night's schedule will have more performances around 9:30, 10:30, and 11:30 p.m. The pianists are acceptable, if nondescript, and play medleys of well-known songs by familiar artists. Some nights have themes, such as '50s and '60s hits, Elvis, or Simon and Garfunkel, and you can always make requests.

During the day, Keys is often used for group seminars on everything from wine and spirits to acupuncture, Chinese herbs, and back-pain treatments. (We sense a "feel better one way or another" theme here.) Check your *Personal Navigator* for details. The bar typically opens anywhere from 5:30 to 6:30 p.m. Children are admitted to Keys until 9 p.m., when it becomes an adults-only venue until its midnight closing.

ACROSS THE SHIPS The *Magic*'s Keys is most similar to the *Wonder*'s **Cadillac Lounge** (see next page). The entertainment is interchangeable between the two, and the retro decor is a toss-up.

O'Gills Pub   LOCATION: Deck 3 Forward

SETTING AND ATMOSPHERE The former Diversions has been rechristened as an Irish bar—the name is a nod to the Disney classic *Darby O'Gill and the Little People*—although it's an "Irish bar" in the same way that Lucky Charms is an "Irish breakfast," which is to say not very. Sure, there's a clover pattern woven into the green carpet and background music that features a lot of fiddle-and-flute and U2, but if you've come expecting Raglan Road at Walt Disney World, you're in for a disappointment.

Nine wall-mounted televisions provide live satellite coverage of whatever sports are being played around the world. Comfortable burgundy-leather banquettes are built into the wall, and padded leather armchairs surround the tables set within the banquettes. In the middle of the room, about a dozen bar-height tables and stools provide the best views of the most TVs.

SELECTIONS The bar menu includes a beer flight of five 5-ounce Irish brews ($9.75). There's also a selection of Irish whiskeys: Tullamore Dew ($9.25), Kilbeggan ($9.25), Middleton ($11.50), and Connemara ($12.50). Beyond these are standard drinks you'll find throughout the ships, including cocktails; red, white, and sparkling wines; and Scotch and other whiskeys. The cocktails are reasonably priced at $5.75 each. Try the **Royal Velvet,** a mix of Guinness stout and sparkling wine.

COMMENTS A comfy spot to sit, sip, and watch the game.

ACROSS THE SHIPS O'Gills Pub on the *Magic* joins the *Fantasy*'s bar of the same name (see page 127). Along with the *Dream*'s **687** (see page 124), these are the DCL fleet's upscale sports bars. The bigger televisions at the *Magic*'s O'Gills make it easier to watch events from across the room. The open seating at **Diversions** on the *Wonder* (see page 117) means that you're more likely to interact with other guests, whereas you can more easily keep to yourself at 687 and both O'Gills.

ON THE *WONDER*

Cove Café   LOCATION: Deck 9 Forward

COMMENTS See profile of Cove Café on the *Magic* (page 111) for details.

Outlook Café   LOCATION: Deck 10 Forward

SETTING AND ATMOSPHERE What makes the Outlook Café special is that its seating area is surrounded by large glass windows, making it the perfect venue in which to get some sun in a climate-controlled environment. This means air-conditioning when the *Wonder* is in the Caribbean and heat when it's plying the waters off Alaska.

SELECTIONS Coffees, teas, wine, beer, mixed drinks, and Champagne by the glass. Complimentary snacks are also offered.

COMMENTS An extension of the Cove Café, the Outlook Café, found upstairs via a spiral staircase, is a lovely place to while away some time.

ACROSS THE SHIPS The Outlook Café is unique to the *Wonder*. As at the Cove Cafés, guests must be age 18 to enter, 21 to drink.

Promenade Lounge   LOCATION: Deck 3 Aft

COMMENTS See profile of Promenade Lounge on the *Magic* (page 112) for details.

Signals   LOCATION: Deck 9 Midship

COMMENTS See profile of Signals on the *Magic* (page 112) for details.

Route 66

This is the designation for the bars and lounges found on the *Wonder*'s Deck 3 Forward. As you might guess from the name, the theming is a nostalgic tribute to what was once America's premier highway: road signs, old-timey gas pumps, and murals depicting billboards and postcards from the days before the Jet Age.

Route 66 has a dance club, **WaveBands,** that also hosts games and entertainers such as magicians at night. A piano bar, the **Cadillac Lounge,** and a sports bar, **Diversions,** round out the area. Of these, we like Cadillac Lounge the most, but we find all the clubs far too large and impersonal to be truly enjoyable. Some Route 66 lounges, such as WaveBands, are home to family-oriented entertainment during the day, but all usually have an adults-only policy after 9 p.m.

Route 66's bars have substantially the same drink menus, but the Cadillac Lounge is the only club of the three that serves Champagne by the glass.

Cadillac Lounge   LOCATION: Deck 3 Forward

SETTING AND ATMOSPHERE This is the *Wonder*'s piano bar. The decor pays tribute to 1950s-era Cadillac cars by way of leather-upholstered barstools and chairs, couches made to look like automobile rear seats, and a bar built into a replica of the front of a Cadillac Coupe de Ville, complete with working headlights.

"Designed by General Motors" isn't something we normally listen for when discussing bar theming, but it works here. The furnishings—with dark woods; carpets in burgundy, gold, and fuchsia; leather-covered walls; chrome accents; and those butter-and-chocolate-colored leather barstools—clearly indicate that this is a bar meant to evoke a very specific time and place.

The best seats in the house are in the far corner, opposite the main entrance and to the right of the piano player. These include a comfortable leather couch and two leather armchairs, plus a side table to hold drinks. From here you can listen to the music and watch some of the action at the bar, tucked away in your own discreet corner of the lounge.

SELECTIONS The Cadillac Lounge serves beer, wine, spirits, and cocktails, and it's the only bar in Route 66 that serves Champagne by the glass (outside Route 66, the **Outlook Café** also serves Champagne; see page 115). Coffee, cappuccino, and espresso are available as well, but we'd recommend the Cove Café if you're looking for those. Free snacks and appetizers, including caviar, are available all evening.

COMMENTS Live entertainment usually begins with a show around 7:30 p.m.; a typical night's schedule will have more performances around 9:30, 10:30, and 11:30 p.m. The pianists are acceptable, if nondescript, and play medleys of well-known songs by familiar artists. Some nights have themes, such as '50s and '60s hits, Elvis, or Simon and Garfunkel, and you can always make requests.

During the day, the Cadillac Lounge is often used for group seminars on everything from wine and spirits to homeopathic treatments such as acupuncture. Check your *Personal Navigator* for details. The bar typically opens anywhere from 5:30 to 6:30 p.m. Children are admitted to the Cadillac Lounge until 9 p.m., when it becomes an adults-only venue until its midnight closing.

ACROSS THE SHIPS The Cadillac Lounge is most similar to the *Magic*'s **Keys** (see page 114). The entertainment is interchangeable between the two, and the retro decor is a toss-up.

Diversions LOCATION: Deck 3 Forward

SETTING AND ATMOSPHERE Diversions is the *Wonder*'s sports bar. Large LCD screens are mounted on walls and columns all around the room, allowing you to watch multiple games in progress at the same time. There's plenty of seating—mostly large fabric-covered and upholstered chairs, plus a handful of semicircular booths in the back—to accommodate large crowds. If you're interested in playing a few games, Diversions has tables for checkers, chess, and backgammon too.

SELECTIONS Diversions usually has a hot-appetizer bar available during games, with nachos, hot dogs, wings, and other bar food. A full drink menu is available, and waitstaff serve you at your seat so you don't have to miss any of the game.

COMMENTS We've had a good time watching basketball at Diversions. Given the size of the ship, the odds are good that you'll be able to find other fans of your favorite teams too. And because Diversions' satellite feed pulls in sporting events from around the world, there's always something to watch. If there's a specific game that you want to see, show up at least 30 minutes before the game and ask a member of the crew to find the right station—with literally hundreds of channels, it sometimes takes a while to find the right one.

Besides televised sports, Diversions hosts family-oriented and adult activities throughout the day, ranging from Disney-character-drawing classes for kids to trivia contests and afternoon beer tastings. Check your *Personal Navigator* for the schedule.

ACROSS THE SHIPS Diversions is the least interesting sports bar in the DCL fleet, with decor more likely to be found in an Omaha Marriott than on a billion-dollar cruise ship. **687** on the *Dream* (see page 124) and the Irish-themed **O'Gills** on the *Magic* and *Fantasy* (see pages 115 and 127, respectively) are a little more upscale. Diversions' open floor plan means that you're more likely to interact with other guests, whereas you can keep to yourself more easily at 687 and O'Gills.

WaveBands   LOCATION: **Deck 3 Forward**

SETTING AND ATMOSPHERE This is the *Wonder*'s dance club. The idea behind the theming is that you're supposed to be inside a radio. Lightning bolts line the ceiling, representing the flow of electricity, and illuminated green photographs of computer circuit boards line the bar and railings. Padded chairs surround small, round tables, and because WaveBands doubles as an activity space for families during the day, there's plenty of room to sit.

SELECTIONS The usual wine, beer, spirits, and mixed drinks. Free hors d'oeuvres and snacks are available all evening.

COMMENTS The ship's crew sometimes dons costumes and leads dances on WaveBands' dance floor. Thus, you may see crew members barely old enough to drink doing their best imitation of John Travolta in his white polyester suit from *Saturday Night Fever*. Depending on how much the people around you are participating—which is probably linked to how much the people around you are drinking—this is either funny or sad. Do the young 'uns a favor and jump out on the dance floor.

ACROSS THE SHIPS WaveBands doesn't have an identical sibling on the other ships, but it's most similar to **Fathoms** on the *Magic* (see page 113), **Evolution** on the *Dream* (see page 122), and **The Tube** on the *Fantasy* (see page 130). WaveBands' theming is the oldest and least sophisticated, which makes sense because the *Wonder* is the second-oldest ship and hasn't undergone refurbishment as the *Magic* has.

ON THE *DREAM*

Bon Voyage   LOCATION: **Deck 3 Midship**

SETTING AND ATMOSPHERE Sitting just off the atrium, Bon Voyage is one of the prettiest, if not smallest, of the *Dream*'s bars, with just 10 seats at the counter plus 4 covered armchairs a few feet away. The two highlights here are the gorgeous Art Deco mural behind the bar—which shows well-heeled passengers in 1920s formal wear departing their touring cars to board the *Dream*—and the swirled, maize-yellow illuminated bar face, which reflects gold light off the beige-marble floors.

SELECTIONS Bon Voyage's bar menu is similar to that in The District (see page 121) and includes draft and bottled beer, wines by the glass and bottle, spirits, and mixed drinks, including a few special fruit-flavored martinis. Service is excellent.

COMMENTS Open from around noon to 11 p.m. daily, Bon Voyage is a good spot for groups to meet before dinner or to have a nightcap before departing for the elevators. Because it's in a heavily trafficked area, there's no live entertainment, and it isn't our first choice for a quiet drink or conversation, but it is a good place to fortify yourself while standing in those character-greeting lines. Sometimes you need a little liquid courage to face Chip 'n' Dale.

ACROSS THE SHIPS The *Fantasy* also has a Bon Voyage just off the Deck 3 atrium; the *Dream*'s Bon Voyage is more appealing, even without live entertainment. The **Promenade Lounge** is the comparable bar on the *Magic* and *Wonder* (see page 112).

Cove Café   LOCATION: Deck 11 Forward

COMMENTS See profile of Cove Café on the *Magic* (page 111) for details.

Currents   LOCATION: Deck 13 Forward

SETTING AND ATMOSPHERE This outdoor area has the best views of any bar on the *Dream*. Built behind and into the structure supporting the forward stairs and elevators, the curved, glossy white face of the bar mirrors the curve along the opposite deck rail and provides some shade during the day. Currents is beautiful at night, when a royal-blue neon sign (which calls to mind the nameplate on a 1950s car) lights up the bar and bar shelves, accented with matching blue tile.

Ten stationary barstools are spaced far enough apart for easy access to walk-up traffic. Most guests take drinks back to their lounge chairs, but there's also plenty of (unshaded) armchair seating around Currents.

SELECTIONS Currents serves bottled and draft beer, cocktails, and frozen drinks.

COMMENTS The one downside to Currents is that it's next to a smoking section. Depending on the prevailing winds, this is either not an issue at all or a mild annoyance.

ACROSS THE SHIPS Currents is the same on the *Dream* and the *Fantasy*. **Signals** on the *Magic* and *Wonder* is similar (see page 112), but Currents' layout is much more open, with much better views and nicer decor. Also, where Signals is adults-only, Currents welcomes kids and serves nonalcoholic concoctions just for them.

Meridian   LOCATION: Deck 12 Aft

SETTING AND ATMOSPHERE Situated between the restaurants Palo and Remy, Meridian is the *Dream*'s martini bar. It's also one of our favorite bars on the ship.

Sitting high up on Deck 12 Aft, Meridian has windows on three sides of its relatively small, square room. Panoramic views of the sunset await early diners who stop in around dusk. Antique ship-navigation maps and instruments adorn the walls and shelves. Meridian's furnishings include rich brown-leather couches and armchairs, and cocoa-colored teak floors with brass inlays. Meridian also has outdoor seating on a teak deck that runs along one wall of Remy. It's lovely on warm summer evenings—and in demand around dusk, so don't be surprised if it's standing room–only.

SELECTIONS Meridian's bar menu emphasizes mixed drinks and spirits over beer and wine, although those are also available, as are coffees. The best thing about Meridian is the bartending staff, who will often offer to make a custom martini for you on the spot. This usually starts with the bartender—ask for Alexandra if she's working—inquiring whether you like fruit- or herb-based drinks and what kinds of liquors you usually prefer. A couple of minutes of muddling, shaking, and stirring, and you have the first draft of your new drink. And if it's not quite what you expected, they'll be happy to start over.

COMMENTS We recommend stopping by Meridian for its martini experience alone, even if you don't have reservations for Remy or Palo (see Part Seven). If you're dining at Remy, though, beware of the combined effect of Meridian's martinis and Remy's wine pairings—as Len found out, it may be more than you bargained for.

Meridian usually opens around 5 p.m. and stays open until midnight. It's one of the few DCL nightspots with a dress code: Inside the lounge, men should wear dress shirts and pants, and women should wear dresses, skirts and blouses, or pantsuits. If you're just visiting the outdoor area, jeans and shorts are allowed, but swimwear, T-shirts, or tank tops are verboten.

ACROSS THE SHIPS Both the *Dream* and the *Fantasy* have nearly identical Meridian lounges; the *Magic* and *Wonder* do not.

Vista Café   LOCATION: Deck 4 Midship

SETTING AND ATMOSPHERE A small, Art Deco–themed nook in a corner of Deck 4.

SELECTIONS Vista Café serves everything from coffee and complimentary pastries in the morning to beer, wine, cocktails, and light snacks at night.

COMMENTS With only four seats at the bar, this isn't the place for large groups. It's most useful as a place for a family to get a drink and a bite to eat on their way to one of the day's activities on Decks 3 or 4.

ACROSS THE SHIPS Vista Cafés can be found on both the *Dream* and the *Fantasy* but not the *Magic* or *Wonder*. Both cafés offer the same food and drink and are about the same size; the only significant difference is the decor—the Vista on the *Fantasy* has that ship's Art Nouveau theme rather than the Art Deco styling of the *Dream*. The marble floor of the *Fantasy*'s version is a bit bigger than the *Dream*'s, making the former Vista Café seem more of an intentionally designed space versus one carved out of an underutilized corner.

Waves   LOCATION: Deck 12 Aft

SETTING AND ATMOSPHERE Tucked behind the rear smokestack, Waves is an outdoor bar catering primarily to sunbathers on Deck 12. Waves' eight fixed barstools are arranged around an attractive white tile face, and the back of the bar is decorated with small tiles in varying shades of blue. An overhang above the bar provides shade for guests seated or standing at the bar, but most of the seating—upholstered blue cushions on glossy, curved-back teak booths, plus various sets of tables and chairs—is directly in the sun.

SELECTIONS The most popular drinks at Waves are bottled beers, frozen cocktails, and mixed drinks. Nonalcoholic smoothies and fruit juices are available for children and teetotalers.

COMMENTS Waves' hours vary, but it's usually open from late morning to late evening. Most visitors are coming from the lounge chairs or sports activities on Deck 13; some are just looking for a quiet spot away from the crowds.

ACROSS THE SHIPS Both the *Dream* and the *Fantasy* have Waves bars, and they're essentially identical. **Signals** is the outdoor bar on the *Magic* and *Wonder* (see page 112); Waves, however, is quieter, has nicer decor, and welcomes kids (Signals is 21-and-up only).

The District

This is the designation for the five bars and lounges on the *Dream*'s Deck 4 Aft: **District Lounge,** in a hallway connecting the different venues; **Evolution,** a dance club; **Pink,** a Champagne bar; **687,** an upscale sports bar; and **Skyline,** a cosmopolitan watering hole.

The theming is meant to evoke images of exclusive urban nightlife. Along the faux-brick walls and behind velvet ropes are black-plastic silhouettes of couples "waiting" to get in. Other walls have black-plastic images of paparazzi, or simply the logos of the clubs illuminated in a repeating pattern.

Most of The District's bars open between 5 and 5:30 p.m. and stay open until midnight. District Lounge usually opens a little earlier; Evolution usually operates from around 10 p.m. to 2 a.m. Hot snacks are usually provided throughout the evening in one of The District's circular pedestrian walkways.

Evolution, Pink, and Skyline only admit guests age 18 and up. Families are welcome at District Lounge and 687 until 9 p.m., when they become adults-only.

District Lounge   LOCATION: Deck 4 Aft

SETTING AND ATMOSPHERE An attractive, contemporary bar and seating area are bisected by a walkway connecting The District's bars. The bar seats six along its curving, white-stone front. Lights hidden beneath the black-marble top point down, creating smoky gray shadows in the stone. Behind the bar is a bronze-colored wall; orange lighting illuminates the bottles and provides this side of District Lounge with its most prominent color.

A lounge with couches and armchairs sits across the walkway opposite the bar, and although it's not perfect, it's one of the more stylish places on the *Dream*. While the lounge is completely open (and exposed to noise from) guests going from club to club, off-white leather couches, champagne-colored metal poles, and cocoa-colored carpeting provide a visual boundary marking its border. Deeper inside are U-shaped armchairs, covered outside in the same white leather and inside in deep-brown leather, arranged in groups of four around small tables. A curving, chocolate-colored, illuminated wall provides a backdrop.

SELECTIONS The bar menu has a bit of everything: draft and bottled beer, cocktails, frozen drinks, whiskeys and tequilas, and wine and Champagne by the glass and bottle. There's also a special martini menu

($8.50–$9.50) not found at other clubs in The District. A few non-alcoholic drinks and coffee are available as well.

COMMENTS The best seats are along the lounge's inside wall, where you can relax in those deep armchairs while watching everyone else shuttle between clubs. This is also the best vantage point from which to watch the District Lounge's entertainment, which includes live singers and pianists later at night. The lounge is also a good meeting place to start out the evening, especially for groups who haven't decided which of The District's bars to visit.

ACROSS THE SHIPS The District Lounge roughly corresponds to the Venice-themed **La Piazza** lounge on the *Fantasy* (see page 128) but has no relative on the *Magic* or *Wonder*. We like the District Lounge more than La Piazza: Its recessed seating allows you to enjoy a drink away from the bustle of clubgoers walking to their next destination.

Evolution   LOCATION: Deck 4 Aft

SETTING AND ATMOSPHERE The *Dream*'s dance club, Evolution is, according to Disney, designed as "an artistic interpretation of the transformation of a butterfly . . . emerging from a chrysalis." What this entails is a lot of yellow, orange, and red lights arranged in the shape of butterfly wings and hung around the club. Pairs of wings hang above the dance floor, and we'll forgive you for comparing the slightly tipsy, dancing tourists to wriggling pupae. A couple of the walls are wing-patterned too, bathing guests seated at the leather couches alongside in hues of ginger and crimson.

Fortunately, most of the butterfly theming is concentrated around the dance floor and along a couple of back walls. Between the two it's not as noticeable; plastic-shell chairs sit in the dimly lit sections, occasionally alongside high-backed couches. Short barstools line the outside edge of the room, surrounding small, round tables. The circular bar has gold-leather seats on one side, allowing guests a view of the dance floor while they drink; the other half of the bar is for walk-up traffic.

SELECTIONS Evolution's drink menu is similar to District Lounge's, offering draft and bottled beer, cocktails, spirits, and wine and Champagne by the glass and bottle.

COMMENTS Because it's one of the largest venues on the *Dream*, Evolution is the site of family activities throughout the day, holding everything from hands-on craft-making seminars to tequila tastings to time-share presentations. Evolution's adults-only entertainment usually starts later than at other bars in The District, around 10 or 10:30 p.m.; check your *Personal Navigator* for details.

Live entertainment include magicians, comics, singers, and more. In addition to live acts, Evolution's DJs sometimes dedicate an entire night's music to a specific genre. Common themes include classic rock, disco, and something called urban country. Evolution also hosts get-togethers for adults ages 18–21, in an event helpfully called Club 18*21.

ACROSS THE SHIPS Evolution is most similar to **The Tube** dance club on the *Fantasy* (see page 130), **Fathoms** on the *Magic* (see page 113), and

WaveBands on the *Wonder* (see page 118). We rate Evolution as the second-best dance club on Disney Cruise Line, behind The Tube. Theming, lighting, and seating are nicer than at Fathoms and WaveBands, while The Tube's London Underground ambience is better executed than Evolution's more-conceptual "caterpillar to butterfly" idea.

Pink LOCATION: Deck 4 Aft

SETTING AND ATMOSPHERE Pink, the *Dream*'s Champagne bar, is our favorite nightspot on the ship. Decorated in silvers, whites, and golds, the space is intended to make you think you're sitting inside a glass of Champagne. In the walls are embedded round lights of white and pink, tiny near the floor and larger near the ceiling, imitating the carbon dioxide fizz inside a flute of bubbly. The silver carpet's starburst pattern calls to mind bubbles rising from below, and the rounded, glossy white ceiling is meant to represent the top of the glass. The light fixtures are upside-down Champagne flutes. Behind the bar are a multitude of glass "bubbles," expanding as they rise from the bar shelf to the ceiling.

Around the bar are half a dozen stools, with silver legs and clear, oval plastic backs that continue the bubble theme. Beyond the bar, a couple of burgundy chairs sit among their silver-velvet sisters. After a few drinks, we're pretty sure these are supposed to represent rosé Champagne, of which several are served at the bar. The best seats in the house, though, are on the padded couch inside a dome-shaped cubby in the wall at one end of the lounge. Move a couple of those big chairs in front and you have a private little cocoon, or slide them away for a view of the entire room.

SELECTIONS Pink's Champagne menu includes many recognizable names: Cristal, Moët et Chandon, Taittinger, Veuve Clicquot, and the requisite Dom Pérignon. Champagne-based cocktails are also available; most include fruit juices such as mango, pomegranate, and peach, while a few include other liquors—the **Elderbubble** ($10.50), for example, contains raspberry vodka along with Champagne and elderflower syrup. A small selection of white, red, and dessert wines is available by the glass (more by the bottle), along with a dozen or so whiskeys and Cognacs.

unofficial **TIP**
Look carefully inside a few of the bubble lights on the wall, and you'll see a tiny pink elephant from Disney's *Dumbo*. A little odd, because Dumbo is the mascot of the *Fantasy*, which has its own Champagne bar, the French-themed **Ooh La La** (no elephants).

COMMENTS If you love Champagne, Pink is a relative bargain. Its markup is generally less than twice the average retail price—usually considerably less than what Disney charges at its theme park resorts. For example, a bottle of Taittinger La Française sells for about $35 plus tax at your local wine store. The same bottle costs $69 at Pink: a fairly standard double bar markup, but a far cry from the $108 per bottle (a triple markup) charged on Disney property. Similarly, Pink's Dom Pérignon, at $225 per bottle, is marked up a little more than one-and-a-half times over retail—at Walt Disney World's Grand Floridian Resort, it's nearly $300 a bottle.

ACROSS THE SHIPS Only the *Dream* and the *Fantasy* have Champagne bars, and this is one of the main reasons we prefer these ships over the *Magic* and the *Wonder*. However, we like Pink's relatively understated theming better than the *très feminine* French-boudoir decor of **Ooh La La** on the *Fantasy* (see page 127).

687 LOCATION: Deck 4 Aft

SETTING AND ATMOSPHERE Anytime you see a venue with a dozen flat-panel TVs, there's a good chance that it's a sports bar. On the *Dream* it's 687, and the screens are set in rows above the bar, in a cluster at a far end of the room, and individually in some seating areas.

The bar is set in the middle of 687's rectangular floor. Four porthole windows across from the bar provide light during the day, and moss-colored couches beneath them work to separate the wall into group-size partitions. The scarlet, green, and gold carpet and burgundy-painted, wood-paneled walls give 687 a more masculine feel than the sports bars on the *Fantasy, Magic,* and *Wonder.*

Besides the couches, barstools and tables are arranged around the room to provide good views of either set of televisions. A few leather-covered armchairs are also arranged around the screens and across from the couches. There's plenty of room to stand between these too, in case you want to just catch up on some scores. Couches arranged in some of the corners provide quieter spots to unwind.

SELECTIONS Bar and table service are excellent. The menu is similar to District Lounge's and includes both draft and bottled beer, cocktails, spirits, and wine and Champagne by the glass, plus coffees and non-alcoholic drinks. Unique to 687 is a selection of "Beercktails" (a word that no self-respecting adult would ever use): cocktails of beer, spirits, and fruit juice. The most popular of these is the **Baha Fog** ($5.75), which adds a shot of tequila to a glass of Corona with lime.

COMMENTS We've spent a few evenings watching games at 687. The seating is comfortable, and it's easy to see and hear the action on the screens. Because of the way the seating is arranged, however, we've found it difficult to start conversations with other patrons. Try sitting at the bar if that's important to you.

Besides sporting events, 687 hosts family activities during the day, including movie, music, and sports trivia. A selection of board games is available in case you want to play rather than watch. Finally, this is usually where runners meet before debarking for the start of the Castaway Cay 5K run when the *Dream* is docked there.

ACROSS THE SHIPS We find 687 more upscale than **Diversions** on the *Wonder* (see page 117) or **O'Gills** on the *Magic* and *Fantasy* (see pages 115 and 127, respectively). While its seating isn't as open, it's a posh place to catch up on the day's highlights in relative quiet.

Skyline LOCATION: Deck 4 Aft

SETTING AND ATMOSPHERE Along with Pink, Skyline is one of our two favorite bars on the *Dream*. The concept is that you're in a lounge high on the edge of some of the world's most famous cities. Behind the bar are seven "windows"—large high-definition television screens—affording panoramic views of New York City, Chicago, Rio de Janeiro, Paris, and Hong Kong.

Each city is shown for about 15 minutes across all seven screens; then the scene changes to another locale. The foreground of each view includes close-up views of apartments and offices, while the middle and background show each city's iconic architecture and landscape.

That would be mildly interesting scenery on its own, but Disney has added special effects that make Skyline beautiful. Each view shows the city in motion: Cars move along streets, neon signs blink to illuminate sidewalks, and apartment lights go on and off as their residents come and go. (Look closely and you can even see Mickey Mouse waving to you from inside a tiny apartment in Paris.) A second effect is that the scenery changes depending on the time of day you're inside. If you get here in late afternoon, you'll see the sun setting on these towns. Stay long enough—and we have—and dusk turns to evening, then evening to night.

Last, Skyline has mirrors on the walls perpendicular to the video screens. Because the mirrors are set at right angles to the screens, they reflect the videos and make the bar look longer than it is. It's a well-known decorating trick for making a small room seem larger, but it's still nice to see included here.

The rest of the decor is natural surfaces: wood panels, ceiling, and floors, in colors ranging from honey to mahogany; dark marble countertops; and leather chairs.

SELECTIONS The specialty is "around the world" cocktails themed to the featured cities. For example, the **1914** ($8.50), representing Chicago, pairs Absolut Vanilla and Absolut Kurant vodkas with fresh blackberries and raspberries; the **Zen-Chanted** ($10.50), representing Hong Kong, is made with 3Vodka (distilled from soybeans), Zen green-tea liqueur, Cointreau, and guava and lime juices.

COMMENTS Adding movement to the scenery means the view at Skyline doesn't get boring. It also means that the club doesn't need a television to hold its patrons' attention. And the cityscapes are a great way to break the ice with fellow cruisers.

ACROSS THE SHIPS Although there are Skylines on both the *Dream* and the *Fantasy,* their drink menus are mostly different. Drinks at the *Dream*'s Skyline tend toward the fruity, whereas drinks at the *Fantasy*'s Skyline make more use of herbs and spices, such as basil, thyme, coriander, cilantro, and paprika.

ON THE *FANTASY*

Bon Voyage   LOCATION: Deck 3 Midship

SETTING AND ATMOSPHERE Just off the atrium and done in the same Art Nouveau style as the rest of the ship, Bon Voyage is one of the prettiest bars on the *Fantasy.* Behind the bar are two gold-and-white peacocks etched in glass, while the bar's face is a translucent gold marble. Cinnamon-colored wood accents complete the look. Bon Voyage has just 10 seats at the counter, plus 2 fabric-covered couches and 6 armchairs a few feet away.

SELECTIONS The bar menu is similar to that at La Piazza (see page 128) and includes draft and bottled beer, wines by the glass and bottle, spirits, and mixed drinks, including a few special fruit-flavored martinis.

COMMENTS Near the atrium and open from around noon to 11 p.m. daily, Bon Voyage is a good spot for groups to meet before dinner or have a nightcap before departing for the elevators. Because it's in a heavily trafficked area, there's no live entertainment at the bar, and it's not our first choice for a quiet drink or conversation.

ACROSS THE SHIPS The *Dream*'s Bon Voyage is done in Art Deco rather than the *Fantasy*'s Art Nouveau version and is more appealing, even without live entertainment. The **Promenade Lounge** is the comparable bar on the *Magic* and *Wonder* (see page 112).

Cove Café　LOCATION: Deck 11 Forward

COMMENTS See profile of Cove Café on the *Magic* (page 111) for details.

Currents　LOCATION: Deck 13 Forward

COMMENTS See profile of Currents on the *Dream* (page 119) for details.

Meridian　LOCATION: Deck 12 Aft

COMMENTS See profile of Meridian on the *Dream* (page 119) for details.

Vista Café　LOCATION: Deck 4 Midship

COMMENTS See profile of Vista Café on the *Dream* (page 120) for details.

Waves　LOCATION: Deck 12 Aft

COMMENTS See profile of Waves on the *Dream* (page 120) for details.

Europa

This is the designation for the five nightspots on the *Fantasy*'s Deck 4 Aft: **O'Gills Pub,** a sports bar; **Ooh La La,** a Champagne bar; **La Piazza,** an Italian-inspired lounge; **Skyline,** a cosmopolitan watering hole; and **The Tube,** a London subway–themed dance club.

While the nightlife districts on the other three ships have distinctive theming, Europa has next to none. The ostensible theme is Europe, but the decor consists mostly of just shiny gold walls, with each club's name illuminated and repeated in a pattern. That said, one nice touch found only at Europa lies in the round black-and-white photos on the walls: The images, which feature European icons including the Eiffel Tower, London's Big Ben, and the Leaning Tower of Pisa, turn into short animated videos. Also, for what it's worth, the bathrooms here are decorated fabulously and worth a special trip.

Most of Europa's bars open between 5 and 5:30 p.m. and stay open until midnight. La Piazza usually opens a little earlier than that; The Tube usually operates from around 10 p.m. to 2 a.m. Hot appetizers are usually provided throughout the evening in one of La Piazza's circular pedestrian walkways.

Ooh La La, Skyline, and The Tube only admit guests age 18 and up. Families are welcome at La Piazza and O'Gills Pub until 9 p.m., when they become adults-only.

O'Gills Pub   LOCATION: Deck 4 Aft

SETTING AND ATMOSPHERE The *Fantasy*'s sports bar, O'Gills lies just off one side of La Piazza (see next page). It's ostensibly an Irish pub, but it's the least visually interesting bar in Europa. The attempts at theming—Irish music and liberal use of four-leaf clovers—are halfhearted at best; with some paint, antiques-store scavenging, and the right "beer of the month" subscription, O'Gills could pass as a Chicago-, Dallas-, or Green Bay–themed bar.

The centerpiece is a huge high-def video screen in the back corner, which shows sporting events and sports news all day long. Several other smaller screens are distributed throughout the room, and there's plenty of seating and standing room.

SELECTIONS The bar menu includes bottled and draft beer, including a house draft lager and several Irish brews. Wine is available by the glass and bottle, and the friendly bartenders can mix up any cocktail you want. The specialty is Irish whiskey and Scotch; a private-label Irish cream liqueur is on the menu too. The mixed drinks are reasonably priced at $5.75 each. Try the **Royal Velvet,** a mix of Guinness stout and sparkling wine.

COMMENTS You wouldn't come here for the Irish ambience, but as a generic sports bar, O'Gills isn't bad.

ACROSS THE SHIPS There's another O'Gills on the *Magic* (see page 115). As a sports bar, however, it's similar to **687** on the *Dream* (see page 124) and **Diversions** on the *Wonder* (see page 117). We prefer 687, O'Gills on the *Magic,* and Diversions because they have better sight lines to the TV screens from the seats.

Ooh La La   LOCATION: Deck 4 Aft

SETTING AND ATMOSPHERE This is the *Fantasy*'s Champagne bar. The French-boudoir theme is enough to make you break out in "Lady Marmalade" from *Moulin Rouge:* rose-colored upholstery on the walls, purple carpet, and chairs lined with gold fabric. Along one wall are a series of padded couches in ivory and green. Gold-edged mirrors and fleurs-de-lis line the walls. A single red chair and a couple of small, red-topped side tables provide a touch of bold color.

The bar, at the far end of the lounge, seats six around its black marble top. In keeping with the boudoir theme, the mirror behind the bar looks like an oversize version of one you'd find on the dressing table of a fashionable Frenchwoman at the *fin de siècle*. And because it's a Champagne bar, hundreds of small glass bubbles fill the mirrors.

SELECTIONS Ooh La La serves reasonably priced Champagnes by the glass and bottle. A couple of these, such as Pommery Rosé Brut and Bollinger La Grande Année, aren't found at Pink, the Champagne bar on the *Dream*. Available along with these are such familiar names as Taittinger and Dom Pérignon. A glass of bubbly starts at around $6 and goes up to $18; bottles cost anywhere from around $50 to $500.

Champagne cocktails, with fruit juices and other liquors, cost around $11, but remember the Second Law of Champagne: If it needs another ingredient, you're drinking the wrong Champagne. (The First Law: Champagne goes with everything!) Sparkling wines, along with reds and whites, are available by the glass and bottle, and the fully stocked bar can furnish virtually any cocktail you like.

COMMENTS The best seats in Ooh La La are on the L-shaped silver couch near the main entrance. It's the perfect private place to do some people-watching. Another nice touch is the use of area rugs to mark off sections of seats—it's possible to mingle within that small area, having individual conversations while still being part of the group. The club has three porthole windows—which we didn't expect—with ocean views and seating below. If you visit during the late afternoon, the light from outside provides a gentle transition from day to dusk.

ACROSS THE SHIPS Only the *Dream* and the *Fantasy* have Champagne bars, and this is one of the main reasons we prefer these ships over the *Magic* and the *Wonder*. However, we like the relatively understated theming of **Pink** on the *Dream* (see page 123) better than the over-the-top decor of Ooh La La.

La Piazza   LOCATION: Deck 4 Aft

SETTING AND ATMOSPHERE This Venetian-themed lounge sits near the front of Europa. Appropriately, La Piazza ("The Plaza") serves as the walkway to O'Gills and Ooh La La, whose entrances sit just off this venue; farther beyond are Skyline and The Tube, so you'll walk by La Piazza on the way.

The bar sits in the middle of a bright circular room. It's themed to look like an Italian carousel, its ceiling decorated with hundreds of carousel lights. Around the bar are rose-colored barstools; lining the wall are golden, high-backed, upholstered couches with small tables for drinks. The couches are separated, elevated, and set into niches in the walls, making them good vantages from which to watch people walk between the clubs.

SELECTIONS La Piazza's bar menu features Peroni and Moretti, two Italian beers, as well as prosecco (Italian sparkling wine) and *limoncello* (an Italian lemon-flavored liqueur). These ingredients also make their way into La Piazza's five signature cocktails—the **Mercutio** ($5.75), for example, features Absolut Pears vodka, limoncello, grappa, and fresh lemon juice, with the sweetness of the pear and grappa balancing out the tartness of the citrus.

COMMENTS The couches are good spots for watching La Piazza's live entertainment, which has been an up-tempo jazz trio on each of our cruises. If you're not into music, our favorite pastime at La Piazza takes place starting at 11 p.m., when we start to wager a round of drinks on the number of couples who will stop to take photos on La Piazza's Vespa motorcycle-and-sidecar prop in the next 10 minutes. The over–under on that bet is usually 2.5, and the rules prohibit shouting encouragement to the *ubriachi.*

ACROSS THE SHIPS Somewhat similar to **District Lounge** on the *Dream* (see page 121), La Piazza has a better drink menu, while District Lounge has a better layout. Neither the *Magic* nor the *Wonder* has a comparable bar.

Skyline LOCATION: Deck 4 Aft

SETTING AND ATMOSPHERE Skyline is our favorite bar on the *Fantasy.* The concept is that you're in a lounge high on the edge of some of the world's most famous cities. Behind the bar are seven "windows"—large high-definition television screens—affording panoramic views of seven cities: Athens, Barcelona, Budapest, Florence, London, Paris, and St. Petersburg.

Each city is shown for about 15 minutes across all seven screens; then the scene changes to another locale. The foreground of each view includes close-up views of apartments and offices, while the middle and background show each city's iconic architecture and landscape.

That would be mildly interesting scenery on its own, but Disney has added special effects that make Skyline beautiful. Each view shows the city in motion: Cars move along streets, neon signs blink to illuminate sidewalks, and apartment lights go on and off as their residents come and go. (Look closely and you can even see Mickey Mouse waving to you from inside a tiny apartment in Paris.) A second effect is that the scenery changes depending on the time of day you're inside. If you get here in late afternoon, you'll see the sun setting on these towns. Stay long enough—and we have—and dusk turns to evening, then evening to night.

Last, Skyline has mirrors on the walls perpendicular to the video screens. Because the mirrors are set at right angles to the screens, they reflect the videos and make the bar look longer than it is. It's a well-known decorating trick for making a small room seem larger, but it's still nice to see included here.

The rest of the decor is natural surfaces: wood panels, ceiling, and floors, in colors ranging from honey to mahogany; dark marble countertops; and leather chairs.

SELECTIONS The specialty is "around the world" cocktails themed to the featured cities. For example, **El Conquistador** ($8.50), representing Barcelona, pairs Tanqueray gin and Absolut Peppar vodka with fresh muddled strawberries, basil, and cracked black pepper; the **Aquincum** ($10.50), representing Budapest, is made with 901 Tequila, Grand Marnier, paprika, and freshly squeezed lime juice.

COMMENTS Adding movement to the scenery means the view at Skyline doesn't get boring. It also means that the club doesn't need a television to hold its patrons' attention. And the cityscapes are a great way to break the ice with fellow cruisers.

ACROSS THE SHIPS Although there are Skylines on both the *Dream* and the *Fantasy,* the latter one features two more cities in its "windows" than the one on the *Dream.* Also, their drink menus are mostly different. Drinks at the *Dream*'s Skyline tend to be flavored with fruits and fruit juices, such as cranberry, pomegranate, lemon, and lime; drinks on the *Fantasy*'s Skyline are made with fruits too, but also herbs and spices such as basil, thyme, coriander, cilantro, and paprika. We find that these extra ingredients add another layer of flavor and cut some of the fruits' sweetness. If you're unsure about ordering one of these cocktails, ask the bartender to make the drink without the herbs or spices, and take a sip. Then have the remaining ingredients added and sip again.

The Tube LOCATION: Deck 4 Aft

SETTING AND ATMOSPHERE With a London subway–meets–*Austin Powers* theme, The Tube is the *Fantasy*'s dance club. Its decor includes leather couches with prints that look like Underground tickets, 1960s-mod egg-shaped chairs, and a floor painted like a London subway map. We especially like the upholstered leather couch set deep inside the lounge, because it's under a set of lights in the shape of a crown and across from two shiny silver armchairs designed to look like thrones. A couple of red phone booths are set on either side of the dance floor. *Yeah, baby!*

SELECTIONS The Tube's circular bar, set under Big Ben's clock face, serves a typical menu of bottled beer, mixed drinks, spirits, and wine and Champagne by the glass. The Tube also serves six signature drinks, several of which are made with sodas or sparkling wines. Our favorite is **Mind the Gap** ($8.50), a mix of whiskey, Drambuie, and Coke.

COMMENTS The Tube usually opens around 10 p.m. and sometimes gets things going with a quick game of Match Your Mate (think *The Newlywed Game,* only groovier). Dancing usually gets started around 10:30 or 11 p.m. Most of the music is contemporary dance, but there are themed nights with disco and, of course, British hits.

ACROSS THE SHIPS The club's closest counterparts are **Fathoms** on the *Magic* (see page 113), **WaveBands** on the *Wonder* (see page 118), and **Evolution** on the *Dream* (see page 122). The Tube, though, is our favorite dance club on any of the ships.

PART NINE

ACTIVITIES, RECREATION, *and* SHOPPING

BESIDES EAT, DRINK, BE ENTERTAINED, AND EXPLORE PORTS, there's lots to do on every Disney Cruise Line (DCL) itinerary:

- Family activities are held throughout the day and include trivia contests, bingo, deck parties, and more.
- Children's programs, the strength of Disney Cruise Line, begin as early as 7 a.m.
- It wouldn't be a Disney cruise without character greetings, including Mickey, Minnie, and the Disney princesses.
- Each ship's pools and water-play areas are the center of activity during the day on most cruises.
- Onboard seminars are inexpensive (some are free) and cover everything from cooking demonstrations to wine tastings.
- Runners and sports fans will find a measured track on each ship, plus basketball, volleyball, miniature golf, and more.
- After a tough day on shore, you can relax at the spa.
- Shopping opportunities are available on board and in port.

FAMILY ACTIVITIES

BINGO

DCL IS ONE OF THE FEW CRUISE LINES that have no casino gambling on board. What it does have is bingo, played most days on most ships, with at least two 90-minute sessions per day. The cost to play is about $10 per paper card per game, with four to six games played per hour. Prizes range from duffel bags filled with DCL swag to actual cash jackpots of several thousand dollars.

With that much money at stake, it's no surprise that many people take these games seriously. Games are fast-paced, and players are expected to keep up. If you're bringing along your family, consider renting an electronic bingo machine for about $20 (plus the cost of the cards). These machines receive signals from the bingo console, telling them which numbers have been called. Because the machines keep track of the state of the game, there's no need to be hypervigilant every second.

DECK PARTIES

FEATURING DISNEY CHARACTERS, deck parties are usually held several times per cruise, usually near the family pool or in the ship's main lobby. The first party, known as the **Sail-Away Celebration,** happens as you leave port on embarkation day. Expect to hear every Black Eyed Peas song ever recorded over the rest of your cruise.

All outdoor parties are high-energy affairs, with loud music, dancing, games, and other activities, plus videos displayed on the ship's giant LED screen. The indoor versions omit only the giant video screens. Check your *Personal Navigator* for dates and times.

FAMILY NIGHTCLUBS

IN ADDITION TO ITS MYRIAD adult-entertainment offerings (see Part Eight), DCL has what would be an oxymoron in any other context: the family nightclub. Set up like grown-up nightspots, with snazzy decor and their own bars, tables and chairs, and dance floors, these lounges offer daytime and nighttime entertainment, including comedy shows, trivia contests, cooking demos, karaoke, line dancing, and more. (Many of the same activities are also offered during the day at some adult lounges.) Refreshments are served, including cocktails for Mom and Dad and smoothies and sodas for the kids (all at an extra charge).

Family nightclubs are found on each ship's Deck 4 Midship. On the *Wonder,* it's **Studio Sea;** on the other three ships, it's **D Lounge.** Hours vary, so check your *Personal Navigator* for details.

SPORTS AND FITNESS

THE DISNEY SHIPS have several sports options available for families, covered later in this chapter, beginning on page 154.

CHILDREN'S PROGRAMS *and* ACTIVITIES

WHEN IT COMES TO ENTERTAINING CHILDREN, Disney Cruise Line has no equal. Youth clubs, designed for infants to 17-year-olds, open as early as 7:30 a.m. for babies and close as late as 2 a.m. for teens. Kids can participate in organized activities ranging from craft-making to trivia contests and dance parties, or they can play individually with computer games, board games, books, and craft materials. Most of the organized activities last 60–90 minutes, so a new event will likely start soon after your child arrives; this means kids become part of the group quickly. Based on reader feedback, it's far more likely that your child will not want to leave his or her kids' club than not want to go to it in the first place.

Outside of the kids' clubs, there's plenty for children and families to do. Much like the Disney theme parks, the DCL cruise ships offer a contained environment that allows tweens and teens to enjoy some autonomy to roam on their own. Wave Phones (a mobile phone you may use free of charge on the ship and Castaway Cay for calls, voice mail, and text messaging, only from Wave Phone to Wave Phone) mean that you'll always be able to reach your children, and the food offerings on the pool deck mean that there's no worrying about finding something to eat (or how to pay for it).

Younger children (and older ones who aren't yet pretending they don't know you) and their families have activities scheduled throughout the day, from karaoke to character greetings; check your *Personal Navigator* for times and locations. Even the not-yet-walking crew can get in on the fun, with "diaper derbies" that happen in the ships' atria—these are lots of fun to watch even if you don't have a child participating.

Other activities include minigolf (*Dream* and *Fantasy*), the arcade (**Quarter Masters** on the *Magic* and *Wonder*; **Arr-cade** on the *Dream* and *Fantasy*), and the sports decks, all topside.

SPECIAL CONSIDERATIONS

TWEENS AND TEENS Don't worry that your preteen or teenager is "too cool" for a Disney cruise. Based on both our own experiences and those of other parents, teens will practically forget you exist once they get a feel for the clubs and activities. In fact, before you even set foot on the ship, you should set some ground rules for how often your teen needs to check in with you. Our rule was that everyone had to eat two meals per day together during sea days and stay together during shore excursions. On Castaway Cay, we reserved morning activities for family time, and the teens were allowed to explore the island on their own after lunch.

unofficial **TIP**
Be careful about cruising during times when school is in session: Some cruises have so few teens and tweens traveling that the youth clubs can be kind of a bust.

ONLY-CHILD SITUATIONS The middle- and high-school kids' clubs are seamless for kids who are traveling with similarly aged siblings, cousins, or friends. They have a built-in companion for activities and can sample the club offerings at will, with no fear of being the odd man out. Our (multiple) children were able to pop in and out of the teen clubs whenever an activity seemed interesting, never feeling alone or out of place.

For a middle-schooler or teen traveling as the only one of his/her age group in the family, the youth clubs can be more challenging, as was the case with one of our teens on a recent trip. She was completely fine joining in the introductory games during the Sail-Away Celebration, where the fun was orchestrated by a counselor. Several other times, however, she dropped in at Vibe and found just a few kids obviously paired off into subgroups. Because of this—coupled

DCL Youth Clubs in Brief

FLOUNDER'S REEF NURSERY *Wonder*

LOCATION Deck 5 Aft **AGES** 3 months–3 years

OPENS Varies **CLOSES** 11 p.m.

FEE $9/hour for first child, $8/hour for each additional child

MEALS Bring your own food, milk, and formula.

IT'S A SMALL WORLD NURSERY *Magic, Dream, Fantasy*

LOCATION Deck 5 Aft **AGES** 3 months–3 years

OPENS Varies **CLOSES** 11 p.m.

FEE $9/hour for first child, $8/hour for each additional child

MEALS Bring your own food, milk, and formula.

OCEANEER CLUB/OCEANEER LAB *All ships*

LOCATION Deck 5 Midship **AGES** 3–12 years

OPENS Varies **CLOSES** Midnight

FEE None **MEALS** Lunch and dinner

EDGE *All ships*

LOCATION Deck 2 Midship (*Magic, Wonder*), Deck 13 Forward (*Dream, Fantasy*)

AGES 11–14 years **OPENS** Varies **CLOSES** 1 a.m.

FEE None **MEALS** None

VIBE *All ships*

LOCATION Deck 11 Midship (*Magic, Wonder*), Deck 5 Forward (*Dream, Fantasy*)

AGES 14–17 years **OPENS** Varies **CLOSES** 2 a.m.

FEE None **REFRESHMENTS** Sodas (free), smoothies (extra charge)

EXTRAS Sun deck with splash pools (*Dream, Fantasy*)

with the fact that the counselors at the tween/teen clubs occasionally seem more invested in stamping out juvenile delinquency and covert smooching than actively engaging the kids—our normally social and extroverted daughter had trouble slotting herself in.

Our teen's observation was that the "single" kids who did best at Vibe were the ones who participated in absolutely every activity there, including the teen activities on Castaway Cay, thus giving them the opportunity to pair off with someone. Because she was doing so much stuff with us, she found it harder to participate at Vibe on an ad hoc basis. For solo teens and tweens, then, the youth clubs might best be thought of as an all-or-nothing proposition: Those who just want to sample the clubs, as opposed to immersing themselves in the activities, should expect the social scene to be harder to break into.

YOUTH CLUBS

THE BULK OF DCL'S CHILDREN'S ACTIVITIES take place at the youth clubs on the ships. They're organized by age group, as follows:

- **Flounder's Reef Nursery** (*Wonder*) and **It's a Small World Nursery** (*Magic, Dream, and Fantasy*), for infants and toddlers up to age 3
- **Oceaneer Club** and **Oceaneer Lab**, for children ages 3–12
- **Edge,** for ages 11–14
- **Vibe,** for ages 14–17

We provide profiles of the clubs starting on the next page, organized by ship and ordered from the youngest to oldest age groups.

Children in the following age groups may choose which club they wish to participate in: 3-year-olds can choose the nursery or (as long as they're potty-trained) Oceaneer Club/Lab, 11- and 12-year-olds can choose between Oceaneer Club/Lab and Edge, and 14-year-olds can choose Edge or Vibe. This flexibility is helpful when siblings who are close in age want to be in the same club. Once a choice is made, however, it may not be changed. Disney is also strict about making sure that kids stick to the club for their age group—that is, no sneaking into Vibe if they're not old enough.

Children in the nurseries, Oceaneer Club, and Oceaneer Lab will be asked to wear a wristband while they're on the premises, and parents will be given an electronic pager. Sensors at each club's doors will trigger an alarm if your child tries to leave without a parent to deactivate the wristband. In the event that Disney or your child needs to contact you, the club staff will call you on your Wave Phone, a mobile phone you can use while aboard the ship.

All kids must be registered to use the clubs. Parents can sign up their children either before boarding through online check-in (see page 19) or on embarkation day in the clubs' open houses. Signing up online has the advantage of giving busy cruisers one less thing to worry about after boarding the ship. Open houses are a great way to check out the various clubs. (*Warning:* The spaces are so well themed that adults will be sad when they have to leave.) Once a child is registered for a club, he or she may use its facilities for the entire cruise.

Nurseries

These operate under a reservation system and charge an hourly rate for services; parents will need to book specific times. The charge is $9 an hour for the first child and $8 an hour for each additional child in the same family. You should bring milk, formula, and baby food, along with diapers and wipes, a change of clothes, and a blanket and pacifier if your child needs these to nap.

Space is limited at each nursery; reservations are required and are first come, first served:

- Concierge guests and Platinum Castaway Club members can make reservations 120 days in advance.
- Gold Castaway Club members can make reservations 105 days in advance.

- Silver Castaway Club can make reservations 90 days in advance.
- All other guests can make reservations 75 days out.

If you haven't made nursery reservations by the time you board, either stop by before dinner or call from your stateroom: Dial ☎ **7-5864** on the *Magic*, *Dream*, and *Fantasy* or ☎ **7-18500** on the *Wonder*.

Hours vary, especially when the ship is in port, but on most sea days the nurseries are open 9 a.m.–11 p.m., with open-house tours 8–9 a.m.; check your *Personal Navigator* for details. The nurseries are sometimes open noon–3 p.m., and usually 5:30–11 p.m. on the first afternoon of your cruise.

The *Magic*'s Youth Clubs

It's a Small World Nursery LOCATION: Deck 5 Aft

OVERVIEW This is the *Magic*'s onboard nursery for infants and toddlers age 3 months–3 years. Trained staff play with the children throughout the day. Unlike the activities at the clubs for older kids and teens, activities at the nursery are unstructured but may include movies, story time, crafts, and occasional visits from Disney characters.

DESCRIPTION AND COMMENTS Too cute. Decorated with brilliantly colored murals inspired by the art of Mary Blair, the Disney animator who designed It's a Small World at Disneyland and Walt Disney World, the nursery is cleverly divided into three sections. Up front is the "acclimation zone," a welcome area where kids can get used to their surroundings; this leads to a long, narrow, rectangular, brightly lit play area, off of which is a darkened, quiet room for naps. The play area is stocked with pint-size activities, including a 2-foot-tall playground slide on a padded floor, a small basketball hoop, plenty of leg-powered riding vehicles, play mats with large toys, and adorable miniature craft tables that you'd swear came from the Lilliput IKEA. A one-way mirror lets parents check up on their tots discreetly.

Around the corner, at the far end of the nursery, is the resting room, with six cribs and three glider chairs (sort of like rocking chairs, except they move linearly). Murals in soothing blues and golds adorn the walls. This room is kept dark most of the day, and the staff ensures that activities in the main room happen far enough away that noise isn't a problem. Just outside are a sink and changing area.

ACROSS THE SHIPS The *Dream* and the *Fantasy* also have It's a Small World Nurseries. The only real difference from the version on the *Magic* is that the nap room is larger, with more than twice as many cribs. The *Wonder* has **Flounder's Reef Nursery** (see page 139)—the basic setup is the same, but the theme is *The Little Mermaid* and the nap room is smaller.

Oceaneer Club and Oceaneer Lab LOCATION: Deck 5 Midship

OVERVIEW The Oceaneer Club and Oceaneer Lab are connected spaces that host the 3- to 12-year-old set. Activities for older kids usually take place in the Lab and are often educational or participatory in nature (such as cooking demonstrations or science experiments). Younger children's programs are generally held in the Club and include story time, character greetings, and movement activities. Disney designates 7 as the border age for the Club and Lab and provides details in your *Personal Navigator* about each area's different activity tracks. During open houses, one side remains open for activities while the other side is open to the public. Lunch and dinner are provided.

Parents must check kids up to age 7 years in and out of the club. With parental permission, 8- to 12-year-olds may check themselves in and out—just designate your preference when you register your kids.

DESCRIPTION AND COMMENTS Newly redesigned on the *Magic,* the Oceaneer Lab and Club are separate areas connected by a short private hallway, allowing children to go from Lab to Club and back. Besides providing kids twice as much space, this arrangement separates younger and older children while giving siblings of different ages the chance to stay in contact.

The Oceaneer Club consists of four distinct sections branching off from a central "library" decorated with oversize children's books and outfitted with a huge plasma TV for movie screenings. **Andy's Room** is *Toy Story*–themed and is for smaller children. Its main feature is a tall, circular, gentle playground slide in the shape of Slinky Dog. There's also a large pink Hamm (the piggy bank) sitting in the middle of the play floor, and a giant Mr. Potato Head with equally large plug-in pieces, all scattered about.

The **Mickey Mouse Club,** the second themed room, serves as the Oceaneer Club's primary activity center. Done in black-and-white square tiles, with red tables and accents and pictures of Mickey and friends on the walls, the room has a large video screen on one wall and game consoles lining another.

The Mickey Mouse Club connects to both Andy's Room and **Marvel Avengers Academy.** In the academy you'll find Thor's hammer, Captain America's shield, and a life-size Iron Man suit, as well as another video screen and computer collection.

Disney is using the *Magic* to try out a new concept, also called Marvel Avengers Academy. The activities follow a multiday story in which kids embark on a recruitment experience that has them team up with various Avengers, hang out with Captain America, and suit up like Iron Man to battle the evil Red Skull. (No word yet on whether you can rent out Captain America's costume for private parties.)

Opposite Marvel Avengers Academy is **Pixie Hollow,** a Tinker Bell–themed dress-up and play area with costumes, an activity table, and a few computer terminals with themed games.

The Oceaneer Lab is done in a 19th-century nautical theme, with lots of exposed woods, red-leather chairs, navigation maps, and sailors' tools. More than a third of the space consists of one long room, filled with kid-size tables and stools, which serves as the primary area for arts and crafts. At the far end of this space is a set of computer terminals.

Next to the craft space, in the middle of the Lab, is a large screen for watching movies. Facing the screen is a collection of comfortable beanbags. Finally, the left side of the Lab is a set of small rooms. A couple have computer terminals or video-game consoles; one is a smaller arts-and-crafts room, and another is an animation studio where kids can learn to draw Disney characters and create their own computer animations.

ACROSS THE SHIPS All DCL ships have an Oceaneer Club/Lab. On the *Dream* and the *Fantasy,* the Club is also subdivided into themed areas, but they differ somewhat from those on the *Magic.* The Lab has a similar nautical theme and layout but is distinguished by a central "interactive floor," composed of individual video screens surrounded by foot-operated touch pads and used to play different interactive games.

On the *Wonder,* the Club is *Peter Pan*–themed and doesn't have the individual themed areas of the Clubs on the other three ships; the Lab has a *Toy Story* theme and a more open layout. Also, given that the *Wonder* is the second-oldest ship and hasn't yet benefited from a renovation, both areas seem slightly dated. Finally, where kids on the other three ships can roam between the Club and Lab as they wish, kids on the *Wonder* must be escorted by a counselor from one space to the other.

Edge LOCATION: Deck 2 Midship

OVERVIEW Tweens and early teens rule at Edge. Unlike at the Oceaneer Club/Lab, kids can come and go as they please. Activities range from drawing and cooking classes to scavenger hunts and computer games. Parents may be surprised to see that things are scheduled past midnight on some nights.

DESCRIPTION AND COMMENTS A three-section activity area, Edge is the basement rec room your kids dream of. One entire wall is stacked with computer terminals hooked up to various video-game consoles; another section of the room is filled with couches and pillows around a video screen for movies and television; a large middle section for playing board games and other activities rounds out the space.

Edge is likely to be the first of the youth clubs in which the staff will treat your kids as peers to interact with rather than as children to be supervised. The staff generally does a great job of getting to know each child and will even compete in games alongside the kids. If you ever want to feel old and slow, watch the cup-stacking competition, where the object is to stack and unstack a pyramid of 15 plastic cups as quickly as possible. Some kids can do both in under 10 seconds total.

ACROSS THE SHIPS All DCL ships have an Edge. The layout and amenities are more or less the same on the *Wonder.* On the *Dream* and the *Fantasy,* Edge is inside the ships' forward (nonfunctioning) smokestack. The decor and atmosphere are ultramodern and high-tech, versus the homier feel of Edge on the *Magic* and *Wonder.*

Vibe LOCATION: Deck 11 Midship

OVERVIEW Vibe is one of the coolest spots on the *Magic.* Even if you don't have a kid traveling with you, it's worth checking out during an open house. Counselors lead the activities (dance parties, karaoke, group games, and the like), but teens are given plenty of autonomy in their structure. Parents should note that the only curfew for teens on board is whatever one they impose themselves. One rule of note that's strictly enforced: no public displays of affection.

DESCRIPTION AND COMMENTS Vibe sits up a flight of stairs in the ship's forward smokestack, but your teens probably won't mind the climb. Inside is a two-story-tall lounge with brick walls; overstuffed leather furniture; a smoothie bar; tons of quirky decorations; and board games, video consoles, and a small room off to the side for activities. It looks more like a well-appointed summer-camp lodge than anything nautical or tropical. We think there should be one of these for adults.

ACROSS THE SHIPS All DCL ships have a Vibe. The layout and amenities are more or less identical on the *Wonder*. On the *Dream* and the *Fantasy,* Vibe is dramatically different but just as cool. The theming and decor are urban ultralounge rather than funky rumpus room, and teens get an indoor/outdoor space, complete with a stylish sun deck and splash pool.

The *Wonder*'s Youth Clubs

Flounder's Reef Nursery   LOCATION: Deck 5 Aft

OVERVIEW This is the *Wonder*'s onboard nursery for infants and toddlers age 3 months–3 years. Trained staff play with the children throughout the day. Unlike the activities at the clubs for older kids and teens, activities at the nursery are unstructured but may include movies, story time, crafts, and occasional visits from Disney characters.

DESCRIPTION AND COMMENTS The cruise industry's first nursery at sea, Flounder's Reef is divided into two sections. One is a narrow, rectangular, brightly lit play area; the other is a darkened, quiet area for naps. The play area is stocked with play mats, toys, books, a playground slide, baby swings and bouncy chairs, and a TV/DVD player. Sea creatures from *The Little Mermaid* (the nursery is named after Flounder, Ariel's best friend) decorate the walls; the floor has a wave motif. A one-way mirror outside lets parents check up on their tots discreetly.

At the back of the nursery is the resting area, furnished with cribs. This room is kept dark most of the day, and the staff ensures that activities in the main room happen far enough away that noise isn't a problem. A sink and changing station are adjacent.

ACROSS THE SHIPS The *Dream, Fantasy,* and *Magic* have **It's a Small World Nursery** (see page 136), with decor inspired by the theme park attraction. Of course, little ones will be too young to care about aesthetics, but It's a Small World is more colorful and creatively themed. Also, the nap area here is small, with room for only a few cribs and a glider, and there's no theming to speak of. Overall, Flounder's Reef feels more like a garden-variety day-care center with a few Disney touches here and there.

Oceaneer Club and Oceaneer Lab   LOCATION: Deck 5 Midship

OVERVIEW The Oceaneer Club and Oceaneer Lab are connected spaces that host the 3- to 12-year-old set. Activities for older kids usually take place in the Lab and are often educational or participatory in nature (such as cooking demonstrations or science experiments). Younger children's programs are generally held in the Club and include story time, character greetings, and movement activities. Disney designates 7 as the border age for the Club and Lab and provides details in your *Personal Navigator* about each area's different activity tracks. During open houses, one side remains open for activities while the other side is open to the public. Lunch and dinner are provided.

Parents must check kids up to age 7 years in and out of the club. With parental permission, 8- to 12-year-olds may check themselves in and out—just designate your preference when you register your kids.

DESCRIPTION AND COMMENTS The Oceaneer Club was designed to look like Captain Hook's ship from *Peter Pan*—wooden-plank floors, hanging ropes, barrels, and netting. The space on the *Wonder* is basically one big room without the individual themed areas of the Clubs on the other ships. Attractions include a "crow's nest" slide; a rope bridge; a computer nook; a stage; a dance floor; an area for arts and crafts; the Captain's Closet (a dress-up room); several TV sets; and, of course, plenty of toys, books, and games. Activities may range from dancing with Snow White to an audience with Captain Hook himself to a "boot camp" with Corporal Green and the Green Army Soldiers from *Toy Story.*

Separated from the Club by a sliding door, the Oceaneer Lab is *Toy Story*–themed, with figures of Buzz Lightyear and the Squeeze Toy Aliens, retro–space age tables and chairs, and floor-to-ceiling columns in the shape of planetary orbs. The open layout includes a reading area, computer stations, a science lab, work spaces for arts and crafts, and a demonstration kitchen. Activities might include cookie-making, building race cars, and learning to draw Disney characters.

ACROSS THE SHIPS We're pretty sure that kids who've experienced the Oceaneer Club/Lab on any of the other three ships would be let down by the *Wonder*'s version. The spaces seem a little worn and dated, and they're positively low-tech in comparison. Also, whereas the themed areas of the Clubs on the *Magic, Dream,* and *Fantasy* are bright and cheerful, the Club on the *Wonder* is a tad gloomy and drab with all that dark wood. Even the Club/Lab's restrooms are nicer on the other ships. We hope to see an upgrade here in the future.

Edge LOCATION: Deck 2 Midship

COMMENTS See profile of Edge on the *Magic* (see page 138) for details.

Vibe LOCATION: Deck 11 Midship

COMMENTS See profile of Vibe on the *Magic* (see page 138) for details.

The *Dream*'s and *Fantasy*'s Youth Clubs

It's a Small World Nursery LOCATION: Deck 5 Aft

COMMENTS See our profile of It's a Small World Nursery on the *Magic* (see page 136) for details.

Oceaneer Club and Oceaneer Lab   LOCATION: Deck 5 Midship

OVERVIEW On the *Dream* and *Fantasy,* the Oceaneer Club and Oceaneer Lab are connected spaces that host the 3- to 12-year-old set. Activities for older kids usually take place in the Lab and are often educational or participatory in nature (such as cooking demonstrations or science experiments). Younger children's programs are generally held in the Club and include story time, character greetings, and movement activities. Disney designates 7 as the border age for the Club and Lab and provides details in your *Personal Navigator* about each area's different activity tracks. During open houses, one side remains open for activities while the other side is open to the public. Lunch and dinner are provided.

Parents must check kids up to age 7 years in and out of the club. With parental permission, 8- to 12-year-olds may check themselves in and out—just designate your preference when you register your kids.

DESCRIPTION AND COMMENTS The Oceaneer Lab and Club are separate areas connected by a short private hallway, allowing children to go from Lab to Club and back. Besides providing kids twice as much space, this arrangement separates younger and older children while giving siblings of different ages the chance to stay in contact.

The Oceaneer Club consists of four distinct sections branching off from a central rotunda painted royal blue; on the ceiling are "constellations" of Disney characters made up of small, twinkling electric lights. **Andy's Room** is *Toy Story*–themed and is for smaller children. There's a crawl-through tube—think a Habitrail for humans—in the shape of Slinky Dog, along with a giant pink Hamm (the piggy bank) sitting in the middle of the play floor, and a large Mr. Potato Head with equally large plug-in pieces, all invariably scattered about.

The next area is **Monsters Academy,** a brightly colored, *Monsters, Inc.*–themed space filled with all manner of interactive games, along with a climbing structure. Then there's **Pixie Hollow,** a Tinker Bell–themed dress-up and play area with costumes, an activity table, and a few computer terminals with themed games. Finally, **Disney's Explorer Pod** is a scaled-down submarine inspired by *Finding Nemo.* Inside are 16 interactive-game stations.

The Oceaneer Lab is done in a 19th-century nautical theme, with lots of exposed woods, red-leather chairs, navigation maps, sailors' tools, and inlaid images of sea horses and compasses on the floor. The main hall features a celestial map on the ceiling and a huge "Magic Play Floor," composed of 16 high-definition video screens surrounded by foot-powered touch pads and used to play interactive games. (If you remember the piano from the movie *Big,* you get the idea.)

Surrounding the main hall are the **Media Lounge,** for relaxing and watching movies; the **Animator's Studio,** where kids can learn to draw Disney characters and create digital animations; **The Wheelhouse,** with computer stations and interactive games; the **Sound Studio,** where kids can record their own music; and the **Craft Studio.**

ACROSS THE SHIPS All DCL ships have an Oceaneer Club/Lab. On the *Magic*, the Club is subdivided into themed areas, but they differ somewhat from those on the *Dream* and *Fantasy;* the Lab has a similar nautical theme and layout but is missing the nifty interactive floor.

On the *Wonder*, the Club is *Peter Pan*–themed and doesn't have the individual themed areas of the Clubs on the other three ships; the Lab has a *Toy Story* theme and a more open layout. Also, given that the *Wonder* is the second-oldest ship and hasn't yet benefited from a renovation, both areas seem slightly dated, and they're positively low-tech in comparison. Finally, where kids on the other three ships can roam between the Club and Lab as they wish, kids on the *Wonder* must be escorted by a counselor from one space to the other.

Edge   LOCATION: Deck 13 Forward

OVERVIEW Tweens rule at Edge. Unlike at the Oceaneer Club/Lab, kids at the Edge can come and go as they please. Activities range from drawing and cooking classes to improv-comedy sessions and ghost-hunting role-playing games. Parents may be surprised to see that things are scheduled past midnight on some nights.

DESCRIPTION AND COMMENTS Built into the *Dream*'s and *Fantasy*'s forward (nonfunctioning) smokestack, Edge has an open layout and a clean 21st-century feel. The walls are papered in a geometric Mickey-head design. The centerpiece of the space is a huge video wall, more than 18 feet wide and nearly 5 feet tall. Across from it are tables with built-in screens for playing interactive games, surrounded by bright-red seating that looks like something out of *The Jetsons;* behind those are cubbyholes outfitted with flat-panel TVs and Wii consoles. Recessed shelves between the game nooks are stocked with books and board games. Next to the game tables are an illuminated dance floor (think *Saturday Night Fever*) and a lounge area with beanbags arranged next to floor-to-ceiling windows. On the other side of the video wall are laptop stations loaded with video games and an onboard social-media app.

Edge is likely to be the first of the youth clubs in which the staff will treat your kids as peers to interact with rather than as children to be supervised. The staff generally does a great job of getting to know each child and getting in on the fun.

ACROSS THE SHIPS All DCL ships have an Edge. On the *Magic* and *Wonder*, it has a totally different layout and atmosphere—more like a family rec room than a high-tech hangout.

Vibe   LOCATION: Deck 5 Forward

OVERVIEW Up a flight of stairs from Deck 4 to Deck 5 Forward, Vibe is one of the coolest spots on the *Dream* and *Fantasy*. Even if you don't have a kid traveling with you, it's worth checking out during an open house. Counselors lead the activities (dance parties, karaoke, role-playing games, and the like), but teens are given plenty of autonomy in their structure. Parents should note that the only curfew for teens on board is whatever one they impose themselves. One rule of note that's strictly enforced: no public displays of affection.

DESCRIPTION AND COMMENTS Accessed through a neon-lit hallway, Vibe has a decidedly adult look and feel—if you didn't know better, you'd think you were in a trendy urban nightspot. The central indoor gathering spot is the theater–cum–TV lounge, accented with soft pink neon lighting and featuring a 103-inch flat-panel television. Two rows of couches are arranged in a semicircle in front of the screen; giant throw pillows scattered on the floor make for additional places to lounge. Behind the couches and built into the rear wall are a row of podlike, porthole-shaped nooks for playing video games, watching videos, or hooking up an iPod. Just off the row of pods is a smoothie bar with a multicolored floor in Day-Glo hues; ultramodern stools with low, curved backs; and white banquette seating.

Off the TV lounge is another sleek space for socializing. The walls are covered in alternating black and silver horizontal bars. Black leather-look benches line the walls; next to those are retro-mod tables and chairs arranged nightclub-style. Video-game booths stand nearby. Across from the seating area are a dance floor and DJ booth, a karaoke stage, and another large video screen.

The main attraction, though, lies outside: the **Vibe Splash Zone,** a private deck with two splash pools, chaise longues, sets of tables and chairs, and recessed seating. Furnishings and decor share the same ultramod style as the indoor spaces.

ACROSS THE SHIPS All DCL ships have a Vibe. On the *Magic* and the *Wonder,* Vibe is dramatically different but just as cool. Built into the ships' forward smokestack, the two-story-tall lounge features brick walls, overstuffed leather furniture, and quirky decor. It looks more like a well-appointed summer-camp lodge than anything you'd find on a cruise ship.

OTHER KIDS' ACTIVITIES ON BOARD

On the *Magic* and *Wonder*

Many activities take place in the **Promenade Lounge** on Deck 3 Aft, including the following:

• *Playhouse Disney* Dance Party	• Pirate Trivia Quest
• Pop Decades Dance	• Wildcat Bingo
• Pirate Scavenger Maps	

On the *Dream* and the *Fantasy*

Midship Detective Agency is an interactive, self-guided game in which kids help Disney characters (the Muppets on the *Fantasy*) solve a mystery. Similar to Sorcerers of the Magic Kingdom at Walt Disney World, this is one of the most fun onboard activities in the fleet. You begin by signing up on a computer inside a small desk on Deck 5 Midship. There you'll obtain a small, numbered cardboard game piece. One side of the game piece holds a 2-D bar code and your agent number; the other side displays a detective's badge icon.

Along with your badge card, you'll receive a pamphlet describing each of the agency's suspects behind the mystery. The pamphlet also includes a map of the ship that shows where to find clues to solve the mystery. Once you've signed up and obtained your game material, you'll watch a short video that explains the mystery you're solving. You'll also be told where to go to find your first clue.

Each clue is presented on an "Enchanted Art" video screen somewhere on the ship. The amazing thing about the video screens is that they look like ordinary wall art to anyone not playing the game— it's only when you hold up your badge that the screen comes alive with video and sound. (The technology embedded behind the screens' frames includes a bar-code reader for your badge, speakers, and a network of computers to keep track of your accomplishments.) To obtain the clue, you'll first have to solve a simple puzzle or win a simple

Height and Age Requirements Around the Ships and Castaway Cay

ON BOARD

AquaDuck (Dream and Fantasy) 42" to ride, 54" to ride alone; kids under age 7 must be accompanied by someone age 14 or older

AquaDunk (Magic) 48" to ride

AquaLab (Magic and Fantasy) All ages; kids must be toilet-trained (no swim diapers)

Donald's Pool (Dream and Fantasy) All ages; children under age 16 must be supervised; little ones must be toilet-trained (no swim diapers)

Family hot tubs All ages; children under age 16 must be supervised; little ones must be toilet-trained (no swim diapers)

Goofy's Pool (Magic and Wonder) All ages; children under age 16 must be supervised; little ones must be toilet-trained (no swim diapers)

Mickey's Pool (Dream, Fantasy, and Wonder) and **Nephews' Pool (Magic)** Age 3 and up; must be toilet-trained (no swim diapers)

Mickey's Slide (Dream, Fantasy, and Wonder) Ages 4–14, 38"–64"

Twist 'n' Spout Slide (Magic) Age 4 and over; at least 38" tall

Mickey's Splash Zone (Wonder), Nemo's Reef (Dream and Fantasy), and **Nephews' Splash Zone (Magic)** Age 3 and younger only; swim diapers required

Quiet Cove Pool (all ships) Age 18 and over only

Satellite Falls (Fantasy) Age 18 and over only

ON CASTAWAY CAY

Pelican Plunge waterslide No height requirement listed; life jackets encouraged

The Hide Out Ages 14–17; must be registered for Vibe

Scuttle's Cove Ages 3–12; must be registered for the Oceaneer Club/Lab game. You do this by using your badge as a sort of game controller while you're playing, tilting and moving the badge to guide the action on the screen. It takes a little practice to get used to, so tell your kids before they start that their first try at each screen is just a dry run. You can repeat the action as often as needed.

Once you've obtained the clue, you can eliminate one of the suspects from the mystery; then it's off to another section of the ship to get another clue. Make no mistake: Playing this game involves climbing a lot of stairs. However, you get to see a lot of the ship, and it's good exercise for the kids. You'll see them playing at all times of the day and night, and lines often form in front of each video screen, especially on sea days.

The *Dream* has two separate games: **The Case of the Plundered Paintings** and **The Case of the Missing Puppies.** Both feature Mickey Mouse and his friends. On the *Fantasy,* the Muppets star in **The Case of the Stolen Show.** We think the latter is the most fun—the game's designers expertly incorporate the Muppets' humor into the scenes.

Exclusive to the *Fantasy*

Borrowing from Walt Disney World, the *Fantasy* added the very popular **Bibbidi Bobbidi Boutique** (Deck 5 Midship) for girls ages 3–12 who want the princess treatment. Makeover variations include Disney Diva, Pop Princess, and Fairy Tale Princess. Young princes may sign up for the **Royal Knight Package.** On Pirate Night, the boutique becomes **The Pirates League** and gives buccaneer-themed makeovers to guests age 3 and up (guests 17 and younger must be accompanied by an adult). Packages range from $15.95 to $184.95 and can be prebooked; note that these slots fill fast. The other ships offer a less extensive version of these experiences in **Skulls & Scurry** and **Glitter & Go** on theme nights.

For the princess who has everything, there's the **Royal Sea Package,** which gets you three nights of makeovers plus a gift delivered to your stateroom. It can be yours for $595 and must be booked by e-mail; download a reservation form from **tinyurl.com/royalseaorderform,** or ask your travel agent for details.

CHILDREN'S ACTIVITIES IN PORT

WHEN BOOKING PORT EXCURSIONS, look for activities that are specified for families. Some tours will be specially designated for those traveling with kids. All excursion descriptions (see Part Twelve) include a recommendation for ages (or a requirement, depending on the type of activity) and an indication of the amount of stamina needed to participate. Another option for days when you're in port is to stay aboard and enjoy the lower crowds at the pools and waterslides.

CHILDREN'S ACTIVITIES AT CASTAWAY CAY

DCL'S PRIVATE ISLAND (see Part Ten) has designated areas just for children and families. The teen area, **The Hide Out,** is tucked away, though not on the beach, and offers sports such as volleyball and table tennis and scheduled activities. **Scuttle's Cove,** a play area for young children, has youth-club counselors on hand to direct activities. Both The Hide Out and Scuttle's Cove are monitored by Disney cast members to ensure that only children and their parents enter.

CHILL SPA FOR TEENS

INSIDE SENSES SPA & SALON on the *Dream, Fantasy,* and *Magic,* Chill Spa is for guests ages 13–17. Services can be booked at Senses after boarding. If you don't want your teen to be offered any extra products to buy after treatment, note that when you make your reservation—we found this out the hard way. Read more about the spas on page 156.

WHERE TO MEET CHARACTERS

DISNEY CHARACTERS ARE AVAILABLE for photos and autographs several times per day at various locations on the ships; they also make occasional visits to the nurseries and kids' clubs. A complete schedule is usually available at the Character Information Board in your ship's atrium. The schedule is printed in the "Character Appearances" section of each day's *Personal Navigator*; it's also available by calling ☎ 7-PALS (7257) from your stateroom phone.

unofficial **TIP**
Arrive at least a half-hour ahead of time to meet the Disney princesses. We've arrived 45 minutes ahead to get a spot for our kids to meet Belle, and we weren't the first people in line.

Lines can get very long to meet the most popular characters, such as the Disney princesses, and appearances are limited to around 30 minutes each. The line to meet a character will be closed once it's been determined that no more guests can be accommodated in the character's remaining time. If your child is intent on meeting a specific character, your best bet is to get in line 15–30 minutes before that character is scheduled to appear.

One of the most popular greetings is one that Laurel calls "The Princess Bomb," which explodes in the atrium several times per cruise. Your kids can meet and pose for photos with four to six of the usual suspects from the Princess Hit Parade. On some cruises each princess will have her own line, while on others everyone will queue for one big royal receiving line. Ask the character attendants when you arrive if it's not obvious which is happening on your night. The princess greetings often have the longest lines, with some guests lining up more than 30 minutes before they start, as this reader found out:

> We had a princess event at 9:30 in the morning. Parents started gathering in the atrium an hour ahead. Some hadn't had their coffee yet, and they were NOT happy.

On the afternoon of your first day on the ship, many characters will be on stage at the family pool. On other days, you may see princesses in the ship's lobby around 11:30 a.m. An assortment of characters, including everyone from Mickey and Minnie to Captain Jack Sparrow, usually gathers in the ship's lobby starting about 75 minutes before each dinner seating—that is, 4:30 p.m. for the 5:45 p.m. dinner seating and 7 p.m. for the 8:15 p.m. seating.

Character photo ops including the Fab Five (plus Chip 'n' Dale) in beach attire and Captain Jack Sparrow happen on Castaway Cay close to the ship dock and family beach.

POOLS *and* WATER-PLAY AREAS

EACH SHIP HAS SEPARATE FRESHWATER POOLS designed for small children, families, and adults. All are heated to a minimum temperature of 75°F. Health regulations require that children be toilet-trained to use the pools, while swim diapers are mandatory in the water-play areas. You may bring water wings and other Coast Guard–approved flotation devices into the pools, but not rafts, floats, or those foam noodles you see every summer, nor are snorkels.

THE *MAGIC'S* POOLS

THE SHIP'S NEWEST WATER FEATURE is the **AquaDunk** waterslide, a variation on the AquaDuck slide found on the *Dream* and *Fantasy.* Short and mildly fast, with a vertical start, the AquaDunk starts with your entering a vertical tube. You lean against one side of the tube while a clear Plexiglas door closes opposite you to seal the tube. Suddenly, the floor drops away and you plunge nearly vertically down the tube, through a quick 270-degree turn and into a braking pool of water. The entire experience takes perhaps 7 or 8 seconds, but the initial sensation of falling is fun enough to make it worth repeating. The AquaDunk usually opens at 9 a.m. and closes around 11 p.m.

Because the AquaDunk has an hourly capacity of only around 120 riders, long lines will develop quickly; we've seen 80-minute waits posted. If you're not there first thing in the morning, try during lunchtime or the first dinner seating around 6:15 p.m.

AquaLab, the *Magic*'s water-play area for small children (age 3 and up), is on Deck 9 Aft. It consists of four areas: AquaLab, the Twist 'n' Spout waterslide (age 4 and up and over 38 inches tall), the Nephews' Pool, and the Nephews' Splash Zone.

Every inch of AquaLab is covered in water, which comes out from both vertical and horizontal surfaces. Overhead buckets, slowly filling with water, will dump their contents periodically on anyone standing below, while sprays from faux ship-plumbing will drench anyone walking within 10 feet. Your kids will probably spend hours here, so it's a good thing that both covered seating and refreshments are available nearby.

Next to the main AquaLab area is the **Nephews' Splash Zone,** a water-play area for kids up to 3 years old. This plexiglass-enclosed area has water spouting from pint-size Huey, Dewey, and Louie figures. Padding on the ground allows kids to jump and run around safely, and you'll find parents sitting and relaxing nearby while the little ones get soaked.

A new three-story spiral waterslide, **Twist 'n' Spout** is a lot longer and slower than AquaDunk, making it perfect for kids not quite tall enough for the big slide. Twist 'n' Spout starts above Deck 11 and ends on Deck 9 next to AquaLab. The top part of the slide isn't usually staffed, but a camera system there allows the attendant at the bottom of the slide to monitor both the start and the end simultaneously. Kids must be 4–14 years old and 38–64 inches tall to ride. There's plenty of nearby seating for parents to get some sun while watching the little ones splash around.

The **Nephews' Pool** is a shallow, circular pool in the middle of the deck, touching both AquaLab and the Nephews' Splash Zone. Small children can splash around to their hearts' content while parents sit on ledge seating. Just past the forward end of AquaLab is **Pete's Boiler Bites** snack bar, and on the aft end is **Daisy's De-Lites.**

Goofy's Pool, the *Magic*'s family pool, is on Deck 9 Midship. It's the focal point of outdoor activity on the ship. The pool is 4 feet deep at every point, and deck chairs and lounges are arranged on both sides along its length. At the forward end of the pool is the **Funnel Vision** LED screen, which plays movies, TV shows, and videos almost constantly. At the aft end are **Pinocchio's Pizzeria** and two covered whirlpools. Both Goofy's and Nephews' Pools are typically open 8 a.m.–10 p.m. every day; check your *Personal Navigator* for specific hours.

The adults-only **Quiet Cove Pool** is on Deck 9 Forward. Like Goofy's Pool, it's 4 feet deep throughout, and two adults-only whirlpools are nearby. Teak lounge chairs are provided for relaxing. Just past the aft end of the pool are **Signals** bar and **Cove Café.**

THE *WONDER*'S POOLS

ON THE *WONDER* YOU'LL FIND **Mickey's Pool,** for children age 3 and up, toward Deck 9 Aft. Divided into three smaller pools corresponding to Mickey's face and ears, the pool has a maximum depth of 2 feet, and the bright-yellow spiral **Mickey's Slide** rises about one deck high (about the same level as Deck 10). Kids must be 4–14 years old and 38–64 inches tall to use the waterslide. There's plenty of nearby seating for parents to get some sun while watching the little ones splash around.

*un*official **TIP**
The *Wonder*, alas, doesn't have anything like the AquaDuck or AquaDunk waterslides.

Just past the forward end of Mickey's Pool is **Pluto's Dog House** snack bar, and on the aft end is **Goofy's Galley.**

Children who don't meet the requirements for Mickey's Pool can play in the nearby **Mickey's Splash Zone,** on the port side of the pool.

Surrounded by short walls and themed to *The Sorcerer's Apprentice*, this water-play area for kids age 3 and under features gurgling sprays, jets, and sprinkles of water bubbling up from fountains in the floor. Best of all, there's plenty of covered seating nearby. Kids playing in Mickey's Splash Zone must be supervised.

Goofy's Pool, the family pool, is on Deck 9 Midship. It's the focal point of outdoor activity on the ship. The pool is 4 feet deep at every point, and deck chairs and lounges are arranged on both sides along its length. At the forward end of the pool is the **Funnel Vision** LED screen, which plays movies, TV shows, and videos almost constantly. At the aft end are **Pinocchio's Pizzeria** and two covered whirlpools. Both Goofy's and Mickey's Pools are typically open 8 a.m.–10 p.m. every day; check your *Personal Navigator* for specific hours.

The adults-only **Quiet Cove Pool** is on Deck 9 Forward. Like the corresponding pool on the *Magic,* it's 4 feet deep throughout, and two adults-only whirlpools are nearby. Teak lounge chairs are provided for relaxing. Just past the aft end of the pool are **Signals** bar and **Cove Café.**

THE *DREAM*'S POOLS

LIKE THE *FANTASY* AND *WONDER*, the *Dream* has **Mickey's Pool** for children age 3 and up, roughly midship on Deck 11. Divided into three smaller pools corresponding to Mickey's face and ears, the pool has a maximum depth of 2 feet, and the bright-yellow spiral **Mickey's Slide** rises about one deck high (about the same level as Deck 12). Kids must be 4–14 years old and 38–64 inches tall to use the waterslide. There's plenty of nearby seating for parents to get some sun while watching the little ones splash around.

Children who don't meet the requirements for Mickey's Pool can play in the nearby **Nemo's Reef,** toward the aft end of the pool. Larger and wetter than the Nephews' Splash Zone on the *Magic* and Mickey's Splash Zone on the *Wonder,* this *Finding Nemo*–themed water-play area for kids age 3 and under features gurgling sprays, jets, and sprinkles of water bubbling up from fountains in the floor, as well as from kid-size replicas of some of the movie's characters. A set of restrooms is just behind Nemo's Reef.

Found on Deck 11 Midship is the *Dream*'s family pool, **Donald's Pool.** Like Goofy's Pool on the *Magic* and *Wonder,* it's the center of outdoor activity on the ship. The rectangular pool is about a foot deep close to its edges; in the middle is a roughly circular section that drops to a maximum depth of around 5 feet. The different depths allow younger swimmers to relax in the shallows without having to get out of the pool.

Deck chairs and lounges line both sides of Donald's Pool. At the forward end of the pool is the **Funnel Vision** LED screen, which plays movies, TV shows, and videos almost constantly. At the aft end is the Mickey Pool. Just beyond the Funnel Vision stage are the counter-service restaurants: **Fillmore's Favorites, Luigi's Pizza,** and **Tow Mater's Grill** on the starboard side and the **Eye Scream** ice-cream station on the port side. Both Donald's and Mickey's Pools are typically open 8 a.m.–10 p.m. every day; check your *Personal Navigator* for specific hours.

The adults-only **Quiet Cove Pool** is on Deck 11 Forward on both the *Dream* and the *Fantasy*. This pool is 4 feet deep throughout. Rather than wasting space on whirlpools, the *Dream*'s designers wisely placed an outdoor bar, **Cove Bar,** at one end of the Quiet Cove Pool. The area around the bar is a splash-friendly, nonslip surface, with white bench seating and a round ottoman-like seat in the middle; there are also a few seats directly at the bar. Behind the pool is the lovely **Cove Café;** on either side is covered seating with lounges and chairs.

Both the *Dream* and the *Fantasy* have an **AquaDuck** waterslide, a 765-foot-long clear-plastic tube that's almost as popular as the Disney princesses. Riders board an inflatable plastic raft at the aft end of Deck 12. The raft is shot forward through the plastic tube by high-pressure water faucets below and to the sides, making the AquaDuck a water-powered miniature roller coaster. There's enough water pressure here to propel your raft up two full decks' worth of height, followed by a descent of four decks into a landing pool. Guests must be at least 42 inches tall to ride, and children under age 7 must ride with someone age 14 or older who also meets the height requirement.

unofficial **TIP**
The best time to visit the AquaDuck is between 5 and 7 p.m., when most families are either at dinner or getting ready to go. You'll also find smaller crowds on days when the ship is in port.

The AquaDuck's track sits at the outside edge of Deck 12 and goes as high as one of the ship's smokestacks. If you can keep your eyes open (and your wits about you), it offers some awesome views of the surrounding ocean and any nearby islands.

THE *FANTASY*'S POOLS

LIKE THE *DREAM* AND *WONDER*, the *Fantasy* has **Mickey's Pool** for children age 3 and up, roughly midship on Deck 11. Divided into three smaller pools corresponding to Mickey's face and ears, the pool has a maximum depth of 2 feet, and the bright-yellow spiral **Mickey's Slide** rises about one deck high (about the same level as Deck 12). Kids must be 4–14 years old and 38–64 inches tall to use the waterslide. There's plenty of nearby seating for parents to get some sun while watching the little ones splash around.

Children who don't meet the requirements for Mickey's Pool can play in the nearby **Nemo's Reef,** toward the aft end of the pool. Larger and wetter than the Nephews' Splash Zone on the *Magic* and Mickey's Splash Zone on the *Wonder*, this *Finding Nemo*–themed water-play area for kids age 3 and under features gurgling sprays, jets, and sprinkles of water bubbling up from fountains in the floor, as well as from kid-size replicas of some of the movie's characters. A set of restrooms is just behind Nemo's Reef.

Found on Deck 11 Midship is the *Fantasy*'s family pool, **Donald's Pool.** Like Goofy's Pool on the *Magic* and *Wonder,* it's the center of outdoor activity on the ship. The rectangular pool is about a foot deep close to its edges; in the middle is a roughly circular section that drops to a maximum depth of around 5 feet. The different depths allow younger swimmers to relax in the shallows without having to get out of the pool.

Deck and lounge chairs line both sides of Donald's Pool. At the forward end of the pool is the **Funnel Vision** LED screen, which plays movies, TV shows, and videos almost constantly. At the aft end is the Mickey Pool. Just beyond the Funnel Vision stage are the counter-service restaurants: **Fillmore's Favorites, Luigi's Pizza,** and **Tow Mater's Grill** on the starboard side and the **Eye Scream** ice-cream station on the port side. Both Donald's and Mickey's Pools are typically open 8 a.m.– 10 p.m. every day; check your *Personal Navigator* for specific hours.

Like the *Magic,* the *Fantasy* has an **AquaLab** water-play area. On Deck 12 Aft, it's similar to Nemo's Reef in that its entertainment is provided by water splashing out at you, but where the water comes up from the floor at Nemo's Reef, it comes from the sky at AquaLab. High above your head are water pipes filling buckets and buckets of water, which are counterbalanced so that they spill down on unsuspecting (and suspecting) kids below. In fact, water comes at you from every angle in AquaLab, and that's exactly the appeal. AquaLab is for kids too old or too large to play in Nemo's Reef.

The adults-only **Quiet Cove Pool** is on Deck 11 Forward on both the *Dream* and the *Fantasy.* This pool is 4 feet deep throughout. Rather than wasting space on whirlpools, the *Fantasy*'s designers wisely placed an outdoor bar, **Cove Bar,** at one end of the Quiet Cove Pool. The area around the bar is a splash-friendly, nonslip surface, with white bench seating and a round ottoman-like seat in the middle; there are also a few seats directly at the bar. Behind the pool is the lovely **Cove Café;** on either side is covered seating with lounges and chairs.

Both the *Fantasy* and the *Dream* have an **AquaDuck** waterslide, a 765-foot-long clear-plastic tube that's almost as popular as the Disney princesses. Riders board an inflatable plastic raft at the aft end of Deck 12. The raft is shot forward through the plastic tube by high-pressure water faucets below and to the sides, making the AquaDuck a water-powered miniature roller coaster. There's enough water pressure here to propel your raft up two full decks' worth of height, followed by a descent of four decks into a landing pool. Guests must be at least 42 inches tall to ride, and children under age 7 must ride with someone age 14 or older who also meets the height requirement.

The AquaDuck's track sits at the outside edge of Deck 12 and goes as high as one of the ship's smokestacks. If you can keep your eyes open (and your wits about you), it offers some awesome views of the surrounding ocean and any nearby islands. The best time to visit is between 5 and 7 p.m., when most families are either at dinner or getting ready to go. You'll also find smaller crowds on days when the ship is in port.

Besides all this, the *Fantasy* has a water feature not found on any other ship: **Satellite Falls,** an adults-only splash pool and sun deck on Deck 13 Forward. Covered with long, vertical tiles in different shades of blue and green, the pool looks great at night. In the center, a structure that looks like a giant Doppler radar receiver (and mimics a pair of actual satellite receivers on either side of the pool) pours a gentle stream of water into the pool below.

ONBOARD SEMINARS

LED BY CREW MEMBERS and attended by a limited number of passengers, onboard seminars are 30- to 60-minute interactive talks. Topics vary, but most involve food, wine, shopping, fitness activities, or how the ship is run. The shopping seminars and tours of the ship are usually free of charge; some of the cooking demonstrations are also free. A small fee—usually $15 to $25—is charged for seminars involving alcohol, and for some of the fitness activities.

The crew members who lead these seminars generally also have duties related to the subject. Wine presentations, for example, are usually run by either a restaurant sommelier or an experienced bartender; cooking demonstrations are run by one of the ship's chefs. Not surprisingly, the crew members' presentation and speaking skills are the most important factor in determining the quality of the seminar. On one cruise, a well-versed chef butterflied three dozen shrimp in slow motion so we could all take notes on proper knife technique. On another cruise, a bartender apparently not used to public speaking ran us through seven tequila shots and margaritas in 35 minutes, rendering us useless for the rest of the afternoon (not that we minded).

Several **wine-tasting sessions** are usually held on most cruises, especially those of more than four nights. The first session is typically an introduction to wine and covers the basics: grape varietals, flavor characteristics, vocabulary, and such. Subsequent sessions may concentrate on a particular style of wine, or those from a particular region. Most tastings serve 2- or 3-ounce pours from four or five varieties. The Champagne bars on the *Dream* and *Fantasy* hold tastings too. In addition to wine, Champagne, and tequila, cruises may offer Cognac, whiskey, martini, mojito, and beer tastings.

The **cooking demonstrations** are some of the best presentations on board. Like the wine sessions, cooking demos often follow a theme: The first day, for example, may show how to prepare an appetizer; the second involves an entrée; and the third will be dessert. Each of these is led by a member of the kitchen staff, usually a chef. These presentations are typically held in one of the ship's nightclubs so more people can attend. To make it easy for everyone to see what the chef is doing, several video cameras are often mounted above the chef's work table, providing a view of the preparations.

We've attended many cooking demonstrations on the Disney ships, and they've all been presented better and had more interesting foods than comparable classes elsewhere. We're always amazed at the number of ingredients used in some of these dishes too. One shrimp-and-lobster appetizer we prepared involved 31 separate ingredients! You won't be making these for a church potluck.

If you're looking for exercise instead of food or shopping, the **walking tours** of the ships are a great way to keep moving and see the inner workings of the ship. Most tours begin somewhere on the pool deck and wind their way down and back up the ship. Areas covered may include the ship's bridge, engine room, kitchens and restaurants, and entertainment areas. One great thing about these tours is that you get to ask questions of the crew members staffing each section. If you want to know what it takes to prepare 800 appetizers at the same time, you'll find the person to ask on this tour.

Shopping seminars are usually held on sea days when the ship will be docked at a port the following day. (The seminars are also video-taped and available on your stateroom's television 24 hours a day.) Most seminars last 60–90 minutes, with multiple sessions held per day. Each session usually covers one kind of item, such as watches, or a particular kind of gemstone available at the next port. The seminar on diamonds, for example, explains how cut, color, carat, and clarity combine to form the basis of each stone's price.

We don't understand why anyone would attend a shopping seminar. If you're considering a major purchase such as diamonds, jewelry, or an expensive watch, you're almost certainly better off postponing it until you're back at home and can do your own research. Further, with the vast array of goods available on the Internet (usually with better consumer protections), it's unlikely that you'll find many things with prices low enough to justify the risk. (See our "Shopping" section later in this chapter for more information.)

The spa and fitness center host **wellness seminars** most mornings. Topics include everything from stretching exercises and acupuncture to group cycling and Pilates. Many of the sessions, such as stretching and cycling, are free, although space is limited and you're strongly encouraged to sign up well in advance to guarantee a spot. Personal-training sessions, available in 30- or 60-minute increments, cost roughly $45–$80, respectively, before tip.

Finally, the **Disney Vacation Club (DVC)** hosts presentations on its Walt Disney World time-shares during the cruise; check your *Personal Navigator* for the schedule. A DVC representative is often stationed at a desk somewhere just off the lobby. On sea days, you'll probably find the rep roaming the halls of the ship to get the word out on an upcoming seminar. And while you may or may not want to sit through a time-share presentation on vacation, the DVC reps are very generous in giving out free stuff. If you're in need of a cap or backpack during your trip, stop by here before you head to the shops—you may get one for free, as this reader found:

> We didn't want to sit through the DVC sales pitch, but we're suckers for swag. We stopped by the DVC desk and they practically threw goodies at us. Despite me saying that there were just two of us on board, the rep insisted on giving me four DVC baseball caps and four sturdy drawstring backpacks.

SPORTS *and* FITNESS

EACH SHIP OFFERS AN ARRAY of outdoor and indoor sports and fitness options. While it's no substitute for your local megagym, there's enough equipment and variety on board for almost everyone to maintain muscle tone and cardio conditioning during the cruise.

unofficial **TIP**
The Fitness Center is on Deck 9 Forward on the *Magic* and *Wonder,* and on Deck 11 Forward on the *Dream* and *Fantasy.*

Each DCL ship has a comprehensive **Fitness Center** with new, well-maintained weight machines, free weights, treadmills, stairclimbers, elliptical machines, stationary bikes, and more.

These gyms provide yoga mats, large plastic step-aerobics benches, exercise balls, and elastic bands for stretching. Also provided are a water fountain, a basket of fresh fruit, cloth towels, paper towels, and spray bottles of sanitizer to clean the equipment when you're done. Male and female locker rooms have showers, a sauna, sinks, robes, towels, personal-grooming items, and lockers with electric locks. There is no charge to use these facilities.

We've spent a lot of time in the gyms on every ship, and we've been happy with the variety of equipment available. Nautilus-style weight machines are available for working every major and minor muscle group. Virtually all of the electric cardio machines have video monitors so you can watch the ship's television while working out, along with plugs for your headphones.

The Fitness Centers are usually open from around 6 a.m. until 11 p.m.; check your *Personal Navigator* for the exact schedule. They tend to be most crowed in the morning between 8 and 11 a.m., and least crowded between 5 and 11 p.m. Group- and personal-training sessions are available, including weight training, Pilates, and other courses, for an additional fee. Group sessions start at around $12 per workout, typically about 45 minutes each. Individual training sessions cost around $40 per half-hour session.

The only thing we've found disconcerting in the gyms is that the treadmills on the *Dream* and *Fantasy* face the port (left) side of the ship, not the bow. If the ship is moving while you're running on one of these treadmills, the scenery in front of you will be passing from left to right, but your brain expects to see the scenery moving toward you. Some people—including Len—instinctively twist their bodies left in an attempt to line up the scenery with the way their mind thinks they should be going. This makes for awkward running (walking doesn't seem to be much of an issue). If you find yourself unable to run correctly on the treadmill, try the outdoor course described next.

Runners and walkers will appreciate the **0.3-mile track** circling Deck 4 of the *Magic* and *Wonder* and the **0.4-mile track** on Deck 4 of the *Dream* and *Fantasy*. One of the great things about running laps on the ship is the amazing scenery, which (almost) makes you forget that you're exercising while you're seeing it. We've run a few laps on both ships, and the track is certainly good enough to get in a few miles to start your day. Some sections take you through some relatively narrow corridors, and there's a good chance that you'll be running past groups of other tourists who are out enjoying the deck too. Finally, keep an eye open for water on the deck, which can make the track slick.

If running isn't your thing, every DCL ship has **outdoor basketball courts** surrounded by woven rope fencing to keep errant balls from leaving the ship. These are popular with kids and parents looking to shoot around a bit—we've never seen a competitive game played at one. The basketball courts can be converted to a miniature soccer field or volleyball court too, if you can find enough people to play.

unofficial **TIP**
If your itinerary includes a trip to Castaway Cay, Disney usually hosts a 5K run around the island starting at 9 a.m. There's no cost to run. Water is provided at several points throughout the course, and Disney usually hands out Mickey-shaped plastic "medals" to finishers. Check your *Personal Navigator* the night before your stop for where to meet on board.

Each ship also has **shuffleboard courts** near midship on Deck 4; if you're up for a challenge, outdoor **tennis tables** are available too (Deck 9 Forward on the *Magic* and *Wonder*; Deck 13 Aft on the *Dream* and *Fantasy*). Readers report that the windy conditions on deck make it difficult to play, but perhaps your game will benefit from a bit of unpredictability.

The *Dream* and *Fantasy* both have Disney-themed **miniature-golf courses** outdoors on Deck 13 Aft, and these are a lot of fun for the entire family. The *Dream* and *Fantasy* also have **Foosball tables** outdoors. As with the table tennis, we find it helpful to have the following list available when our game fails us:

HANDY EXCUSES FOR RECREATIONAL INEPTITUDE

- Gust of wind changed ball trajectory
- Rough seas caused ship to list suddenly
- Sunglasses aren't made for the UV rays at this latitude (*note:* must be wearing sunglasses when saying this)
- Concentration broken by sound of pirate ship-cannon in distance
- Giant-squid tentacle was seen reaching up behind opponent

If you're looking to get in some individual practice time on the *Dream* and *Fantasy*, **virtual sports simulators** are available on Deck 13 Aft for golf, basketball, soccer, football, hockey, and baseball. These indoor facilities have a large movie screen set up in a dedicated room; a computer projects a simulated soccer field, basketball court, or other appropriate venue on the screen. You're given actual sports equipment to kick, throw, or swing. Your movements, and the movements of the ball, are tracked by computers and displayed on-screen—there's a slight lag in the display, but it's not enough to be distracting. Half-hour sessions cost $25 for golf and $12 for other sports; hour-long sessions are $45 for golf and $20 for other sports.

SPAS

SOME OF THE MOST RELAXING TIMES we've spent on DCL's ships have been in their spas. Whether you're looking for a massage, manicure, new hairstyle, or just some time to unwind in a hot sauna, you'll find it at the spa.

This section summarizes the major spa and salon services offered on each ship, but note that many more are available. We recommend visiting the spa on your first afternoon aboard to sign up for any last-minute treatments and check for specials. *Note:* Prices listed are approximate and do not include a tip, typically 15–20% of the cost of your treatment. There's a 50% cancellation charge if you cancel within 24 hours of your appointment.

unofficial **TIP**
The best time to visit the spa is during dinner or when the ship is in port.

Salon services must be booked after 1 p.m. on your first day aboard—you can't book them online. If you're trying to book spa services before your cruise, Disney's website may not let you book some services, such as facials, for two people at the same time of day. (We think that the website assumes that only one person per ship is qualified to do these tasks, and that this person is unavailable once the first service is booked.) If you run into this problem, try booking the services online one after the other, and then visit the spa in person when you board to explain what you want done.

Along the same lines, one thing that's different about spa treatments on the Disney ships versus on land is that the same person is likely to be your masseuse, facialist, and manicurist—there's simply not enough room on the ship for a whole squadron of beauty experts, so roles have to be combined. Some readers like the continuity of having one person to talk with throughout their treatments; others think that one person can't provide the same level of service as multiple dedicated professionals.

ON THE *MAGIC*

ON DECK 9 FORWARD is **Senses Salon & Spa.** The reception area and check-in desk are just behind the forward elevator lobby, past the adult

Quiet Cove Pool. Senses on the *Dream* and *Fantasy* have a hair salon, treatment rooms for individuals and couples, and a complex of steam baths and showers. Men's and women's locker rooms, shared with the Fitness Center, provide storage lockers with electric locks, showers, robes, slippers, and towels.

Formerly known as Vista Spa & Salon (the name still used for the *Wonder*'s spa), Senses got its current name after the ship's 2013 dry dock. The *Dream*'s and *Fantasy*'s spas are also named Senses, as well as those at the Grand Floridian and Saratoga Springs Resorts at Walt Disney World.

The changes to the *Magic*'s spa were mainly cosmetic, however, and Senses on this ship is much more akin to the *Wonder*'s Vista Spa than the other two Senses. The two major updates are a redesigned lobby and the addition of **Chill Spa** for guests ages 13–17, in line with the teen spas on the *Dream* and *Fantasy*. However, the *Magic*'s Chill Spa is nothing like those two—it's a single treatment room off the beauty salon. To call it a spa is laughable.

Senses' hair salon has services for men and women. Options for men include haircuts (around $35); the **Elemis Express Shave** with hot-towel wrap (around $45); and the wordy **Elemis Pro-Collagen Grooming Treatment with Shave** (around $95), billed as "the shave of all shaves"—an almost hour-long treatment including the towel wrap, a shave, a minifacial, and massages for your face, scalp, and hands. Men who use electric shavers for their daily toilette should be aware that a hand-held razor shaves much closer than an electric blade and can cause razor burn, even on men who aren't normally susceptible. Your face will be as smooth as a baby's bottom, though.

Women can get a literal head-to-toe makeover, starting with hair-styling. A simple shampoo and blow-dry runs about $32–$48 depending on hair length; adding a haircut is about $56–$75. Separate conditioning treatments are available: The **Frangipani Hair and Scalp Ritual,** which sounds like it's part of a tribal initiation, starts at around $30; most other standard conditioning treatments are around $50 each. Senses also offers a treatment for color-treated hair for around $30; hair coloring starts at about $55.

Waxing for eyebrows ($25), legs ($89), arms ($39), upper lip ($19), chin ($19), and bikini line ($29) is available too. If you're headed to Palo for dinner, you can get your makeup done for your big night out, starting at $75.

Manicures (around $50) and pedicures (around $70) come with a heated stone massage of your various digits. There seems to be no discount for doing both together. Additional services include adding polish ($25), removing polish ($20), paraffin baths ($15), and acrylic nails ($82).

Facials and massages are administered in private, individual treatment rooms or in one of the dedicated Spa Villas for singles and couples. Five different facials are offered, including ones with microdermabrasion, fruits and herbs, enzymes, and something that involves "amazing micro-currents applied at a high frequency" to your skin . . . voluntarily. Treatments cost $115–$170 for a 50-minute session.

Some treatment rooms at Senses on the *Magic* (and Vista Spa on the *Wonder*) sit directly under the basketball courts. If someone is playing, you'll hear through the ceiling every time someone bounces a ball or lands after jumping.

Massages include the traditional deep-tissue kind; a variation accompanied by heated, scented stones placed on various parts of your body; and another where warmed bamboo sticks are rolled over you in addition to the massage. Prices range from $129 for a basic 50-minute rubdown to $244 for 100 minutes. Besides these are massages combining hands-on therapy with slatherings of spices, minerals, and herbs designed to make you feel like a Thanksgiving turkey with a healthy glow. Among the offerings are the **Aroma Ocean Wrap with Half-Body Massage** ($188), the **Thai Herbal Poultice Massage ($195),** and the **Exotic Lime and Ginger Salt Glow with Half-Body Massage** (part of two $400-plus treatment packages for couples).

Services in the Chill Spa room for teens range from the **Magical Manicure** at the low end ($29) to the **Hot Chocolate Wrap** at the high end ($141).

unofficial **TIP**
We don't recommend the length-of-cruise Rainforest pass on the *Magic*. Get the cheaper one-day pass instead.

Besides these spa services, 30-minute teeth-whitening treatments are available for individuals (around $150) and couples (around $260). They're not especially popular, though, probably because you're told to abstain from drinking coffee and wine after the whitening.

Our favorite spa experience is the **Rainforest,** which costs around $16 per person, per day. This gets you access to three separate steam rooms, arranged around a quiet tiled room with heated stone lounge chairs. Each steam room has its own scent, temperature, and steam setting. Outside the steam rooms are Rainforest showers, with push-button settings that allow you to vary the intensity, pattern, and temperature of the water flow.

Unfortunately, the Rainforest at Senses on the *Magic* (along with the one at Vista Spa on the *Wonder*) isn't as nice as the versions on the *Dream* and *Fantasy:* It's considerably smaller and less spacious, with fewer showers and lounge chairs, and unlike its larger siblings, it doesn't

unofficial **TIP**
Senses on the *Magic* is smaller and not as pretty as Senses on the *Dream* and *Fantasy,* even after its 2013 refurbishment, but it's nicer than the *Wonder*'s Vista Spa.

have outdoor hot tubs or ocean views. That said, it's still the most relaxing thing you can do on the *Magic,* and because DCL sells a limited number of passes per cruise—we've heard estimates of as few as 20 on the entire ship—you're unlikely to share the Rainforest with more than a handful of other people on any day. Also, a day pass at the Rainforest on the *Magic* and *Wonder* is less expensive than on the *Dream* and *Fantasy*: $16 versus $25 on the larger ships.

ON THE *WONDER*

ON DECK 9 FORWARD, **Vista Spa & Salon** largely mirrors Senses Spa & Salon on the *Magic*. Aside from the name, the only significant differences are that the interiors haven't been refurbished and the Chill Spa treatment room for teens is missing.

ON THE *DREAM* AND THE *FANTASY*

DISNEY'S TWO NEWEST SHIPS each have a **Senses Spa & Salon** on Deck 11 Forward. Both are gorgeous, incorporating dark woods and intricate tile and stonework, with comfortable leather chairs and soft bed linens. Senses on the *Dream* and *Fantasy* is much larger than Vista Spa & Salon on the *Wonder* and slightly larger than the *Magic*'s Senses. Some of the treatment rooms and spa areas afford sweeping views out over the sides of each ship; also, Senses on the *Dream* and *Fantasy* has two covered outdoor whirlpools available to those with a Rainforest pass. On the *Magic* and *Wonder*, ocean views and outdoor features are available only to those who book a pricey treatment in one of the private Spa Villas.

Salon services, facials, and massages are about the same as those offered at the spas on the *Magic* and *Wonder*. Here are the major differences:

More luxurious than its counterparts on the two smaller ships, the **Rainforest** (about $25 per person, per day) gives you access to three saunas with varying levels of heat and humidity: the Laconium, a dry sauna with mild heat and low humidity; the Caldarium, with medium heat and humidity; and the Hamam, a full-on steam bath, with the hottest temperatures and lots and lots of steam. In addition to different levels of steam, each sauna has its own scent and music.

unofficial **TIP**
Bring a towel to sit on in the saunas, and wear sandals—the seats and floors are very hot.

We enjoy hopping between these saunas and the nearby Rainforest showers—tiled circular cutouts hidden behind the walls along the path leading to the saunas. Each shower has different options for water temperature, pressure, and spray pattern, each of which you select by pushing a button. For example, one option might be a light, cool mist, perfect for when you've just jumped out of the sauna. Another is like a warm, steady downpour in a tropical jungle.

Had enough of the steam rooms and showers? Then repair to one of the two covered outdoor whirlpool tubs or one of the stone lounge chairs in an adjacent room. The ocean views here are perhaps the biggest selling point over the Rainforests on the *Magic* and *Wonder*.

unofficial **TIP**
Parents should note that our unaccompanied teens were upsold more than $200 in beauty products during one trip to the spa. When making an appointment for your teen, specify up front whether they can buy products and, if so, how much they can spend.

The best thing about the Rainforest package is that Disney sells only a limited number of them per cruise. We hear that number can be as low as 40 people on the *Dream* and *Fantasy*. Not 40 at a time, not 40 per day—40 people on the entire ship. While we're not sure if that number is correct, we do know that we've never seen more than two other people in this part of the spa on any cruise. It's the single most relaxing thing you can do on board.

Finally, exclusive to the *Dream* and *Fantasy* is the teens-only **Chill Spa,** a spa-within-a-spa entirely inside Senses. (The *Magic* also has something it calls Chill Spa, but it's a single treatment room.) Designed for guests ages 13–17, Chill has its own array of facial, massage, exfoliating, and mani–pedi packages. Prices start at around $90 for a massage, $95 for a facial, and $45 and $65 for manicures and pedicures, respectively. Hairstyling and fitness sessions in the gym are also available.

Parent–child massages are offered as well ($99 for half-body, $195 for full-body). Let us know if you've tried these with your teens, please: When we told ours about them, one replied, "Gross!" and the other gave us a look like she'd prefer being rubbed with angry ferrets.

SHOPPING

WHETHER YOU'RE AT SEA OR IN PORT, your daily *Personal Navigator* handout highlights your shopping opportunities for the day.

unofficial **TIP**
A note about the "Shopping Consultants" on board: You'll note that their name tags look different from other crew members'. This is because they're not Disney employees. Both DCL and the consultants receive money back from shops that have been recommended in the *Personal Navigator* handout when guests buy something there. This is not to say you shouldn't buy from these shops, but remember that the shopping recommendations aren't entirely unbiased.

ONBOARD SHOPPING

ONBOARD SHOPS GENERALLY AREN'T OPEN when the ship is in port. If there's any possibility that you're going to run out of something critical during the day, be sure to stock up on it while the shops are open.

As Disney-theme-park fans, we were surprised at the relatively modest amount of space dedicated to retail stores on the Disney ships. Each ship has dedicated retail spaces for children, women, and men. Look for them on Deck 4 Forward on the *Magic* and *Wonder* and Deck 3 Forward on the *Dream* and *Fantasy*, on either side of the walkway to the Walt Disney Theatre.

The shops sell a little bit of everything, from T-shirts and stuffed animals to snacks, bathing suits, and towels. You'll also find sunscreen, aspirin, toothpaste, diapers, and other travel supplies. In addition, an onboard store sells duty-free alcohol by the bottle, including wines and spirits served on board, though you won't be able to take possession of your purchase until the last night of your cruise.

In case you neglected to pack your eye patch for Pirate Night, the shops can outfit the entire family head to toe, buccaneer-style. You'll find a variety of the same merchandise found in Disney theme parks as well as DCL-specific souvenirs. Some of our favorites are china and spreaders from Animator's Palate—the cynics among us wonder if this wasn't in response to these items walking off the ships on their own—and the DCL-exclusive AquaDuck Vinylmation. A separate retail space sells jewelry, including midpriced watches, earrings, rings, and gold and silver chains by the inch. As we say elsewhere, we're hesitant to buy expensive things on the ship or in port. The concern we have with jewelry is that it's difficult both to comparison-shop for similar items and to assess the quality of what you're looking at.

Besides the retail spaces, each ship has an art gallery with limited-edition Disney-character and theme-park art, along with **Shutters** photo gallery, where you can purchase snaps from your cruise.

The most commonly heard advantage to buying on board or in port is that you don't pay US or local sales taxes, which can be significant on large purchases. US residents are still required to declare these purchases when they return to the States, and they may be subject to import duties. See page 53 for more details.

CASTAWAY CAY

THE SHOPS HERE SELL SOME ITEMS that are exclusive to the island, such as T-shirts and beach towels. We've purchased last-minute cords for our sunglasses, water-resistant pouches for our phones, and other beach supplies on Castaway Cay. Note that no sales tax is charged on the island or on board, which makes purchases cheaper than if you bought them at a Disney park.

IN PORT

MANY TRAVELERS FIND SHOPPING IN PORT as essential to the cruising experience as gambling is to the Las Vegas experience. If you approach buying things with this attitude, you won't be disappointed. You'll be surrounded by retail opportunities at each port from the moment you step off the ship; bargaining is expected, so assume that the price you're quoted the first time you ask isn't the final one. If you need T-shirts, duty-free booze, or handmade woodcrafts to bring back as inexpensive souvenirs, you'll have no trouble finding them within a few hundred yards of the ship.

In fact, you'll find these things at virtually every port, so there's probably no need to rush your purchase. The homogenization of shopping experiences from Ketchikan to Cozumel can only be explained by assuming that people must be buying the stuff being sold. We're fairly certain, therefore, that a large part of the global-tourism trade consists

---

IS IT REAL?

YOU PROBABLY REALIZE that the "Louis Vuitton" bag on sale for $25 at the Straw Market is a fake. Also remember that perfume and sunglasses are among the most counterfeited items out there. Many luxury brands, such as Gucci and the aforementioned Louis Vuitton, do have actual stores in the Caribbean and European ports, so you can buy with confidence there (though to one author's despair, Hermès doesn't have an outpost in the Bahamas). Another thing to look out for is out-of-season merchandise being sold at full price: On one trip to Nassau, we found an authentic Kate Spade bag being sold at MSRP, but it could be found 30–50% off stateside because it was from the previous season. With all purchases, do your due diligence ahead of time to know what a fair price is for anything you're considering buying.

We find that the amount of time spent bargaining in port isn't worth any potential savings, and so we don't spend a lot of time shopping on our cruises. That said, our Ports section (see Part Eleven) highlights any especially good deals we've been able to find along the way.

---

of selling T-shirts and beach towels displaying the Corona beer logo along with the name of the city you're in. And if you've ever been to the Nassau Straw Market, you'll know that an only slightly smaller slice of the trade is made from selling woven baskets bearing a probably unlicensed and definitely disfigured image of Dora the Explorer.

JEWELRY Buying jewelry in port is popular with many cruisers. The problem we have with doing this is that fair prices vary greatly with the quality of the gems purchased, and you really need to be an informed shopper to know what's a good price for an item. Our recommendation is to pre-shop online (**Amazon** and **bluenile.com** are great places to start) to know the going prices for gems of the weight and quality you're interested in. One brand in particular, **Effy,** is already sold on Amazon and through its own website (**effyjewelry.com**), so check it out before you leave.

PART TEN

CASTAWAY CAY

CASTAWAY CAY IS LIKELY TO BE your favorite island on your Bahamian or Caribbean cruise. The weather is almost always gorgeous; the shore excursions are reasonably priced (mostly); and, as is the case with Walt Disney World, there's little of the "real world" to get in the way of a relaxing day. And that's before the free food and (nonalcoholic) drinks. We provide additional coverage of Castaway Cay in Part Eleven, Ports, and Part Twelve, Port Adventures.

▌ WHAT *to* BRING

THE SUN AND HEAT ARE INTENSE, so bring plenty of high-SPF sunscreen and water. Insulated sports bottles are a great idea. Other solar protection you may need includes light-colored, long-sleeved, lightweight shirts; sweatpants; swimsuit cover-ups; hats; lip balm; and sunglasses.

Disney will provide you with medium-size towels for use while on Castaway Cay—as many as you can carry. If you'd prefer a full-size beach towel, bring one of your own or purchase one while you're on the island.

Disney also provides life jackets (free) for use while on the island. Strollers, wagons, and sand-capable wheelchairs are available for rent on a first-come, first-served basis.

OTHER ITEMS YOU MAY FIND USEFUL TO BRING TO CASTAWAY CAY

- **A watch or cell phone** for checking how long everyone has been in the sun and when it's time to reapply sunscreen. Also useful for knowing whether the island's restaurants are open (usually 11 a.m.–2 p.m.).

- **An underwater or waterproof camera** for taking photos while swimming, snorkeling, or participating in other activities.

Continued on page 166

Castaway Cay

ATTRACTIONS

A. Arrival Plaza
B. Post Office
C. Marge's Barges and
   Sea Charters Dock
D. Boating Harbor
E. Scuttle's Cove
F. Boat Beach
G. Monstro Point
H. Castaway Ray's
   Stingray Adventure
I. Gil's Fins and Boats
J. Gazebos
K. Castaway Family Beaches
L. Snorkeling Lagoon
M. Swimming Lagoon
N. In-Da-Shade Games
O. Flippers and Floats
P. Pelican Plunge

ATTRACTIONS

Q. The Hide Out (teens only)
R. Bike Rentals
S. Beach Sports
T. Spring-a-Leak
U. Beach Cabanas 1–17
V. The Windsock Hut
W. Massage Cabanas
X. Serenity Bay Adult Beach
Y. Beach Cabanas 18–21
Z. Observation Tower

FOOD AND DRINK

1. Pop's Props and Boat Repair
   (Covered Seating)
2. Dig In (Covered Seating)
3. Cookie's BBQ
4. Conched Out Bar

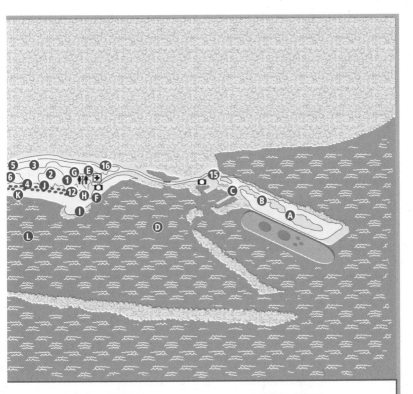

FOOD AND DRINK

5. Outdoor Seating
6. Gumbo Limbo (Covered Seating)
7. Heads Up Bar
8. Grouper (Covered Seating)
9. Sand Bar
10. Cookie's Too BBQ
11. Castaway Air Bar

SHOPPING

12. She Sells Sea Shells . . .
and Everything Else
13. Buy the Seashore
14. Bahamian Retail

MISCELLANEOUS

15. Kargo Handling Tram Stop
16. Scuttle's Cove Tram Stop
17. Pelican Point Tram Stop
18. Serenity Bay Tram Stop

⊞ First Aid
⚦ Restrooms and
   Outdoor Showers
◻ Photo Opportunities
■ Bike/Nature Trail

Continued from page 163

- **A small cooler** to keep medicine, baby formula, and other perishables cool. Fill it with ice before you leave the ship, and refill it from the restaurants' ice machines on the island. The cooler must be soft-sided and no larger than 12 by 12 by 12 inches; larger coolers are not allowed to be brought on the ship when boarding.

- **Water shoes** will protect your feet from sharp rocks and coral and provide some insulation from hot sand and pavement.

- **Small beach toys,** such as a shovel and pail, though pails might present some packing issues. Toys are also available for purchase on the island.

- **Your own snorkeling gear** if you already have it, or if the idea of sharing a snorkel tube just grosses you out. DCL provides flotation vests for free.

- **Swim diapers,** if you have little ones who like the water.

- **A hairbrush or comb.** It's windy on the island, and you'll want to look good in your vacation photos.

- **Insect repellent.** Disney keeps the bug population under control, and we've never been bothered by anything. In case your family is especially sensitive to bites, however, it's a good idea to bring something like Off or Repel.

- **Something to read—a book or e-reader.** Be careful, however, about leaving expensive electronics alone on the island.

- **A portable music player.** Especially useful if you're going for a jog around the island's 5K course.

- **Athletic shoes and socks.** If you want to play basketball on the island, you'll also want proper footwear.

- **A change of clothes.** While Castaway Cay's sun will dry your swimsuit in a hurry, you may want dry clothes to wear while you're walking around the island, sitting down for meals, or riding bikes. You can also return to the ship to change, but going through security takes time.

- **A small amount of cash.** Castaway Cay has its own official Bahamian post office from which you can mail home postcards and letters. The post office takes cash only (no room charges), so bring a few dollars for postage. (This is the only place on the island for which you'll need cash.)

WHAT *to* DO

THERE ARE MORE THINGS TO DO than you'll have time for in a single day or even two. A list of our favorite Castaway Cay shore activities follows; see Part Twelve for details.

- **Castaway Ray's Stingray Adventure** affords you the opportunity to pet and feed small and medium-size stingrays in a dedicated lagoon.

- The **snorkeling lagoon** features underwater sights such as a replica of the *Nautilus* submarine from *20,000 Leagues Under the Sea,* other shipwrecks and shipping artifacts, plus statues of Minnie and Mickey. Common marine life seen in the snorkeling lagoon includes stingrays, blue tang, and yellowtail snapper (plus the occasional barracuda).

- Rent **sailboats or paddleboats, personal watercraft,** or **inflatable floats and tubes.**

- Runners may want to start their day with the **Castaway Cay 5K,** a free (as in no-cost) jog through the developed parts of the island.

- Single-speed **bicycle rentals** allow you to fully explore the island, including the island's observation tower and trails, which can be accessed only on foot or bike.

Castaway Cay's lagoons are shallow, with small, gentle waves. Anchored within a short swim from shore is **Pelican Plunge,** a floating platform with two waterslides and a water-play area. The waterslides begin on the platform's second story (accessed by stairs) and end with a splash back into the lagoon. Each slide offers a different experience: One is a long, open slide with moderate turns, while the other is a shorter, enclosed slide with plenty of tight turns and twists.

Along with the slides, Pelican Plunge's water-play area includes pipes, nozzles, and plumes of water spraying out from every direction. The main feature is a giant overhead bucket, which is constantly being filled with water from the lagoon. The bucket is counterbalanced so that when the water reaches a certain level, the bucket tilts over suddenly, pouring gallons of water on anything nearby.

If you have small children who enjoy water but you're concerned about ocean currents, consider letting the little ones run around at the inland **Spring-a-Leak** water-play area, just beyond the Pelican Point tram stop, near the middle of the family beaches. Like Pelican Plunge, Spring-a-Leak has plenty of burbling, spraying, misting water to keep kids wet and happy all day long.

Scuttle's Cove, an additional area for the little ones, offers supervised activities, yet another water-play area, and a giant-whale-bone excavation site.

Teens have their own dedicated area inland: **The Hide Out,** with volleyball, tetherball, and other activities. Be aware that some teens may not like the fact that The Hide Out is away from the beach and has no water features or water-play areas.

Height and Age Requirements at Castaway Cay

- **Pelican Plunge waterslide:** No official height requirement listed; life jackets encouraged
- **The Hide Out:** Ages 14–17; must be registered for Vibe on board
- **Scuttle's Cove:** Ages 3–12; must be registered for the Oceaneer Club/ Lab on board

WHERE *to* RELAX

CASTAWAY CAY IS ALSO A GREAT PLACE to sit back, listen to the ocean, feel the sea breeze on your face, and smell the salt air. Two family beaches are available, while adults ages 18 and up have **Serenity Bay,** a private beach with its own outdoor barbecue, bar, rental cabanas, and more.

FAMILY BEACHES Most of Castaway Cay's developed beachfront is reserved for families. If you're taking the tram from the dock, get off at the first stop, **Pelican Point,** and you'll find yourself in the middle of both family beaches.

A small, hook-shaped peninsula juts into the lagoon and effectively separates the family beaches. If you're going to rent floats or boats or do some snorkeling, you'll want to head to the left of the peninsula once you're off the tram. If you're going to play in the water, especially at the Pelican Plunge waterslide, bear right.

Both family beaches offer free lounge chairs and towels, with restrooms, food, and drink dispensers a short walk away. The Pelican Plunge side of the beach also has 17 private cabanas for rent ($549 per day; Serenity Bay has 4 cabanas that rent for $399 per day). These are so popular that they're all generally reserved by concierge and Platinum Castaway Club members before the general public gets a crack at them. On the off-chance that a cabana is available, ask at the Port Adventures desk as soon as you board the ship.

PART ELEVEN

PORTS

THE FOLLOWING CHAPTER outlines the ports visited by Disney Cruise Line (DCL). Grouped geographically, each profile summarizes the port's history, weather, tourist highlights, food, and shopping opportunities. See the Itineraries Index (page 221) for maps of the ports.

▌ ALASKAN CRUISES

Juneau, Alaska

LANGUAGES English and Tlingit

HISTORY Juneau began as a mining camp. Gold mining was the major industry from the 1880s until the 1940s, when the last official gold mine was closed. Juneau has been the capital of Alaska since 1906, first as a district and then remaining as the government seat when Alaska became a state in 1959. Growth accelerated in the 1970s with the building of the Trans-Alaska Pipeline. Central Juneau is close to sea level and is surrounded on all sides by natural elements including mountains, glaciers, and the Gastineau Channel. There are no roads leading in or out of town. Travel to other areas is almost exclusively by boat or plane.

WEATHER Cruises dock in Alaska during the summer months. The average daytime high May–September ranges from the mid-50s to the low 60s. Nighttime lows during these months are in the low to mid-40s. Precipitation is fairly steady throughout the year. Typical rainfall is 4–5 inches per month in June, July, and August.

TOURIST HIGHLIGHTS The **Mendenhall Glacier** is a primary attraction. Check at the visitor center for a guide to walking trails maintained by the U.S. Forest Service. In addition to natural features, you may see bears fishing for salmon in glacial streams. The **Mount Roberts Tramway** ferries guests 1,800 feet up the peak for scenic views and hiking. Points of historic interest include the **Saint Nicholas Russian Orthodox Church,** the oldest operating church in Alaska. Also stop by the **Red Dog Saloon,** a remnant of the mining era with an Old West atmosphere.

WHAT TO EAT Fresh fish is a key part of menus throughout the area. Salmon and halibut are most common, but shellfish is also easy to find.

WHAT TO BUY Carved Alaskan jade is abundant in souvenir shops. Also look for native arts and crafts that use natural elements such as stone, wood, and fur.

Ketchikan, Alaska

LANGUAGE English

HISTORY Ketchikan was first settled by native tribes lured by the seaside location. The area has one of the world's largest collections of standing totem poles, found both in town and scattered throughout the region, most created by the town's native founders. In the late 1800s and early 1900s, fishing and fish processing, along with lumber and lumber processing, began to attract settlers from other parts of the world. The town embodied a freewheeling, frontier spirit with plentiful saloons and brothels. Today, Ketchikan is known in Alaska as the Salmon Capital of the World and caters to a booming tourist trade.

WEATHER Cruises dock in Alaska during the summer months. The average daytime high May–September ranges from the mid-50s to the mid-60s. Nighttime lows during these months average from the low 40s to the low 50s. While precipitation is lowest during the summer months, Ketchikan is in a maritime rain forest area, with abundant rainfall and cloud cover. Typical rainfall is 6–9 inches per month during May, June, July, and August. Rainfall may increase to about 12 inches per month in September.

TOURIST HIGHLIGHTS An in-town highlight is the seasonal lumberjack show, where professional lumberjacks demonstrate ax throws, log rolling, and pole climbing. Those wishing to stay near the port can enjoy several small museums, including the **Totem Heritage Center,** the **Tongass Historical Museum,** and the **Southeast Alaska Discovery Center.** Take a ride on the **Cape Fox Lodge** funicular, which affords spectacular views of the port and surrounding areas. Outdoor activities include kayaking, hiking, and wildlife observation.

WHAT TO EAT The local fresh fish is a must-try. Fishermen bring in frequent hauls of salmon, shrimp, crab, octopus, and more.

WHAT TO BUY Alaskan crafts such as miniature carved totems, silver and bronze sculptures, wool clothing, and regional foods are typical Ketchikan souvenirs.

Sitka, Alaska

LANGUAGE English

HISTORY For more than half a century, Sitka was a major Russian port and headquarters of the Russian-American Company traders. In 1867 the Russian Empire ceded the Alaska territory to the United States. During World War II, Sitka played a role in US national defense, with more than 20,000 military personnel stationed in the area. Ruins of the military complex may be explored among the inner islands of Sitka Sound.

WEATHER Summer daytime highs average in the mid-50s to low 60s; summer nighttime lows average in the low 40s to low 50s. Summer is the dry season but still may see substantial rainfall. May–July, expect an average of 2–4 inches of rainfall per month. August rainfall jumps to about 7 inches per month.

TOURIST HIGHLIGHTS Cruises anchor in the sound and use tenders to the mainland. In June and July, take in the **Sitka Summer Music Festival** and listen to classical artists while admiring the spectacular views. Wildlife observation is appealing in any month. Take excursions to see whales, bears, or otters, as well as countless bird species. The **Alaska Raptor Center** allows visitors to see its large collection of wounded and rehabilitating birds of prey. The **Fortress of the Bear** is a habitat for orphaned brown bears and includes public viewing areas and a nearby petting zoo.

WHAT TO EAT It's all about the fish in Sitka. Nearly every restaurant in town features some form of fresh fish, including salmon, halibut, and cod. You may also discover game meats on many menus.

WHAT TO BUY Look for jewelry and carvings in the style of the native inhabitants of the area. Russian items, including nesting dolls, chess sets, and ornaments, are also popular. Epicures will like locally made treats such as jam, honey, and exotic meat jerky.

Skagway, Alaska

LANGUAGE English

HISTORY Skagway was originally settled by the native Chilkoot and Chilkat peoples. Beginning in the late 1800s, Skagway became a center for gold exploration. In 1896 gold was found in the region, leading to an influx of prospectors, miners, and associated service providers. Competition among prospectors was fierce, leading to a lawless, Wild West atmosphere. The gold rush was over by 1900, but the spectacular wilderness inspired many to stay and maintain the new town.

WEATHER Cruises dock in Alaska during the summer months. The average daytime high May–September ranges from the mid-50s to the mid-60s, with nighttime lows averaging from the low 40s to the low 50s. Precipitation is fairly steady throughout the year. Typical rainfall is 1–2 inches per month during May, June, July, and August. Rainfall may increase to about 4 inches in September.

TOURIST HIGHLIGHTS At the **Klondike Gold Rush National Historical Park,** the visitor center has educational materials about the area's mining heyday. For more-hands-on learning, try panning for gold yourself at the **Liarsville Gold Rush Trail Camp.** The **White Pass and Yukon Route Railroad,** a narrow-gauge train line, offers scenic views of mountains, waterfalls, and gorges; in **Haines,** a ferry ride away, you can enjoy watching the whales and American bald eagles. Other outdoor adventures include horseback riding, hiking, rock climbing, and dog sledding.

WHAT TO EAT Fresh fish appears on menus throughout the area. Also try the local Alaskan king crab and elk meat. Due to the cost of shipping nonlocal food to this remote location, prices may be higher than otherwise expected.

WHAT TO BUY Skagway is a small town, catering mostly toward the tourist trade, with abundant small souvenirs. Typical finds include mining and railroad artifacts, hand-knit woolen garments, ceramics, musk-ox yarn, carved wood, and jewelry made by local artisans.

Tracy Arm, Alaska

HISTORY Tracy Arm is a fjord—a long, narrow inlet with steep cliffs on both sides, created by glacial movement. Part of the Tongass National Forest, Tracy Arm is more than 30 miles long, and ice covers about one-fifth of the area. In the summer, the fjord may have significant icebergs floating in its waters.

WEATHER The weather is similar to Juneau's. Average daytime highs May–September range from the mid-50s to the low 60s; nighttime lows during these months are in the low to mid-40s. Precipitation is fairly steady throughout the year. Typical rainfall is 4–5 inches per month in June, July, and August.

TOURIST HIGHLIGHTS Ships do not dock at Tracy Arm—the experience is the view from aboard your ship. Tracy Arm is all about the scenery of the **Sawyer Glaciers.** Take in the granite cliffs, icebergs, and forested mountains. You may spot wildlife such as bears, whales, bald eagles, mountain goats, and more. About once per hour, the glaciers calve, sending massive ice sheets into the waters below.

Vancouver, British Columbia

LANGUAGE English

HISTORY Europeans first visited Vancouver in the late 1700s. The gold rush in the late 1800s brought the initial long-term settlers. Early industry focused on logging, mining, and transportation, due to the natural port. Immigrants came from England, Scotland, Ireland, and Germany, followed by an influx from China and other areas of Asia. Vancouver is now a major industrial center and cosmopolitan city bustling with high-rises, shopping, restaurants, and entertainment.

WEATHER Cruises depart from Vancouver during the summer months. The average daytime highs May–September range from the low 60s to the low 70s. Average nighttime lows during those months range from the mid-40s to the mid-50s. This moderate climate makes Vancouver one of the warmest cities in Canada. Vancouver's rainfall is lowest in the summer, averaging less than 3 inches per month May–September.

TOURIST HIGHLIGHTS The **Vancouver Lookout,** near Harbour Centre, affords a panoramic overview of the city. For additional visual stimulation, check out the **Vancouver Art Gallery,** which displays more than 10,000 pieces of art. Other local attractions include **Science World,** with interactive exhibits and an Omnimax theater, and the **Vancouver Aquarium,** home to 70,000 sea creatures and where whale, dolphin, and sea otter shows happen daily. The **Dr. Sun Yat-Sen Classical Chinese Garden** is the first authentic Chinese garden built outside of China. A 15-minute SkyTrain ride from Vancouver will take you to **Metropolis at Metrotown,** British Columbia's largest shopping center.

WHAT TO EAT You can find nearly every cuisine represented in the restaurants of Vancouver. Local seafood is a must. For authentic Asian dishes, visit the **Chinatown** district. **Granville Island** is a public market with fresh local seafood and produce; walk among the dozens of stalls to taste the best from local vendors.

WHAT TO BUY No trip to Canada is complete without the purchase of something maple—syrup, candy, and even maple mustard. Find silk robes in Chinatown, local crafts at Granville Island, and gear representing the Vancouver Canucks hockey team everywhere.

BAHAMIAN *and*
CARIBBEAN CRUISES

Basseterre, Saint Kitts and Nevis

LANGUAGE English

HISTORY Early native inhabitants of Saint Kitts included the Saladoid people, followed by the Igneri, Arawak, and Caribs. The first European claim, in 1493, was by a Spanish expedition led by Christopher Columbus. About 50 years later, a French settlement ruled the area. In 1623 an English colony replaced the community and was almost immediately usurped by the French again. During the 17th and 18th centuries, island rule repeatedly flipped between the English and French, but in 1783 the British finally wrested control. In 1883 Saint Kitts joined with the islands of Nevis and Anguilla under one independent president, but Anguilla left this arrangement in 1971.

WEATHER Disney cruises visit Saint Kitts in September and October. Average daytime highs during those months are in the upper 80s, with average nighttime lows in the upper 70s. Precipitation may be heavy in autumn, averaging about 8 inches of rainfall per month in September and October.

TOURIST HIGHLIGHTS **Brimstone Hill Fortress** is a well-preserved 17th-century military fortification. During clear weather, you can see six neighboring islands from this point. **Romney Manor** is a colonial estate from the same era. The Carib petroglyphs at **Wingfield Manor Estate** show artwork and communication by the island's native inhabitants. The center of Basseterre, called the **Circus,** is home to art galleries, bookstores, and craft shops. Sun worshippers will find several local beaches of interest.

WHAT TO EAT Fresh fish, often served with rice and beans, is a staple in this island nation. Jerk and Creole seasonings are prevalent on most menus. The national dish is stewed saltfish with plantains and coconut dumplings. Other typical foods include roast pig or goat, goat stew, *rik-kita* beef (marinated with curry and hot pepper), and mango-glazed chicken. Popular side dishes are sweet potatoes, breadfruit, and cassava. Sweets include jam cake, pineapple cake, and tropical fruit. Rum is the adult beverage of choice.

WHAT TO BUY Saint Kitts is home to the **Caribelle Batik Factory,** offering colorfully dyed fabric and clothing. Also look for woven hats and bags, pottery, paintings, and carved statuary. Foodies will want to take home packaged sugar cakes and bottles of local rum.

Bridgetown, Barbados

LANGUAGE English

HISTORY The first Europeans in Barbados were Spanish explorers in the late 1400s, but neither they nor a Portuguese expedition in the early 1500s established permanent outposts. A British ship, the *Olive Blossom*, arrived on the island in 1624, claiming it for King James; Barbados then became a British colony. This is one of the few Caribbean islands that was under constant control by one nation for several hundred contiguous years. As such, the British influence is particularly pronounced here: Cars drive on the left side of the road, and the Anglican church is predominant. Barbados became independent in 1966.

WEATHER Disney cruises visit Barbados in September and October. Average daytime highs during those months are in the mid- to upper 80s, with average nighttime lows in the upper 70s. Precipitation may be heavy, averaging 6–7 inches of rainfall per month in September and October.

TOURIST HIGHLIGHTS Nature enthusiasts should visit **Harrison's Cave,** with natural stalactite formations and waterfalls. **Orchid World** inspires gardeners. History lovers will enjoy the **Barbados Museum,** home to artifacts related to island heritage. For a taste of agricultural history, visit the **Morgan Lewis windmill,** one of only two remaining functional sugar windmills. The **Mount Gay Distilleries,** renowned for its rum, offers factory tours. There are also many nearby beaches for sunning and snorkeling.

WHAT TO EAT The food of Barbados shows influences from England, Portugal, Spain, and West Africa. Fish is in ample supply here. Look for it in flying fish (with a mustard-and-onion sauce) and fish cakes. Other popular dishes include pepper pot (a spicy stew made with beef, chicken, or seafood, plus coconut and hot pepper), peas and rice, candied sweet potatoes, and pudding and souse (pig intestines stuffed with sweet potatoes). Side dishes often include macaroni and cheese or locally grown asparagus and okra. Local sweets are tamarind balls, guava cheese, chocolate fudge, coconut bread, and peanut brittle. A favorite adult beverage is Mount Gay rum.

WHAT TO BUY Popular Barbadian take-home items include replica monkey jars, which were traditionally used to keep water cool. Other desired souvenirs include carved wood, leather goods, jewelry in the shape of fish or dolphins, and handmade soaps and lotions. Epicureans will bring home local rum, bottled local hot-pepper sauce, or packaged rum cake.

Castaway Cay, Bahamas (also see Parts Ten and Twelve)

LANGUAGE English

HISTORY DCL entered into a 99-year lease agreement with the Bahamian government in 1999, giving the cruise line the rights to develop what was then known as Gorda Cay. Renamed Castaway Cay by Disney, the island measures about 1.5 square miles and sits in the Atlantic Ocean, roughly 80 miles north-northeast of Nassau, at about the same latitude as Fort Lauderdale, Florida (100 miles to the west).

WEATHER It's either warm or hot. Average high temperatures gradually increase from around 76°F late December–January to a peak of 89°F in August, before they drop again. Low temperatures are also moderate, from 62°F in late January to 76°F throughout the summer. Rain patterns follow the Atlantic hurricane season, with peak rainfall occurring late August–early November. Precipitation is lightest December–May.

TOURIST HIGHLIGHTS Less than 10% of Castaway Cay has been developed for cruise guests, but Disney packs a lot of activities into that relatively small space, including two family beaches; one adults-only beach; separate lagoons for boating and snorkeling; a teens-only hangout; basketball, soccer, and volleyball areas; and bike trails. Two open-air trams connect the dock with these areas.

WHAT TO EAT Castaway Cay has three all-you-care-to-eat outdoor restaurants: **Cookie's BBQ, Cookie's Too,** and **Serenity Bay BBQ.** Each restaurant serves the same menu of grilled hot dogs, hamburgers, veggie burgers, chicken, fish, and ribs. Sides include corn on the cob, coleslaw, various salads, and similar picnic food, plus cookies and soft-serve ice cream for dessert. They're generally open 11 a.m.–2 p.m. Serenity Bay BBQ is at the adults-only Serenity Bay beach—no guests under age 18.

All of Castaway Cay's bars serve similar drinks. **Conched Out Bar,** near the gazebo, is the largest bar but has only outdoor seating.

Sand Bar, near the Castaway Cay family beach, is a small shack with a couple of serving windows, specializing in beer and frozen drinks. A limited amount of shaded bench seating is available. **Castaway Air Bar,** near the Serenity Bay adult beach, is the quietest of Castaway Cay's bars, and the view is pretty good too. **Heads Up Bar,** near Castaway Ray's Stingray Adventures, sits at the far end of the pier. The one downside to Heads Up is the lack of shade. It can get very hot very quickly out here, so lingering with a drink isn't always possible. The views are great here, though.

WHAT TO BUY Castaway Cay offers minimal opportunities for shopping. Two Disney-operated souvenir stands offer merchandise similar to what you'll find in the onboard shops, such as T-shirts, flip-flops, and baseball caps, as well as fun-in-the-sun basics, including plastic buckets, sunscreen, and goggles. If you're looking for something that specifically says "Castaway Cay" on it, buy it on the island. In addition to the Disney shops, one building houses a few stalls run by Bahamian merchants. You'll find items here much like you'd find at the Straw Market at Nassau: bags, sun hats, and figurines. The one item that many guests find to be a true must is a postage stamp. The island's teeny post office will imprint your letters with a special Castaway Cay postmark. The post office accepts cash only (US currency is fine), not your Key to the World Card, so be sure to carry a few dollars onto the island.

Castries, Saint Lucia

LANGUAGE English

HISTORY The first known setters in Saint Lucia were the Arawak Indians, circa AD 200. The first Europeans in the area were the French, who visited in about 1650, and who remained in place until a massive hurricane 130 years later. British settlers acquired the land in the late 1700s and used the island for sugarcane plantations, worked by enslaved natives and imported Africans. Slavery was finally abolished in the mid-1800s. In 1958 Saint Lucia joined the West Indies Federation, with internal self-government. Saint Lucia is currently a Commonwealth of Great Britain.

WEATHER   Disney cruises visit Saint Lucia in September and October. Average daytime highs during that period are in the mid-80s. Average nighttime lows are in the high 70s to low 80s. Average precipitation is about 8 inches of rain per month in autumn.

TOURIST HIGHLIGHTS   The 18th-century city of **Soufrière** features both charming gingerbread architecture as well as naturally colorful sulfur pools. Near Soufrière is the **Diamond Botanical Gardens and Waterfall,** which allows swimming in mineral baths in a lush setting. **Pigeon Island,** a former pirate lair, has a museum, beaches, a restaurant, and panoramic views. Snorkelers will enjoy **Jalousie Beach** and **Anse Chastanet Beach.**

WHAT TO EAT   West Indian, Creole, African, British, and French cultures influence the cuisine of Saint Lucia. Popular dishes include pepper pot, callaloo (a souplike stew of leafy greens), and fried cod. Fresh seafood is on most menus. Vegetable accompaniments may include cassava, taro, or sweet potatoes. Local fruits include banana, coconut, guava, mango, passion fruit, and pineapple. Common beverages are fruit juices as well as local beer (Piton) and rum.

WHAT TO BUY   The **Castries Market** features stalls with many local vendors. Look for screen-printed clothing, leather goods, carved wood, rag dolls, and handmade jewelry. Gourmands may want to purchase packets of local spices, a jar of the regional banana ketchup, or, of course, rum.

Costa Maya, Mexico

LANGUAGE   Spanish

HISTORY   Mayans resided in the area beginning in about 200 BC. The Mayans first had contact with Spanish explorers in the early 1500s, battling them for control of the area. This was followed by a period of invasion by English pirates. The British claimed the region until the end of the 19th century, when the Mexican Navy came to rule. The Mexicans developed a port system, improving trade and communications. Today the primary industry is tourism. The cruise terminal, built in 2007, was designed to look like an ancient Mayan city.

WEATHER   Temperatures are fairly constant throughout the year. Average daytime highs year-round fall in the mid-70s to mid-80s, while average nighttime lows year-round are in the mid-60s to low 70s. Precipitation is heaviest during the summer months. Average monthly rainfall November–April is less than 2 inches. May–October may see as much as 7 inches of rainfall per month.

TOURIST HIGHLIGHTS   History buffs will want to visit the fourth-century Mayan ruins at **Chacchoben.** Sun lovers should venture to **Uvero Beach** to lounge on the white sands. Animal watchers will enjoy **Uyumil Che,** also known as the Monkey Farm, a rehabilitation facility for injured wild animals. More-adventurous types may want to try diving in the nearby coral reefs.

WHAT TO EAT Seafood prevails on most menus. Try it raw in seviche, prepared in dishes such as fish tacos or fish quesadillas, or simply grilled. Many dishes are served with rice or with corn tortillas and guacamole. *Remember:* Peel all fresh fruits, and drink only beverages in sealed bottles. Sweets include ices and ice creams based on local fruits.

WHAT TO BUY Much of what is sold in Costa Maya near the port is tourist grade. You'll find jewelry and metalwork, but expect it to be silver plate. You will also see fabric, rugs, fragrances, and liquor for sale here. The vendors may be open to bargaining.

Cozumel, Mexico

LANGUAGE Spanish

HISTORY Cozumel was a Mayan outpost from the first century. Mayan legend describes Cozumel as the home of Ixchel, a love and fertility goddess. The story says that when temples were dedicated to her, she released her favorite birds, swallows, as a symbol of her gratitude. (*Cozumel* is derived from *Cuzamil,* Mayan for "Land of the Swallows.") The Spanish arrived in the early 1500s, bringing disease that decimated the Mayan population. For years after this, the region was besieged by pirates. In the late 1800s, Abraham Lincoln briefly explored the possibility of making Cozumel a relocation point for freed American slaves. Popularity as a tourist region exploded in the 1960s after explorer Jacques Cousteau mentioned it in a documentary as one of the most beautiful areas in the world for scuba diving.

WEATHER Temperatures are constant throughout the year. Average daytime highs are in the 80s in every season. Average nighttime lows range from the high 60s to the mid-70s year-round. Precipitation, on the other hand, varies widely during the year. The driest season is October–March, with an average of less than 5 inches of rainfall during each of those months. Rainfall increases to an average of 8 inches per month in the spring, and an average of up to 10 inches per month in the summer.

TOURIST HIGHLIGHTS It's all about the water in Cozumel. Snorkeling and diving in the coral reefs are a popular draw, particularly at **Cozumel Reefs National Marine Park.** For history buffs, the pre-Columbian ruins at **Xelha, Chichén Itzá,** and **Tulum** offer a look into the Mayan culture. **Chankanaab National Park** offers opportunities to interact with marine animals, as well as walking trails that wind among a large iguana population. Cozumel is also the perfect place to enjoy the sun as you lounge at one of its many beaches.

WHAT TO EAT Fish is plentiful here, with grilled mahimahi on many menus. You'll also find familiar Mexican fare such as fajitas, tacos, and enchiladas. Many restaurants offer barbecued pork. Margaritas are found in most watering holes, and you may find that some spots have their own house-made tequila. Also try the local *michelada,* beer mixed with lime juice.

WHAT TO BUY Jewelry, Mexican handicrafts, and tourist T-shirts are all sold close to the cruise terminal. You may find good-quality leather sandals, bags, and hammocks. For food gifts, look for tequila or vanilla, or try the local liqueur Xtabentún, made from honey.

Falmouth, Jamaica

LANGUAGES English and Patois

HISTORY Falmouth was founded in 1769. During the late 18th century, it served as a major distribution point for rum, sugar, coffee, and molasses. In trade for crops, Falmouth received many Africans. The port's business declined with the end of slavery in the 1800s, but tourism brought a resurgence of visitors in the late 1900s.

WEATHER Temperatures in Falmouth are consistent throughout the year. In all months, the average daytime high is in the 80s and the average nighttime low is in the 70s. Falmouth averages less than 3 inches of rain per month January–April. Rainfall picks up later in the year, with an average of about 6 inches per month May–November. Rainfall decreases again in December, to about 4 inches.

TOURIST HIGHLIGHTS The **Good Hope Great House** is a former sugar plantation; estate tours are a highlight of a Falmouth visit. The property also offers horse and buggy rides, dune buggy excursions, river tubing, and zip lining. Many of these activities are also available at **Mystic Mountain** adventure park. **Dunn's River Falls** is a spectacular natural phenomenon. As you walk through town, stop to see the **Water Square Fountain,** the **Anglican Parish Church,** and **Falmouth Court House.** A few beaches are within a 10-minute taxi ride away; **Montego Bay**'s party beaches are about a 30-minute taxi ride away.

WHAT TO EAT Jerk-style preparations are a staple of Jamaican cuisine. Meat, chicken, or fish is rubbed with spices and sugars and then grilled over a wood fire. Rice and beans is a typical side dish. To cool off, try fresh local mango, guava, and the national fruit, ackee. Also look for Jamaican patties, pastries stuffed with meat. With many yam farms nearby, you'll also find yams on many restaurant menus. Rum and rum punches are a potent way to jump-start your relaxation. The national beer, Red Stripe, is served throughout the area.

WHAT TO BUY Many visitors bring home jarred spices and jerk seasonings; rum and coffee are also good souvenirs. Local artwork, jewelry, woodcarvings, and woven goods are also popular items.

Grand Cayman, Cayman Islands

LANGUAGE English

HISTORY Christopher Columbus accidentally discovered these islands during a voyage in 1503. The Caymans came under British control following the 1670 Treaty of Madrid; during this time, they also saw an influx of settlers from Jamaica, and slaves were brought to the island beginning in the 1730s until slavery was abolished in 1834. The region underwent periodic attacks from pirates into the late 18th century. Jamaica (a British colony at the time) governed the islands until 1962, when Jamaica became independent and the Caymans elected to stay under British rule.

WEATHER Temperatures are consistent throughout the year. Daytime highs average in the 80s and nighttime lows in the 70s. Precipitation, however, varies considerably: During December–April, you can expect an average of less than 3 inches of rainfall per month, while May–August experiences an average of about 6 inches of rainfall per month. September–November may have up to 9 inches of rainfall per month.

TOURIST HIGHLIGHTS A smaller vessel called a tender will take you from the ship to the edge of downtown George Town. **Stingray City** offers opportunities to swim with rays. The **Cayman Turtle Farm** is a research facility that studies green sea turtles; here, you'll be able to observe the 16,000 inhabitants and watch the turtle hatchlings feed. Water lovers will find abundant scuba and snorkeling opportunities, including excursions to swim near the wreck of a sunken 1940s schooner. History buffs will enjoy the **Pedro St. James Historic Site** and the **Cayman Islands National Museum.** A nearby seaside village named **Hell** lures many visitors who just want to say they've been there. Numerous nearby beaches afford opportunities for sunning and relaxation.

WHAT TO EAT Seafood—including the traditional national dish, turtle—is plentiful here. Look for rock shrimp and conch in many dishes. Jerked meats are popular on the island, as are many grilled meats. Many of the desserts, such as sticky pudding and rum cakes, have a British influence. Other sweets may include fruit, honey, and coconut.

WHAT TO BUY Decorative conch shells make a nice reminder of the area. If you've interacted with the stingrays or turtles, a carved replica of these creatures may make a good souvenir: Also look for local artwork and woven hats and bags. Gourmets will want to bring home some Tortuga rum cake.

Key West, Florida

LANGUAGE English

HISTORY The original inhabitants of the area were the Tequesta and Calusa peoples. Juan Ponce de León was the first recorded European visitor, arriving in 1521. Cubans and British used the island as a fishing spot before it was claimed by Spain; however, Spain exerted little control over the area. In 1822 Matthew C. Perry claimed the Keys for the United States. The islands became more prosperous when they were connected to mainland Florida by an overseas railway bridge in 1912.

WEATHER Daytime temperatures average in the 80s April–November, with nighttime lows during that time in the 70s. December–March, daytime temperatures average in the 70s, with nighttime lows in the 60s. Precipitation is lowest in the winter and spring, with average rainfall of less than 3 inches per month November–May. The summer gets wetter, with average rainfall of 3–5 inches per month in June and July. August, September, and October average 5–7 inches of rain per month.

TOURIST HIGHLIGHTS The entire island measures only 2 miles by 4 miles. **Mallory Square,** on the waterfront near the docks, offers bars, restaurants, and basic shopping. The **Conch Tour Train** allows visitors to hop on and off for personalized island touring. The must-do for literary types is a stop at the **Ernest Hemingway Home and Museum.** See Hemingway's studio and visit with the colony of cats descended from the author's many feline companions. For excellent views of the Keys, visit the nearby **Lighthouse and Keepers Quarters Museum.** Nature experiences are available at the **Key West Aquarium** and the **Key West Butterfly Conservancy.** And no trip to Key West would be complete without some relaxation time on the beach.

WHAT TO EAT Fresh seafood is abundant here, with oysters, clams, lobster, grouper, and shrimp appearing on many menus. Conch fritters are a specialty at many restaurants. There is a large Cuban influence in the food culture here: Look for sandwiches on Cuban bread stuffed with meats and cheeses. Beef stews, plantains, and yellow rice are all served with a Cuban flair. Of course the most popular regional dessert is Key lime pie, made with the juice of local fruit. In addition to pie, you're likely to find dozens of other lime-accented foods during your visit, including cookies, candy, salsa, and barbecue sauce. Rumrunners, mojitos, and margaritas are all available to help you ease into the island lifestyle.

WHAT TO BUY Most of the shopping is casual and beach-oriented. Look for T-shirts, sunglasses, swimsuits, and surf- and sun-related trinkets. Epicureans may take home a bottle of Key lime juice to use in their own cooking. If you want a permanent souvenir, you could get a tattoo at one of the many shops on the island.

Miami, Florida

LANGUAGES English and Spanish

HISTORY The Tequesta Indians inhabited the area until Spain claimed it in 1566. Spain ceded Florida to the United States in 1819. Miami, named after the Miami River, became a force to be reckoned with following the 1896 southward expansion of Henry Flagler's Florida East Coast Railroad. The population boomed until the Great Depression, and after a pause, the area saw another surge in population from 1960s Cuban exiles.

WEATHER Average daytime highs are in the 80s May–October, with nighttime lows in the 70s. Average daytime highs are in the 70s December–April, with average nighttime lows in the 60s. Precipitation is greatest during the summer. November–April, expect an average monthly rainfall of about 3 inches or less. May, July, and October average 4–5 inches of rainfall per month, while June, August, and September see average rainfall of 6–9 inches per month.

TOURIST HIGHLIGHTS **South Beach** is where the beautiful people go. Take a stroll there to see the Art Deco architecture, and stop in a bar or club for a drink. Another interesting neighborhood is **Little Havana,** imbued with old-world charm. Learn about Miami's immigrant history at the **Cuban Museum of the Americas.** Gardeners will like the **Fruit and Spice Park,** which grows more than 500 species of edibles, while kids will love exploring the **Miami Children's Museum** and the **Seaquarium.** And, of course, you can soak in the sun at the area's many beaches.

WHAT TO EAT Many local establishments serve food with a Cuban flair. Look for stewed chicken or lamb and grilled fish or pork accompanied by tomatoes, vegetables, and rice. Seafood gumbo with rice is also popular, as are stuffed Cuban sandwiches. For a pick-me-up, try strong Cuban-style coffee. For a slow-me-down, try sangria, mojitos, or other fruit-based drinks.

WHAT TO BUY Miami is a major cosmopolitan city with luxury chains and chic boutiques in abundance. There are also the requisite beachside

T-shirt and trinket shops. For off-the-beaten-path ideas, try the **Tropicana Flea Market,** open on weekends. Sports fans may want to pick up a Miami Heat jersey or gear from the University of Miami. Hand-rolled cigars are sold in many areas of Miami. A classic, and classy, choice for gentlemen would be a *guayabera,* the loose-fitting Cuban-style shirt. Ladies can start their cruise with some new swimwear.

Nassau, Bahamas

LANGUAGE English

HISTORY Originally called Charles Town, Nassau was destroyed by fire in 1684 during an attack by the Spanish. It was rebuilt and renamed 10 years later by the Dutch and English. Over the next few decades, the Bahamas became a pirate stronghold. In 1718 the Brits ousted the pirates and reclaimed the area. During the American Revolutionary War, there was a brief occupation by Americans and then another Spanish occupation in 1782. The Spaniards surrendered the land back to England a year later. In 1807 the slave trade was outlawed, and thousands of freed slaves eventually made the island their home. Today, Nassau is a major tourist destination.

WEATHER Daytime highs average in the 80s March–November. Temperatures drop slightly in winter, with daytime highs averaging in the 70s December–February. Nighttime lows average in the 70s June–October and in the 60s November–May. Precipitation is lowest in the winter, with average monthly rainfall of less than 3 inches November–April. A moderate rise occurs in May with average monthly rainfall of less than 5 inches. Precipitation increases substantially in the summer and fall, with up to 9 inches of rainfall per month June–October.

TOURIST HIGHLIGHTS Take a stroll around **Old Town** and see the pink **Parliament Building.** Museum and history lovers will enjoy the **National Art Gallery of the Bahamas,** the **Pirate Museum,** and **Fort Charlotte.** Numerous beach, water-sports, and animal-encounter excursions are available here. Casinos offer the full range of opportunities to lose your shirt.

WHAT TO EAT For a taste of typical Bahamian food, try conch, fish stew, or crawfish. These are often served with a side of grits, rice, macaroni and cheese, or potato salad. Desserts may include pastries flavored with pineapple, guava, or coconut.

WHAT TO BUY There is no shortage of trinket vendors aimed at the tourist trade. You'll find inexpensive T-shirts on every corner. No trip to Nassau is complete without a visit to the **Straw Market**—look for handmade pieces rather than those imported from China. Other popular items include decorated conch shells or carved wood. Foodies may desire rum cakes or guava jams and jellies.

Philipsburg, Sint Maarten

LANGUAGES Dutch, French, and English

HISTORY The island was originally occupied by the Carib Indians. Christopher Columbus later found and named it for the medieval bishop Saint Martin of Tours, which is now aptly fitting. In the early 1600s, Dutch colonists used the island as a source of salt for export. The Dutch were then ousted by the Spanish, who were subsequently removed by the French. In 1648 a treaty divided the area in half, with shared control and occupancy. Parts of the territory changed hands between the Spanish and the Dutch 16 times in about 200 years. At several points in the early 1800s, British pirates attacked and brought the area under English rule. The slave trade was a large part of the island's economy in the 17th and 18th centuries; when slavery was abolished, plantation owners imported low-wage earners from China and the East Indies. The island is currently divided and called by two names: Saint-Martin, controlled by the French, and Sint Maarten, controlled by the Dutch. It is one of the smallest landmasses overseen by more than one country. English is widely spoken on both sides of the island.

WEATHER The climate is mild, with average year-round temperatures between 82°F and 89°F. August–November are typically the wettest months, with 4–5½ inches of rain per month. The water temperature just off the island rarely dips below 80°F.

TOURIST HIGHLIGHTS Gamblers will enjoy the many casinos in Saint-Martin–Sint Maarten. Be sure to brush up on the rules of roulette, baccarat, craps, blackjack, and poker before you arrive. The Boardwalk area on **Great Bay,** on the Dutch side, offers beachside lounging and a long string of bars and restaurants. From **Maho Beach,** also on the Dutch side, watch planes fly incredibly low to land at the nearby airport. Water sports available here include snorkeling, scuba diving, and fishing. **Lucky Stables** offers horseback-riding opportunities. At **Orient Beach,** on the French side, clothing is optional—but the posteriors on display are more Joe the Plumber than Jennifer Lopez.

WHAT TO EAT Seafood, particularly conch fritters, is plentiful here. Other dishes may have West Indian, French, and Dutch influences. More than 40 Chinese restaurants are also on the island. You may encounter the regional favorites callaloo (beef- and crab-based), crab cakes, and johnny-cake biscuits. Dessert often includes coconut pies and guava tarts.

WHAT TO BUY St. Maarten is known for its shopping, particularly electronics, cameras, liquor, fragrances, and cigarettes. These will likely be large European brands. If you're looking for local flavor, you'll find typical tourist souvenirs such as artwork, carvings, and woven goods.

Port Canaveral, Florida

LANGUAGE English

HISTORY In 1929 Congress approved construction of a deepwater port at Port Canaveral, completed and dedicated in 1953. Initially this was a cargo center, with a primary mission of taking orange juice to the North. Concurrent with the rise of shipping in the area was the building of the nearby space center. The first passenger ships arrived in the 1970s to see the area's newly developed theme parks on their ports of call. The first home-ported cruise ship sailed from Port Canaveral in 1982.

WEATHER Expect it to be hot in Port Canaveral during in the summer. May–October, average daytime highs range from the mid-80s to the low 90s. Nighttime lows during that period are in the upper 60s to low 70s.

November–April, expect average daytime highs in the low 70s to low 80s, with nighttime lows in the low 50s to low 60s. Precipitation varies considerably throughout the year. The dry season is November–May, with average monthly rainfall of about 3 inches or less. June–October, monthly rainfall averages 5–8 inches. Summer storms are common.

TOURIST HIGHLIGHTS The main attraction here is the **Kennedy Space Center.** Visitors can tour the facilities, ride in a space simulator, and participate in special programs with astronauts. Beach lovers will want to head over to **Cocoa Beach** and relax in the sun. Twenty minutes away, in Titusville, you'll find the **Brevard Museum of Natural History and Science,** the **Great Florida Birding Trail,** and the **U.S. Space Walk of Fame.** Of course, the Orlando theme parks are about an hour west of Port Canaveral. Many cruisers make a pre- or postvoyage visit to **Walt Disney World, Universal Studios,** or **SeaWorld.**

WHAT TO EAT Seafood is served at most restaurants. Look for oysters, conch, and grouper. Many other cuisines, including Italian, Cuban, Asian, and German, are represented in the waterfront area. Fast food such as burgers and pizza is readily available too.

WHAT TO BUY Look for souvenirs related to the American space program: model rockets, patches depicting moon missions, and pieces of meteorites. For a unique food experience, buy a package of dehydrated astronaut ice cream. Near the beach, stock up on swimsuits, sunglasses, sunscreen, flip-flops, and other last-minute cruising essentials. You'll find that prices on land are significantly lower than in the shops on board. And if you're visiting the theme parks before or after your trip, you'll find a nearly limitless supply of related T-shirts and toys to take home.

San Juan, Puerto Rico

LANGUAGES Spanish and English

HISTORY Juan Ponce de León was the first European explorer to mention visiting the island of Puerto Rico. The city of San Juan was founded in 1521 by Spanish colonists who used it as a stopover on their way to the Americas. Throughout the 17th and 18th centuries, the island withstood various attacks by the English, including Sir Francis Drake, and the Dutch. In 1815 the island was opened to immigration as part of the Royal Decree of Graces. In 1898 United States warships attacked San Juan, eventually resulting in Spanish cession of Puerto Rico to the United States in the Treaty of Paris. In 1917 Puerto Ricans were granted American citizenship. Not quite a state—although 61% of its residents favored statehood in a 2012 referendum—the island sends a nonvoting representative to Congress and also maintains a local legislature.

WEATHER As is the case elsewhere in the Caribbean, weather here stays consistent year-round. Average daytime highs are in the 80s throughout the year, with average nighttime lows in the 70s. Precipitation is lowest in the winter, with an average of less than 4 inches of rainfall per month January–March. During the rest of the year, rainfall averages 4–6 inches per month.

TOURIST HIGHLIGHTS History buffs will want to explore **El Morro,** a fortress built to protect the island from attack by sea, and **El Castillo de San Cristobal,** designed to protect San Juan from overland attacks. Musicians may want to stop by the **Museo de Pablo Casals,** which houses the Spanish cellist's manuscripts and personal documents. The **Museum of Contemporary Art** showcases modern artists from Latin America and the Caribbean. For some fun in the sun, explore the beaches in the nearby towns of **Condado** and **Isla Verde.** Many visitors will want to stop by the **Casa Bacardi** distillery (also known as the Cathedral of Rum) for a tour and a taste.

WHAT TO EAT Puerto Rican cuisine is a melting pot of Spanish, Cuban, Mexican, African, and American flavors. To start your meal, try conch fritters or *empanadillas* (pastry filled with meat or seafood). Entrées include meat or seafood stews, fried steak or veal, barbecued pig, broiled chicken, or grilled seafood. Beans, rice, and plantains are often found as accompaniments. Dessert will likely include coconut or caramel flan (custard). Sweets may also be flavored with guava, papaya, or mango. You'll find that coffee or local rum is the beverage of choice.

WHAT TO BUY Dominoes are a popular game here, and a domino set makes a nice souvenir. Also look for hand-tooled leather, scented soaps, and woven hats and bags. For a take-home treat, buy some rum or coffee. Discount outlet shops for American brands include **Ralph Lauren** and **Coach.**

St. George's, Grenada

LANGUAGE English

HISTORY Grenada's first settlers were the Caribs. Christopher Columbus sighted the island during his third voyage, but this did not result in a European settlement at the time. The first permanent European occupation was begun in 1649 by French explorers from Martinique. French rule continued until the British captured Grenada in 1762, during the Seven Years War. The Brits fended off intermittent attacks but maintained control until 1974, when independence was granted. In 1983 Grenada faced a US invasion related to the island's political ties to Cuba and the USSR. Grenada is currently under democratic self-rule.

WEATHER Disney cruises visit Grenada in September and October. The average daytime high during these months is in the mid-80s. Average autumn nighttime lows are in the mid-70s. Average rainfall in September and October is about 4–5 inches per month.

TOURIST HIGHLIGHTS Grenada is a leading exporter of several spices, including cinnamon, cloves, ginger, mace, allspice, and nutmeg. Though the spice trade took a hit from Hurricane Ivan in 2004, spice-plantation visits are a popular diversion. The **River Antoine Estate** offers tours of local rum production. History lovers will enjoy excursions to **Fort Frederick** and **Fort George. Grand Etang National Park** is home to rain forest hiking trails for many levels of fitness.

WHAT TO EAT The food of Grenada shows the influence of the island's French, Spanish, West Indian, and African history. Local favorites include crab and callaloo, pepper pot, conch, fresh fish, and *roti* (rolled beef or chicken with curry and potatoes). Those with adventurous palates will want to try a dish of *manicou* (wait for it . . . opossum). Side dishes may include rice, vegetables, plantains, peas, and macaroni. Expect to find fresh fruit and fruit juices widely available. Tipplers will enjoy the local rum.

WHAT TO BUY Not for nothing is Grenada nicknamed the Island of Spice. Spices are sold in packets, in baskets, and even in decorative necklaces. Hand-printed fabrics, local carvings, and jewelry are all easy to find. Local chocolates and rums are also popular with gastronomes.

St. John's, Antigua and Barbuda

LANGUAGES English, Spanish

HISTORY This Caribbean nation comprises the inhabited islands of Antigua and Barbuda, along with several uninhabited ones. The first residents were the Ciboney Indians; later settlers included the Arawak and Carib. Christopher Columbus "discovered" Antigua during his second voyage in 1493. The first real European settlement took place in 1632 by an English party vacating Saint Kitts. In subsequent decades, the island became home to massive sugar plantations, farmed by enslaved native peoples. By the mid-1700s, slaves outnumbered their European masters. The American War of Independence in the late 1700s disrupted the sugar trade. Britain abolished the slave trade in 1807, and all Antiguan slaves were emancipated by 1834. In 1981 Antigua and Barbuda cut ties with Britain and are now an independent entity.

WEATHER Disney cruises visit Antigua in September and October. Average daytime highs during these months are in the mid- to upper 80s. Average autumn nighttime lows are in the high 70s. Average rainfall in September and October is 3–5 inches per month.

TOURIST HIGHLIGHTS If you're in the mood to gamble, St. John's is home to several casinos, notably **King's Casino** near Heritage Quay. History buffs will like **Nelson's Dockyard,** which housed 17 Royal Navy warships at one time. **Betty's Hope** is a refurbished sugar planation that depicts life as it was during the 17th century. Several beaches offer surfing, swimming, and snorkeling.

WHAT TO EAT Antiguan food is typical Caribbean. The national dish is pepper pot (a stew of meats, vegetables, greens, and hot peppers) with *fungi* (not mushrooms—it's a cornmeal mush similar to polenta). Other frequent menu items are *ducana* (sweet-potato dumplings), seasoned rice, and fresh seafood. Grilled meats, often served with side dishes of macaroni pie or plantains, are popular. Dessert may include fudge, tamarind stew, or peanut brittle. Locals drink tamarind juice, mango juice, and coconut water. For adult beverages, try local beers and rum.

WHAT TO BUY Many of the goods for sale in St. John's are imported from elsewhere. Look for duty-free perfumes, linen, watches, and electronics. For local flavor, consider hand-carved wood objects, natural soaps, artwork, and pottery. Those with an interest in food may purchase locally produced jams and jellies, as well as local rums.

St. Thomas and St. John, US Virgin Islands

LANGUAGE English

HISTORY The original occupants of the Virgin Islands were the Ciboney people. Christopher Columbus first sighted the islands in the late 1400s, and the Dutch West India Company created a settlement here in 1657. This was shortly followed by occupation by the Danish West India and Guinea Company. Sugarcane, harvested by slaves on St. Thomas and the nearby islands of St. John and St. Croix, became the primary export. In 1848 slavery was abolished and the sugar trade declined. In 1917 the United States purchased St. Thomas, St. John, and St. Croix from Denmark as a means of controlling the Panama Canal during World War I, and the islands remain a US territory today (the other Virgin Islands are now under British control).

WEATHER Temperatures are constant throughout the year. Daytime highs average in the high 80s year-round, with nighttime lows in the 70s. Precipitation is lowest in the winter, with an average monthly rainfall of less than 3 inches December–April. A moderate rise occurs May–August, with an average monthly rainfall of less than 4 inches. Precipitation increases to about 6 inches per month September–November.

TOURIST HIGHLIGHTS The **Paradise Point Skyride** offers views of the harbor. At the top, enjoy lunch and walk along trails inhabited by local wildlife. For another beautiful scene, beachgoers will want to visit the popular **Magens Bay. Coral World** is a nearby attraction with an underwater observatory, animal interaction with sharks and stingrays, and water sports such as parasailing. For history lovers, **Fort Christian** is a great spot. This museum houses local artifacts in a 17th-century Danish fortress. Another historic site is **Blackbeard's Castle,** which was used as a lookout by Danes to protect the harbor from early pirates.

WHAT TO EAT Local dishes include fresh seafood such as conch and lobster. Stewed beef, goat, and chicken are also popular. For a quick bite, try a meat *pate* (pastry filled with ground pork and beef). Side dishes may feature plantains, yams, rice, beans, and lentils. Fruit and fruit juices are available in abundance. If you're drinking alcohol here, it's likely rum made from sugar and molasses grown in the Caribbean.

WHAT TO BUY St. Thomas is the largest shopping port in the Caribbean. Most goods, including electronics, fragrances, jewelry, tobacco, crystal, china, and liquor, are widely available in the States. If you're planning to shop for these, you should be familiar with discount pricing from vendors at home. For local treasures, shop in the open-air markets for artwork, carved wood, and hand-pieced leather. Foodies will want to take home Caribbean rum-ball candy.

CALIFORNIA COAST CRUISES

San Diego, California

LANGUAGE English

HISTORY San Diego is the site of the first European settlement in what is now California, a result of exploration conducted in 1542 by João

Rodrigues Cabrilho of Portugal. Subsequent European visitors were primarily from Spain. The first permanent mission in the area was established in 1769, with a population of Spanish settlers arriving in 1774. In 1821 Mexico claimed the area in the Mexican War for Independence. In 1850 California became part of the United States. Significant American naval presence began in 1901, which solidified San Diego as a major West Coast port. San Diego is now a center of high-tech industry.

WEATHER Disney cruises visit San Diego in May and September. The average daytime high temperature in May is in the high 60s, with average nighttime lows in the high 50s. The average daytime high in September is in the mid-70s, while average nighttime lows are in the mid-60s. Precipitation in both May and September is minimal, with an average of less than 1 inch of rainfall per month.

TOURIST HIGHLIGHTS **Balboa Park** is home to gorgeous gardens and 15 different museums, including the **San Diego Museum of Art** and the **San Diego Natural History Museum.** The **San Diego Zoo** is one of the few places in the United States where you can see pandas. Theme park fans will want to visit **SeaWorld** and **Legoland.** The **Gaslamp Quarter** and the San Diego missions provide insight into the history of the area. **Tijuana, Mexico,** is 17 miles south of San Diego; be sure to check on legal restrictions if you plan to drive there.

WHAT TO EAT San Diego is a major metropolitan area with all major cuisines represented. The offerings at many local restaurants are influenced by nearby Mexico—quesadillas, tacos, burritos, enchiladas, and such. Because of the city's seaside location, fresh fish is another local menu staple. A regional favorite is cioppino, a stew with fish, clams, shrimp, squid, and mussels, often served with toast. Tequila-based drinks and local wines are popular with adult drinkers.

WHAT TO BUY Sports fans will want to purchase jerseys of the local Padres baseball, Chargers football, or San Diego State Aztecs football or basketball teams. Pick up clothing or shell-based jewelry, or choose some art reflecting the surf culture. Local tequila is a common food gift.

San Francisco, California

LANGUAGE English

HISTORY The first European settlers in the area were Spaniards, who arrived in 1769 and established the Presidio of San Francisco in 1776. By the early 1800s, the Bay Area had become part of Mexico. In 1846 the United States claimed California in the Mexican-American War, and two years later, the gold rush brought an influx of miners and prospectors to the West, resulting in massive and rapid growth of the area. In 1906 a major earthquake and fire destroyed much of the city. Many edifices were rebuilt in a grand Beaux Arts style. The Golden Gate and Oakland Bay Bridges were built in 1936–37, allowing further expansion to outlying areas. In the 1950s and '60s, San Francisco's North Beach and Haight-Ashbury neighborhoods became the Meccas of America's counterculture.

WEATHER San Francisco weather is moderate year-round. March–November, you can expect average daytime highs in the 60s and average nighttime lows in the upper 40s to mid-50s. Slightly lower temperatures occur in the winter. Summer rainfall is all but nonexistent, with an average of less than 0.5 inch per month June–September, but what the season lacks in rain, it makes up for in fog.

TOURIST HIGHLIGHTS Watch the ships, eat the snacks, and gaze at the Golden Gate Bridge from **Fisherman's Wharf.** For a look into American penal history, take the nearby ferry over to the infamous **Alcatraz** penitentiary. Wander into **Chinatown** to dine and shop. Take in a museum, such as the **San Francisco Museum of Modern Art,** the **Fine Arts Museum of San Francisco,** or the **Walt Disney Family Museum.** For an outdoor experience, take a hike among the giant redwoods of **Muir Woods National Monument.** Or take a drive out of town for a visit to the Napa and Sonoma wine country. To immerse yourself in the city's famed gay culture, visit the **Castro District.** Of course, no trip to San Francisco would be complete without a ride on a cable car past **Lombard Street,** said to be the crookedest street in the world.

WHAT TO EAT Virtually all major cuisines are represented in San Francisco. Along Fisherman's Wharf, look for seafood in all forms, particularly chowder. Sourdough bread is an area specialty, often serving as a chowder bowl as well as a side dish. The vineyards north of the city make San Francisco a wine lover's paradise. Authentic Chinese dishes abound in the Chinatown district. The Ghirardelli chocolate factory no longer offers tours, but the ice-cream shop is still out of this world.

WHAT TO BUY For children, a toy cable car is a fun gift. Pick up some silks or carved stone in Chinatown. Sports fans will want jerseys representing the local teams, and foodies will want to pick up some Ghirardelli chocolate, a sourdough starter, or a fabulous bottle of wine.

Vancouver, British Columbia See page 172 for full profile.

Victoria, British Columbia

LANGUAGE English

HISTORY British settlement in Victoria began in the mid-1840s as a Hudson Bay trading post. Not long after this, the Fraser Canyon Gold Rush brought an influx of prospectors. The port then became a naval base and the commercial center of British Columbia. Victoria was designated the capital of British Columbia after the territory became a Canadian province in 1871. Today the city is home to thriving fishing and shipbuilding industries and is a nascent technological hub. The scenic harbor is also a major tourist destination.

WEATHER Cruises visit Victoria during the summer months. May–September, daytime highs average from the high 50s to high 60s, with nighttime lows in the low 40s to low 50s. Summers are dry, with typical rainfall of less than 1 inch per month during the summer.

TOURIST HIGHLIGHTS For lovers of flora, the sunken garden at **Butchart Gardens** is just one of the popular destinations in Victoria, known as the City of Gardens. Many remnants of Victoria's British heritage—including double-decker buses and horse-drawn carriages—remain, and the **Empress Hotel** serves a proper English tea. **Craigdarroch**

Castle, a 19th-century edifice, boasts panoramic city vistas and an impressive collection of antique furnishings. For a dose of history, visit the **Royal British Columbia Museum,** which owns more than 7 million artifacts, including an intact woolly mammoth. Outdoor enthusiasts will enjoy walking trails along the Pacific Ocean, as well as scuba diving, kayaking, and marine life observation. Victoria is also home to a vibrant **Chinatown.**

WHAT TO EAT Victoria is a modern city, with restaurants featuring most major cuisines. Pacific cod, salmon, and halibut are on menus throughout Victoria. For Asian favorites such as noodles and broth, venture into Chinatown.

WHAT TO BUY Look for native crafts such as jewelry and carvings. You can find tea and tea-service items in the Anglophile shops. **Fort Street** is known as Antique Row due to the many older trinkets for sale in the shops along this thoroughfare. Visit Chinatown for silks, fans, and Asian ornaments.

EUROPEAN CRUISES

Barcelona, Spain

LANGUAGES Catalan and Spanish

HISTORY Barcelona was founded as a Roman city. Subsequently, Visigoths and then Moors controlled the area until the early 800s. Franks held the region through the 10th and 11th centuries. From the 12th century, Barcelona and Catalonia became allied with the Kingdom of Aragón, and the Port of Barcelona became a trading thoroughfare. A period of decline ensued with the arrival of the Black Death in the 14th century, followed by the expansion of the Hapsburg monarchy as well as the rise of Turks in the region. The early 1700s brought a rejuvenation of the Barcelona dock system and then the arrival of the industrial age in the 1800s. By the mid-1800s, Barcelona was again a flourishing European port. Periods of unrest and rebuilding took place throughout the early 1900s, with stability constant since 1977, when the Catalan government was restored. Barcelona hosted the 1992 Summer Olympics, a boon for the entire region.

WEATHER Daytime highs average in the low 70s to low 80s May–September, with nighttime lows in the low to upper 60s. Even when temperatures peak, coastal breezes typically keep things comfortable. Precipitation is usually minimal during the summer, with an average of less than 3 inches of rain per month May–September.

TOURIST HIGHLIGHTS **La Rambla** is a pedestrian mall lined with restaurants, boutiques, and major international clothing chains. The premier attraction is **La Boqueria,** an open-air market with dozens of food stalls. The influence of artist Antonio Gaudí is in evidence throughout the area, principally in the can't-miss **Sagrada Família** cathedral and the **Park Güell** garden complex. Gothic architecture abounds in the old section of town. Art aficionados will enjoy the **Salvador Dalí Theatre and Museum,** the world's largest Surrealist object (*trippy* doesn't begin to describe it). Foodies will relish the **Museu de la Xocolata** (Museum of Chocolate). The **Poble Espanyol,** a walled city within the city, showcases architecture, artisans, and food from each of Spain's 15 regions. Sun worshippers appreciate the city's public beaches.

WHAT TO EAT In a word: ¡*Tapas!* Most restaurants offer some version of these small plates. Look for seafood, olives, artichokes, egg dishes, breads, and local hams and sausages. La Boqueria's many sweets vendors offer intricately shaped chocolates and marzipans.

WHAT TO BUY You can find almost anything in Barcelona, from high-end leather goods and shoes to handblown glassware. Great choices are packaged foodstuffs, such as candy, olives, olive oil, and wine, or sportswear featuring the local football (soccer) teams and Antonio Gaudí–inspired artwork.

Catania, Italy

LANGUAGES Sicilian and Italian

HISTORY Catania began as a Greek colony circa 700 BC. Several hundred years later it was taken by Rome, followed by periods of rule by the Byzantine Empire, the Arabs, Normans, Vandals, Ostrogoths, and others. In the early 16th century, Sicily and Catania became part of the Spanish Empire. In the 1860s Catania was included in a unification of Italy, where it remains today. The history of Catania is punctuated by seismic activity, including major earthquakes in 1169 and 1693, and several significant eruptions of nearby Mount Etna.

WEATHER Catania is hot in the summer. Average daytime highs in June, July, and August are in the 80s; average nighttime lows during those months are in the low to mid-60s. Precipitation is minimal during the summer, with average rainfall of less than 1 inch per month May–August.

TOURIST HIGHLIGHTS Chief among the area's natural wonders is **Mount Etna,** the largest active volcano in Europe. Another attraction is the Baroque architecture, particularly in the downtown area. Ancient ruins include the **Roman Forum** and the **Odeon.** A central point is the **Piazza del Duomo** and its elephant fountain, carved from black lava. Of course, the **Mediterranean Sea** is a wonderful background for beach lovers.

WHAT TO EAT Naturally, Italian food reigns in Catania. Try *arancini di riso* (fried rice balls) and *pasta alla Norma* (with eggplant, tomatoes, and ricotta) to begin your meal. Fresh fish will be featured on many menus. *Scacciata* is a bread-dough pie stuffed with local cheese, anchovies, or vegetables. Fresh blood oranges are a refreshing treat. For dessert, try cannoli stuffed with sweetened ricotta along with chocolate flakes or candied fruit. Many other pastries will include almonds or lemon flavoring. Strong coffee is served in abundance.

WHAT TO BUY *Pupi* (marionettes) are classic souvenirs of the area. You can also find many craft objects made from native lava stone. For decorative items, look for Baroque-style candelabras carved from wood. Connoisseurs will want to take home wine, olive oil, dried fruits, and spices.

Civitavecchia, Italy

LANGUAGE Italian

HISTORY Rome is a major metropolis with a lengthy past. Legend has it that the city was founded by the mythological twins Romulus and Remus, who were abandoned as infants and suckled by a wolf until a shepherd found them and raised them as his own. From 290 BC to AD 235, Rome was the dominant force in the Western world, controlling most of Europe and the Mediterranean. Later the Bishop of Rome (the Pope) established the city as the center of the Catholic Church. During the Renaissance, Rome became a hub for art and invention.

WEATHER Summers in Rome are hot. Average daytime highs June–September are in the low to upper 80s; temperatures in the high 90s are not unusual. Nighttime summer lows average in the low 60s. Summer is the dry season in Rome, with monthly rainfall in June, July, and August averaging less than 2 inches per month, and September averaging less than 3 inches per month.

TOURIST HIGHLIGHTS Civitavecchia is a 90-minute journey to Rome via bus or train. The walk from the pier to the train station is about 10 minutes.

It's impossible to take in all Rome has to offer in a day—choose one or two highlights and plan to come back. Among the main attractions are **Vatican City,** with the **Sistine Chapel** and **Saint Peter's Basilica;** the **Colosseum;** the **Spanish Steps;** the **Pantheon;** the **Trevi Fountain;** the **Catacombs;** the **Arch of Constantine;** and the numerous museums.

If you choose not to visit Rome or the countryside, you'll find smaller sights in **Civitavecchia** itself. The most popular local attraction is **Fort Michelangelo,** built in 1503 to protect the village from invaders. Another spot in town is the ancient baths, **Terme Taurine,** which were built around natural hot sulfur springs. A seafront market—offering souvenirs, food, and, of course, gelato—is open during the summer. A public beach is near the Civitavecchia promenade.

WHAT TO EAT Pizza is available almost everywhere, as is pasta in almost every conceivable shape and size. Roasted or fried artichokes are a popular side dish. Salt cod, zucchini blossoms, and fresh and aged cheeses may be served as an appetizer. For dessert, gelato is a specialty—look for unique flavors such as licorice, melon, apple, or hazelnut.

WHAT TO BUY With every major fashion designer represented in Rome, haute couture and leather goods abound. In and around the Vatican, you'll find religious artifacts, books, and artwork for sale. Sports enthusiasts will want to purchase jerseys of the local soccer teams.

Corfu, Greece

LANGUAGE Greek (English widely spoken)

HISTORY According to ancient myth, Corfu was where the god Poseidon fell in love with and subsequently abducted the nymph Korkyra. Corfu's tangible history is equally colorful, with long periods of Venetian and British control. It became part of modern Greece in 1864 as part of the Treaty of London.

WEATHER Corfu is hot in the summer. Daytime highs in June, July, and August average in the 80s. Average nighttime lows during those months are in the low to mid-60s. Precipitation is minimal during the summer, with average rainfall of less than 1 inch per month June–August.

TOURIST HIGHLIGHTS Corfu's **Old Town** is home to the historically significant **Old Fort,** with panoramic views; the **Agios Spyridon Church;** and an archeological museum. For theme park–style fun, try **Aqualand,** a small water park with slides and tubing. Sun lovers will want to head south of Old Town to **Mon Repos,** which features a beach area as well as Roman baths and historical sites.

WHAT TO EAT Traditional meal starters are dips made with eggplant or yogurt served with bread and vegetables. Other light bites include fried meat or fish balls. *Numbulo* (smoked ham) and *bourdouni* (blood sausage) are traditional meat dishes. Salads loaded with Feta cheese and olives are easy to find. Hearty appetites will be satisfied by souvlaki meat sticks, minced-meat pies, grilled lamb, or fish stew. A traditional dessert is *sykomaïtha,* a cake with dried figs, almonds, oranges, black pepper, cinnamon, and ouzo.

WHAT TO BUY Carved wood is a typical Corfu find. Look for bowls, boards, and picture frames. For clothing, you'll want items decorated with handmade lace or embroidery. Other crafts such as local jewelry and pottery are readily available. Connoisseurs will enjoy locally made wine, *limontselo* (a lemon liqueur that's more or less identical to Italian *limoncello*), ouzo, olive oil, honey, or kumquat marmalade.

Dubrovnik, Croatia

LANGUAGES Croatian and Italian

HISTORY Called the Republic of Ragusa in the Middle Ages, Dubrovnik became the only maritime city-state to rival Venice. From the 14th century to 1808, Dubrovnik was a free state, although it had to pay some monetary tribute to the Ottoman Empire. The 15th and 16th centuries marked a period of rapid development due to an influx of trade. The area has long attracted innovative thinkers and was one of the first municipalities to create modern laws and public-service institutions, including hospitals, an orphanage, and a clean water supply. In the Hapsburg period, Dubrovnik fell under Austrian rule. More recently, Dubrovnik underwent extensive shelling during the breakup of Yugoslavia.

WEATHER Summer daytime highs range from the low 70s to the low 80s, and summer nighttime lows range from the low 50s to the low 60s. The dry season in Dubrovnik, summer averages less than 2 inches per month in June, July, and August.

TOURIST HIGHLIGHTS High walls surround the **Old City,** dating from the Middle Ages; walk along them to view the Gothic, Baroque, and Renaissance architecture as well as the Adriatic Sea. Within the walls, visit the **Franciscan Monastery,** which houses a pharmacy that's been in continuous operation since 1391. Culture mavens will enjoy the **Rector's Palace,** the former residence of the governor of

Ragusa, which now houses a museum. Beyond the city, you'll find beaches for relaxing.

WHAT TO EAT Fresh fish (sea bass, grouper, mackerel, squid, and sea bream) and locally grown vegetables and olives are on menus throughout the area. Fish will often be grilled with garlic and lemon. Boiled or baked lamb is popular, including *pašticada,* a meat stew served with gnocchi. Locally cured ham makes an appearance at many restaurants. There is a strong Italian influence to the food here, so you'll find plenty of pasta and risotto.

WHAT TO BUY Typical souvenirs from Dubrovnik include packaged foods such as candied almonds or candied orange peel, wine, and olive oil. You can also find natural soaps and lotions scented with lavender and rosemary. Local craftspeople work with gold and leather. Handmade silk ties are popular, as are decorative painted eggs.

Heraklion, Greece

LANGUAGE Greek

HISTORY The Saracens founded present-day Heraklion (Iraklion) in the early 800s. About 100 years later, the Greeks burned the existing city to the ground and claimed the area. This was followed by periods of control by the Romans, Venetians, and Ottomans. The autonomous Cretan State was created in 1898, and in 1913 it was incorporated into the Kingdom of Greece.

WEATHER Average daytime highs in June, July, and August are in the low 80s, with average nighttime lows in the upper 60s to low 70s. Precipitation is minimal during the summer, with average rainfall of less than 1 inch per month May–September.

TOURIST HIGHLIGHTS Heraklion hosts several museums, including the **Heraklion Archaeological Museum,** the **Historical Museum of Crete,** the **Natural History Museum of Crete,** and the **Museum of Visual Arts.** For those with other historical interests, try the ruins at **Gournia** or the **Palace of Knossos.** The **Venetian Walls** and **Castello del Molo** also attract visitors. Several nearby beaches offer sunning along the Mediterranean Sea.

WHAT TO EAT Food in Crete is notable for its fresh herbs and vegetables. A typical starter is *dakos,* a dried bread topped with tomato, olive oil, cheese, and oregano. Other starters may include *dolmas* (stuffed grape leaves), *fasolakia* (beans with olive oil), and marinated vegetables. Greek cheeses and yogurts are found in abundance in restaurants and markets. Look for stews of pork or fish, as well as grilled lamb and seafood. Desserts may include candied fruits, *loukoumades* (like doughnut holes), and *bougatsa* (fried dough filled with sweet cream). Local wines and herbal teas are found throughout the region.

WHAT TO BUY Typical souvenirs include Cretan head scarves (*sariki*), ceramics, hand-decorated tablecloths, and replicas of local historical sites. Cretan knives are a popular gift, but be aware of travel regulations with a purchase like this. Connoisseurs will want to bring home jarred olives or olive oil, spices, wines, herbal teas, and Greek coffees.

Ibiza, Balearic Islands, Spain

LANGUAGES Catalan and Spanish

HISTORY Phoenicians settled Ibiza (*Eivissa* in Catalan) in 654 BC. Periods of control by the Greeks, Assyrians, and Carthaginians followed. During the Roman era, the island served as an imperial outpost. After the fall of Rome, Vandals and Byzantines ruled in turn. Later occupations came from Norway, Sicily, Aragón, and Spain. Democracy came to Ibiza during the 1970s, leading to the Statute of Autonomy of the Balearic Islands.

WEATHER Average daytime highs in June, July, and August are in the low to mid-80s; average nighttime lows during those months are in the mid-60s to low 70s. Precipitation is minimal during the summer, with average rainfall of less than 1 inch per month May–August.

TOURIST HIGHLIGHTS **Dalt Vila** (or D'Alt Vila) is the oldest part of town. It's quite hilly, so wear sturdy shoes. Start touring here by noting the **Portal de Ses Taules,** a 16th-century drawbridge. Dalt Vila is surrounded by fortified walls and honeycombed by secret tunnels. Museum lovers will appreciate the **Museu d'Art Contemporani d'Eivissa** and the **Museu Arqueològic d'Eivissa.** Beach lovers may want to venture to the western tip of the island to visit **Cala Conta Beach** for the exquisitely clean water. Finally, Ibiza's vibrant nightlife attracts fun seekers from around the globe.

WHAT TO EAT Spanish classics such as gazpacho and paella will be on many Ibiza menus, as will simply prepared fresh seafood. Tapas available here are similar to those found on the Spanish mainland. Look for vegetables, fried squid, and garlic prawns. Local meats include sausages such as *botifarra* and *sobrasada*. Also look for stews made with lamb, pork, chicken, sausage, and potatoes. For a sweet treat, try *ensaïmada de Mallorca,* a light pastry served plain with a dusting of sugar or filled with chocolate or cream.

WHAT TO BUY Shoppers shouldn't miss the **Hippie Market,** which is like a giant 1970s street fair. Hand-painted plates make a nice souvenir display item. Handmade pottery and jewelry are good local finds. Also look for leather goods, carved wood, and wickerwork. Foodies search for the local salts, red wine, or liqueurs made from local herbs or almonds.

Katakolon, Greece

LANGUAGE Greek

HISTORY Olympia, near Katakolon, is a cornerstone of Greek history. The ancient Greeks honored the god Zeus with athletic competitions called the Olympics, which began in 776 BC. Only men, with exceptions made for the priestesses of Hera, attended the original games. Competition winners had life-size statues created in their honor. After 1,200 years of games, the ancient Olympics ended in AD 393. The modern version of the games was reinstated in Athens in 1896.

WEATHER Average daytime highs in June, July, and August are in the mid- to high 80s, with average nighttime lows in the low to mid-60s. Precipitation is minimal during the summer, with average rainfall of less than 1 inch per month June–August.

TOURIST HIGHLIGHTS The main attraction for visitors is the village of **Olympia,** the original home of the Olympic games, about 20 miles to the east. Here you can see the ruins of the **Sanctuary,** with remnants of stadia, temples, and athletic areas. Then move on to the **Olympia Archaeological Museum.** Note that the flame for each modern Olympic Games is still lit in Olympia by a reflection of sunlight in a parabolic mirror. The flame is then carried by torch to the new game site. If you want to stay in Katakolon, be aware that the town is quite tiny, with only minor shopping and a small beach area. A local winery is the other sightseeing option.

WHAT TO EAT Katakolon likewise has minimal dining options. If you're staying in town, expect the food to be directed at the tourist trade. Typical dishes will include squid or octopus cooked in a wine sauce or a gyro platter served with onions, *tzatziki,* and pita bread. Desserts may include walnut cake or other nut-based pastries. For a refreshing beverage, try Mythos Hellenic Lager.

WHAT TO BUY Typical purchases in Katakolon might include pottery, woodcarvings, or local handcrafted jewelry. Visitors to Olympia may want to buy Olympic-themed paraphernalia.

Kusadasi, Turkey

LANGUAGE Turkish

HISTORY The region of Ephesus was founded by the Leleges people in about 3000 BC. Other early inhabitants included Aeolians, Ionians, and Persians. The Roman Empire colonized the area in the second century BC. Byzantine, Venetian, and Genoese traders stopped here on their journeys. In 1086 the Turks took control, followed by the Crusaders and the return of the Byzantines. Kusadasi became part of the Ottoman Empire in the early 1400s. The area remained a popular trading outpost until the 1800s. In the early 20th century, Italian and Greek forces briefly controlled the region. Tourism has been a primary industry only since the 1980s.

WEATHER Kusadasi has baking-hot summers. Average summer daytime highs are in the mid-80s to low 90s; nighttime lows average in the mid-60s to low 70s. Precipitation is almost nonexistent during the summer, with an average of less than 1 inch of rainfall per month during May and September and less than 0.1 inch in June, July, and August.

TOURIST HIGHLIGHTS A trip to **Ephesus,** 8 miles from Kusadasi, is the must-do. Ephesus is the best-preserved ancient Roman city in the Eastern Mediterranean. The **Temple of Cybele at Artemis** here was one of the Seven Wonders of the Ancient World. Nearby, see the **House of the Virgin Mary,** said to be the where she lived at the end of her life. If you want to stay in town, try sampling a *hammam,* or traditional Turkish bath. Beaches are accessible by taxi about 2 miles south of the city. Kusadasi also has three nearby water parks.

WHAT TO EAT Local fish appear on many menus; a specialty is salt-baked fish. *Meze* (appetizers) include stuffed grape leaves, stuffed eggplant, yogurt dips, and marinated tomatoes. Look for bulgur salads, meatballs, and kebabs for more substantial fare. Popular dessert items include baklava (pastry with nuts and honey) and *kadayıf* (pastry with pistachio filling). Turkish teas and coffees are potent beverages well worth trying.

WHAT TO BUY Turkish honey makes a great gift, and you can find it in many flavors. Also look for Turkish delight candy and local teas and spices. Rugs are a common purchase, but be sure to inquire about delivery options if you choose to buy a larger item. More-portable items include copper and ceramic pots, leatherwork, and local jewelry. You'll find lemon-scented colognes and soaps available throughout the region.

La Spezia, Italy

LANGUAGE Italian

HISTORY Florence and Tuscany are considered the birthplace of the Italian Renaissance. From about 1300 to 1500, it was the most important city in Europe. Its factious history includes several changes of government, including a period of rule by the storied Medici family. For a part of the 1700s, Tuscany became an Austrian territory and then later a prefecture of the French *département* of Arno. In the 1800s Italian rule returned. In modern times Tuscany has been a center of tourism, trade, and financial services.

WEATHER Summer temperatures are hot, with average daytime highs in the mid-70s to upper 80s. Temperatures approaching 100°F are not uncommon. Precipitation is fairly constant throughout the year, with average rainfall being about 2–4 inches per month in every season.

TOURIST HIGHLIGHTS La Spezia is a sweet town with several cafés and public beaches. The most popular attraction in the port city is the **Cinque Terre,** five small villages built into the rocks between the water and the hills. The villages are connected by a walking trail at Riomaggiore, a brief train ride away. La Spezia is also easily accessible by boat to the elegant resort of **Portofino.** Florence is a 2-hour auto trip from the port; Pisa is a 1-hour auto trip.

Museums abound in Florence, with the most famous being the **Uffizi Gallery.** Other museums include the **Bargello, Pitti Palace, Museo dell'Opera del Duomo,** and **Gucci Museum.** The symbol of the city is the **Duomo di Firenze.** For a fee, you can climb to the top of the cathedral for a bird's-eye view of the city. A stroll along the **Ponte Vecchio** is perfect for romance. The **Boboli Gardens** offer lush plantings and an interesting sculpture garden. In Pisa you must see the **Leaning Tower.** The cathedral there is constructed of colorful hand-carved marble.

WHAT TO EAT Try antipasto, often thinly sliced salami, pickled vegetables, and crostini. Most menus will include pasta or risotto, salads, grilled meats, and olives. Florentine desserts may include gelatos, *schiacciata con l'uva* (a sweet grape bread), or *castagnaccio* (chestnut cake).

WHAT TO BUY Florence is a city of high fashion, with most major luxury retailers in evidence. Leather goods are sold everywhere. Look for jackets, gloves, wallets, briefcases, and handbags in traditional and boldly colored dyes. Gold jewelry is often lovely here, but watch for extreme pricing. Crafty types may enjoy hand-marbled papers or wax letter

seals. Murano glassware and jewelry are popular purchases. Marionettes are wonderful takeaway items for kids.

Mykonos, Greece

LANGUAGE Greek

HISTORY The earliest inhabitants of Mykonos were the Carians. They
were followed by the ancient Egyptians, the Phoenicians, the Cretans,
and the Ionians. Greek mythology describes Mykonos as the site of the
battle between the god Zeus and the Titans (the island is named after
Mykons, a son of the god Apollo). Since the 1950s, the principal industry has been tourism.

WEATHER Summer in Mykonos is hot. Average daytime highs May–
September are in the high 70s, but temperature spikes into the 90s and
100s are not unusual. There is minimal nighttime cooling, with average
summer nighttime lows only in the low 70s. Summer is the dry season.
Typically there will be less than 0.5 inch of rain per month May–
September.

TOURIST HIGHLIGHTS Walking the narrow, winding streets is a primary
activity for visitors; these roads were specifically constructed to confuse
pirates. Animal lovers can interact with the island's many pelicans. For
fun in the sun, find beaches catering to every niche: solitude seekers,
partiers, families, water-sports enthusiasts, couples, gays, and naturists.
Be sure to seek the one that suits your needs. Nearby **Delos Island** is
home to an archeological museum and ancient ruins.

WHAT TO EAT Most international cuisines are found here. For Greek
dining, seafood, crepes, and gyros are available throughout the island.
Most Mykonos menu staples include Greek yogurt with honey, cheese
pies, grilled meats, *meze* (appetizers), and salads. For beverages,
look for wine, retsina, and ouzo, and be sure to try some of the thick
Greek coffee.

WHAT TO BUY You'll find posh international brands catering to the
beautiful people alongside stalls manned by local artisans. Jewelry,
bags, and hats can be found everywhere. Greek ceramics and sandals
are popular purchases. For a bit of local culture, pick up some *kombolói*
(worry beads). Be aware that most shops close for several hours during
the late afternoon.

Naples, Italy

LANGUAGE Italian

HISTORY Naples has been continuously inhabited since at least the second
millennium BC. During the first century BC, Naples played a role in the
merging of Greek and Roman cultures. Following the fall of the Western
Roman Empire, Naples became the capital city of the Kingdom of Naples
and remained so from the late 1200s to the early 1800s. During World
War II, Naples was the most bombed Italian city. Many of the outer buildings in the area were constructed as part of the restoration.

WEATHER Daytime highs during the summer months range from the
mid-70s to the mid-80s. Nighttime lows during that period fall into the
low 60s. Precipitation is fairly low in the early part of the summer,

averaging fewer than 2 inches per month May–August. Rainfall picks up to about 3 inches per month in September.

TOURIST HIGHLIGHTS In the city of Naples, see the **Museo Archeologico Nazionale.** Other historic sites include the **Castel Nuovo,** the **Museo di Capodimonte,** and the **Duomo di Napoli.** Fifteen miles southeast of Naples are the ruins of **Pompeii,** where you can wander the streets of an ancient town preserved in time by the volcanic eruption of Mount Vesuvius. If you're in the mood for a beach day, take a hydrofoil boat to the island of **Capri.**

WHAT TO EAT Naples is the birthplace of pizza, and **Antica Pizzeria Port'Alba** (founded in 1738) is the first establishment to serve it, though certainly not the only one you should consider. The classic version is the *pizza margherita,* a simple pie of tomato, basil, and fresh mozzarella. Neapolitan cuisine is also rich in seafood, often sauced with tomatoes, garlic, and olive oil. You will find house-made mozzarella available in many shops. *Limoncello* (lemon liqueur) is the adult beverage of the region; sip it alone or mixed into juices for a refreshing cocktail. Regional desserts include *baba* (a cake, perhaps soaked in liqueur), *zeppole* (like a doughnut, often filled with custard), and *sfogliatelle* (shell-shaped pastry). The local chocolatier, **Odin-Gay,** is a city favorite.

WHAT TO BUY Bring home some of the local limoncello if you want to taste Naples at home. If you're looking for jewelry, artisans here work in 18-karat gold and carved coral. Many visitors bring home replicas of the historical artifacts they see in Pompeii. Various shops sell locally carved wooden Christmas ornaments. In Capri, handmade sandals are a popular find.

Palma, Balearic Islands, Spain

LANGUAGES Catalan and Spanish; English and German widely spoken

HISTORY Like Ibiza (see page 194), Majorca is one of the Balearic Islands, an autonomous region of Spain, and Palma is its capital. Majorcan rule has changed hands numerous times over the centuries. The island's first inhabitants were peoples of the prehistoric Talaiotic Period. Palma was founded in 123 BC as a Roman camp upon the remains of a Talaiotic settlement; it later came under the rule of the Byzantines and the Moors. In 1229 James I of Aragón renamed the city Palma de Mallorca. Over the centuries it has weathered attacks from the Vandals and from Turkish and Berber pirates. In the 18th century, commercial activities and trade with the Spanish colonies and the Americas blossomed, which eventually led to the expansion of maritime tourism. Since the 1950s, Majorca has been a popular tourist destination, particularly with Britons and Germans. In fact, so many of the latter vacation here or live here during the winter that some call it "the 17th German state."

WEATHER Mid-June–mid-September is the warm season, with daytime highs typically in the low 80s and nighttime lows typically in the low 60s. This is also the driest time of the year, with only a 16% chance of precipitation during the summer.

TOURIST HIGHLIGHTS **La Seu** is a great place to start your touring. Located in the oldest part of town, the cathedral affords views of the seaside **Parc de la Mar,** a wonderful picnic venue. Also nearby is the **Avinguda d'Antoni Maura,** a street lined with cafés and snack shops, and **Passeig des Born,** a major shopping thoroughfare. Keep an eye out for Gothic, Moorish, and Renaissance architectural influences. To see the countryside, take the breathtaking 1-hour train ride through the mountains to the **Port de Sóller.**

WHAT TO EAT Mediterranean staples abound. For a sit-down meal or snack, go with tapas, the traditional Spanish small plates. Cured meats, ham, fresh fish, figs, almonds, and olives are often prominently featured on the menus. The Majorcan countryside is known for its orange and lemon groves, so many dishes will have a citrus element.

WHAT TO BUY Palma is renowned for its cultured-pearl trade and leather goods. Jewelry and bags should be the focus of your shopping. Also look for carved wood bowls and decorative objects made from felled agricultural trees.

Piraeus, Greece

LANGUAGE Greek

HISTORY Athens was named for Athena, the Greek goddess of wisdom. It is one of the world's oldest cities, considered by many to be the cradle of Western civilization and the birthplace of democracy. Since its first settlement circa 3000 BC, Athens has experienced intermittent periods of prosperity and unrest. Modern Athens emerged in the early 1800s, when the city became the capital of independent Greece. Following World War II, the area had a burst of rapid expansion and industrialization. Currently, Athens is a world center for archeological inquiry.

WEATHER Athens is hot and dry. Summer daytime highs are in the mid-80s to low 90s, and summer nighttime lows are in the low 70s. Precipitation is minimal during the summer, averaging less than 1 inch of rain per month May–September.

TOURIST HIGHLIGHTS Piraeus is just 7 miles from Athens, and a train can take you into the city's Pláka district (beware of unscrupulous taxi drivers). The **Acropolis,** a UNESCO World Heritage Site and a must-do for any visitor, is the most storied landmark in all of Greece; its marble shrine to Athena, the **Parthenon,** is one of the world's most recognizable ancient structures. Another UNESCO World Heritage Site worth visiting is the Byzantine **Monastery of Daphni,** renowned for its mosaic-tile work. The site has been under ongoing restoration since it sustained extensive damage in the 1999 Athens earthquake, and visiting hours are erratic. If you can catch it when it's open—try going on a Tuesday or Friday in the late morning or early afternoon—it's well worth the cab ride there.

Museum enthusiasts have numerous options, including the **National Archeological Museum,** the **Agora Museum,** the **National Art Gallery,** the **Benaki Museum,** and several others. Sports fans will want to see the **Panathenaic Stadium,** the site of the first Olympiad as well as the site of the 2004 Olympic Games.

WHAT TO EAT For a quick bite, try souvlaki (grilled pork or chicken) served with vegetables and the spiced yogurt-based *tzatziki,* held together by thin pita bread. You'll find that french fries are wrapped in the bread with the meat, instead of being served as a side dish. Cheese and spinach pies are a popular delicacy. Vegetables and salads are usually made with fresh local ingredients. Lamb and fish can also be found on most menus. Café culture is alive and well in Athens, with ouzo and wine popular in the evenings. *Opa!*

WHAT TO BUY Olives, olive oil, herbs, spices, and honey are popular purchases. For something more substantial, look for handwoven carpets or hand-tooled leather goods and jewelry. Copper coffeepots are often a good value. You can also find replicas of vases and ancient Greek statuary; the museum gift shops often have the highest-quality merchandise. Shops typically close for several hours during the afternoon as well as all day on Sunday.

Rhodes, Greece

LANGUAGE Greek

HISTORY Rhodes has been inhabited since Neolithic times. During the classical period, sculptor Chares built the Colossus of Rhodes, a tribute to the sun god Helios, which became one of the Seven Wonders of the Ancient World. In 164 BC, the Romans gained control of Rhodes. This was followed by periods of occupation by the Byzantines, the Knights Hospitaller, the Ottoman Empire, and the Italians. Rhodes sustained significant bombing during World War II. The Greeks have made a concerted effort to excavate and protect the impacted area, particularly the medieval town structures.

WEATHER Average daytime highs in June, July, and August are in the mid- to high 80s, with average nighttime lows in the high 60s to low 70s. Precipitation is minimal during the summer, with average rainfall of less than 1 inch per month May–August.

TOURIST HIGHLIGHTS The **Acropolis** of ancient Rhodes is a short distance outside town. This site includes the Temples of Athena and Apollo, along with a small theater. In **Old Town,** the **Palace of the Grand Masters** houses a museum focusing on the history of the island. The nearby **Knight's Hospital** houses the **Archaeological Museum,** which is also close to the Byzantine Museum. The **Mosque of Süleyman the Magnificent,** notable for its pink color, is a remnant of the Ottoman occupation. The beaches offer a great place to work on your tan or to view the many beautiful sailboats in the harbor.

WHAT TO EAT Typical Greek dishes are served throughout Rhodes. In particular, look for *hilopites* (pasta with red sauce or meat), *moussaka* (a baked casserole with potatoes and eggplant), and *pitaroudia* (chickpea fritters). You can also find grilled meats and fish, as well as fish stews, on many menus. Traditional accompaniments include onions and potatoes. Local sweet treats include baklava, *kataifi* (sweet shredded dough), and *belekounia* (made with sesame and honey). Ouzo is the adult beverage of choice here.

WHAT TO BUY The best shopping area is on **Sokratous Street** in Rhodes's Old Town. Typical souvenirs include ceramics decorated with a deer, the symbol of the city. Also look for leather goods, furs, and gold and silver jewelry. Turkish-influenced rugs are also a popular purchase, but look into shipping costs before committing. For foodies, local wines and olive oil are popular choices.

Santorini, Greece

LANGUAGE Greek

HISTORY The island of Santorini is principally a caldera formed from the remnants of a cataclysmic volcanic eruption, often called the Minoan eruption. Early settlers of the region included the Phoenicians, Dorians, Romans, and Byzantines. During the Crusades, the Franks settled on Santorini. Later they were usurped by Venetians and then by the Ottomans. Santorini broke from Ottoman rule in 1821 and then was united with Greece in 1830 as part of the Treaty of London.

WEATHER Average daytime highs in June, July, and August are in the low to mid-80s; average nighttime lows during those months are in the high 60s to low 70s. Precipitation is minimal during the summer, with average rainfall of less than 1 inch per month June–August.

TOURIST HIGHLIGHTS Ships anchor off Santorini and tender passengers to the small port of Skala Thíra (also called Thera or Fira). To get to the town itself, you must travel up a 1,000-foot cliff, either by funicular or by donkey. Simply getting to civilization is an adventure here.

The town of **Thíra** is especially picturesque, with whitewashed buildings and ancient cobbled streets. Museum lovers will enjoy the **Archaeological Museum of Santorini,** home to Roman and Hellenic artifacts, and the **Megaro Ghisi Museum,** which displays manuscripts, maps, and photos documenting the history of Thíra. The main shopping street is **Erythrou Stavrou,** featuring both designer shops and local craft merchants. **Akrotiri** is a partially excavated city that was encased in lava during a volcanic eruption in 1450 BC. Several local wineries give tours and tastings.

WHAT TO EAT The food in Santorini comes primarily from the agriculture on the island. Typical ingredients include fava beans, tomatoes, white eggplant, cucumbers, capers, watermelon, local cheeses, and fresh seafood. You'll find these items along with moussaka, fried fish or meatballs, grilled lamb, and meat casseroles. Desserts may include baklava, *loukoumades* (similar to doughnut holes), nougat, and *halvah,* a super-sweet, fudgelike candy popular across eastern Europe and the Middle East. Beverages include local wines and the ubiquitous ouzo.

WHAT TO BUY Gold merchants are everywhere in Santorini. Prices tend to be higher as you move north in the gold district. Look for jewelry featuring insects embedded in amber. Other finds include pottery, replicas of antiquities, cotton and linen clothing, and paintings by local artists. Oenophiles will want to bring home bottles of Santorini wine.

Valletta, Malta

LANGUAGES English and Maltese

HISTORY The Phoenicians originally colonized the Maltese Islands in the 800s BC, but the islands have also been under the control of the Greeks, Romans, Carthaginians, Byzantines, Arabs, Normans, Spanish, French, and British. In 1530 Emperor Charles V gave the islands to the Knights

Hospitaller in a lease arrangement; in exchange, the Knights gave the emperor a Maltese falcon each year. During this period, the Knights resisted control by Turkey's Ottoman Empire in what would later be known as the Great Siege. The Knights' reign ended in 1798 with the capture of the island by Napoleon. Malta became part of the British Islands in 1814 in the Treaty of Paris and became independent in 1964. It joined the European Union in 1990.

WEATHER Summers in Malta can be intensely hot. Summer daytime highs average from the low to upper 80s, though spikes into the upper 90s are not uncommon. Average summer nighttime lows are in the low 70s. Precipitation is minimal during the summer. Rainfall averages less than 1 inch per month May–August.

TOURIST HIGHLIGHTS The **Upper Barrakka Gardens** provide a lovely view of the harbor. **St. John's Co-Cathedral** houses wonderful artwork, including the Caravaggio masterpiece *The Beheading of St. John the Baptist.* The **Palace of the Grand Master** offers a look into the Great Siege of Malta. Other sites also help visitors learn more about the island, including the **National Archeology Museum,** featuring artifacts from the country's Neolithic temples, and the **National Library of Malta,** containing manuscripts related to the Order of St. John (also known as the Knights of Malta), a Catholic humanitarian, chivalric, and diplomatic order dating from the late 11th century.

WHAT TO EAT The national dish of Malta is stewed rabbit, often cooked with wine and garlic. Pork is readily available in the form of grilled steaks or sausages. *Pastizzi,* meat-filled pastries, are sold in markets and stalls throughout Malta. You can also find plentiful cheeses and breads topped with cheese. Honey and almonds play a prominent role in the nation's sweets.

WHAT TO BUY Malta is overwhelmingly Roman Catholic. You'll find gold and silver filigreed crosses for sale throughout the area. Handmade glassware is another popular choice. You'll also find handwoven cloth and intricate lacework in many shops.

Venice, Italy

LANGUAGE Italian

HISTORY Venice comprises 118 small islands linked by an intricate collection of canals and bridges. The city's name comes from the Veneti, an ancient people who were among the area's earliest inhabitants. In the sixth century, the Germanic Lombards drove mainland Italians into the Venetian islands. Byzantine control lasted until about AD 815. From the 9th to 12th centuries, Venice was one of four Italian city-states. In 1204 Venice conquered Constantinople, leading to a period of prosperity. Shifting political alliances in the 1400s in Europe eroded much of Venice's power. Subsequent blows came from the Black Plague and Napoleon's reign. A later period of Austrian rule gave way to Italian control.

WEATHER Summer in Venice is slightly cooler than in some of the other Italian ports. Daytime highs May–September average in the mid-70s to low 80s. Nighttime lows average in the low 60s. Precipitation is fairly constant throughout the year, with an average rainfall of about 3 inches per month.

TOURIST HIGHLIGHTS Automobiles are prohibited in Venice, so all transportation is via waterway and walkway—a gondola or *vaporetto* (water bus) ride is a must. The **Piazza San Marco** is the classic tourist spot. Nearby you'll find the clock tower, the **Doge's Palace,** and **Saint Mark's Basilica.** The **Bridge of Sighs** connects the Doge's Palace to the old prison. The **Rialto Bridge** area is known for its open-air markets. Museums include the **Gallerie dell'Accademia,** the **Guggenheim Collection,** and the **Museo Correr.**

WHAT TO EAT Venice is a city of seafood, with rice, vegetables, and polenta also prominent on local menus. Easy bites include pizza and pasta. For a sweet treat, enjoy refreshing Italian ices. **Harry's Bar** on the Piazza San Marco offers famed Bellinis for sipping, and Italian wine, of course, is in abundance everywhere.

WHAT TO BUY Most major fashion houses have outposts in Venice. Luxury goods are abundant, as are leather goods, antiques, and jewelry. Murano glass is a classic souvenir. Venetian masks are also easy to find on the streets.

Villefranche, France

LANGUAGES French and Italian

HISTORY The Greeks were the first organized human presence on what is now known as the French Riviera. They were followed by the Romans in the eighth century BC. Before the Dark Ages, the region saw invasions from Visigoths, Burgundians, and Ostrogoths, which were later followed by threats from the Saracens and Normans. Stability came in the 13th century with the House of Grimaldi, which took power in what is now Nice, Antibes, and Monaco. Tourism became a major influence in the area beginning in the late 1700s, when wealthy Brits began arriving to take advantage of the climate and fine air quality.

WEATHER Summers along the French Riviera are warm and dry. Summer daytime highs average in the low 70s to low 80s. Summer nighttime lows average in the mid-60s. Precipitation is low during the summer, with less than 2 inches of rainfall per month averaged May–August.

TOURIST HIGHLIGHTS Disney cruises anchor in the harbor and tender to the terminal in central Villefranche. A soap factory in town, **La Savonnerie de Villefranche,** lets visitors watch its work. If you're staying in port and looking for relaxation, the public beach is about a 10-minute walk away from the old town.

Most major and minor points on the French Riviera are accessible with less than an hour of travel away from the port. In **Nice,** stroll along the **Promenade des Anglais** or visit the **Cours Saleya** market for sweet and savory treats. In **Cannes,** look for art galleries on the **Rue d'Antibes. Monte Carlo** is famous for luxury shopping, the upper crust, and the **Grand Casino.** Try your hand here if you're in the mood for gambling. **Èze** is a medieval-era hilltop village from which you can see into France, Monaco, and Italy. Nearby **Grasse,** known as the fragrance capital of the world, offers tours of the **Fragonard** perfume factory.

WHAT TO EAT You'll find less butter and cream in food along the French Riviera than you would in other parts of France. Look here for *bouillabaisse* (fish stew), *salade niçoise* (a composed salad of tuna, tomato, eggs, and olives), the pizzalike *pissaladière*, crepes, and, of course, plenty of pastry.

WHAT TO BUY In Monte Carlo, look for souvenirs associated with Princess Grace and other members of the Grimaldi family, as well as trinkets representing the Grand Prix auto race. In Cannes, you'll find many items emblazoned with the film-festival logo. Throughout the area, look for wines, linens, and fragrances.

PANAMA CANAL CRUISES

Cabo San Lucas, Mexico

LANGUAGE Spanish

HISTORY Native inhabitants of the Cabo San Lucas region include the Pericu peoples. European influence was minimal until the early 1800s. Industry and trade took hold in the early 1900s, when commercial fishing companies began to capitalize on the local tuna. The 1970s saw a surge in tourism, due in part to the completion of Mexican Federal Highway 1, linking Cabo to other parts of Mexico.

WEATHER Disney cruises visit Cabo San Lucas in May and September. Average daytime highs during those months are in the mid-80s to low 90s. Average nighttime lows during that time are in the low to mid-70s. Precipitation is typically low in May, averaging about 1 inch per month. Late summer is the rainy season, with September precipitation averaging about 9–10 inches of rainfall per month.

TOURIST HIGHLIGHTS The cruise ship anchors in the harbor and tenders guests into the marina, where nearby lie a large mall and luxury brand outposts. White-sand beaches are the major attraction—relax on the sand or take part in active water pursuits such as snorkeling, sailing, parasailing, or sport fishing. For those wishing to be active and dry, Cabo is a golf paradise, boasting numerous world-class courses. Zip lining is a wonderful excursion for guests with a daredevil streak. Whale watching and interactive dolphin experiences are popular activities. Those looking to enjoy art and culture will want to visit the **Vitrofusion Glass Blowing Factory** to watch artisans create recycled glassworks, or stay in town to explore the **Iglesia de San Lucas,** a Spanish mission with many original features still intact.

WHAT TO EAT While you can find food from many nationalities, the local Cabo cuisine is, of course, Mexican. Try the street-vendor versions of tacos, quesadillas, and tortas. Rocker Sammy Hagar's **Cabo Wabo Cantina** is a must-stop spot for many visitors. The menu features a dozen different shrimp dishes, as well as catch-of-the-day specials, served with a heaping earful of rock and roll on the side.

WHAT TO BUY Along with typical seaside tourist trinkets, shirts, caps, and shot glasses emblazoned with the Cabo Wabo logo are an obligatory purchase for many visitors. Foodies will want to take home the local hot sauce, a Mexican tequila, or Damiana, a liqueur made with an herb known for its supposed aphrodisiac qualities. Look for soaps and lotions made with imitation turtle oil or scented with local spices.

Cartagena, Colombia

LANGUAGE Spanish

HISTORY Cartagena has been inhabited since 4000 BC. Spanish explorers founded the city proper during the early 1500s. This was followed by periodic plundering by pirates and privateers from France and England, and later by a major invasion from Englishman Sir Francis Drake. During the 17th century, the Spanish constructed a series of fortresses to protect the city. Throughout the 17th and 18th centuries, Cartagena was a major trading outpost. In 1811 the region declared its independence from Spain, resulting in nearly a century of crisis. Today Cartagena is a prosperous tourist destination.

WEATHER Cartagena is hot year-round. Expect daytime highs in the upper 80s throughout the year. Average nighttime lows are in the 70s year-round. Average precipitation varies from 1 inch or less per month December–April to a moderate 3–4 inches per month May–August, culminating in the rainy season of up to 8 inches per month September–November.

TOURIST HIGHLIGHTS **Old Town** is a popular exploration spot. Look for the **Plaza de Bolívar** and the giant bronze statue of Simón Bolívar, who helped Colombia and other South American countries secure independence from Spain. Nearby are the **Museo del Oro y Arqueologia** and a 16th-century cathedral. The fortress **Castillo San Felipe de Barajas** presents a look into the area's past. The **Palacio de la Inquisición** exhibits artifacts from the Spanish Inquisition, including some very creative torture devices. For outdoor fun, Cartagena offers many beaches within a 10- to 20-minute taxi ride away from town. Divers will find scuba and snorkel equipment available for rent.

WHAT TO EAT Restaurants here serve food from most major cuisines. Traditional foods include grilled fish, meat, and rabbit; rice, cassava, and plantains are common side dishes. Street vendors sell *butifarras* (meatballs), *buñuelos* (cheese balls), and *arepas de huevo* (fried dough with an egg inside). Try the *mote de queso,* a local soup made from yams, eggplant, and cheese. Fruit juices are available in abundance, both in restaurants and in street shacks. The local beer is Club Colombia.

WHAT TO BUY You'll find plenty of jewelry, particularly emeralds, for sale here. Many vendors are open to bargaining. Ornate (and often obscene) woodcarvings are common finds. For local flavor, search out loose-fitting traditional dresses, baskets, or handmade musical instruments. Java junkies will naturally want to take home some Colombian coffee.

Cozumel, Mexico   See page 177 for full profile.

Key West, Florida   See page 179 for full profile.

Miami, Florida   See page 180 for full profile.

Panama Canal, Panama

HISTORY The Spanish government initially authorized construction of the Panama Canal in 1819. Progress was scattershot for several decades thereafter, with planning beginning in earnest in 1876 and construction starting in 1881. Engineering struggles plagued early efforts to dig the canal, eventually resulting in the plan for a system of raised locks. Continued disease and construction difficulties caused the bankruptcy of the original funders and a long stall in the work process. The project was revived following strategic interest from US President Theodore Roosevelt, with the United States taking formal control over the region in 1904. Several years were spent creating an infrastructure capable of supporting the materials and labor force required to complete the task. Lock building commenced in 1909 and was finished in 1913. In 1914 a French boat, the *Alexandre La Valley,* became the first to completely traverse the canal. The Panama Canal subsequently revolutionized world trade patterns, cutting nearly 8,000 miles off a sea journey from New York to San Francisco. In 1977 the United States began to reduce its role in the region, and today the Panama Canal Authority oversees the canal, which continues to be improved. Currently the locks cannot accommodate the size of the largest ships, and in 2007 a project began to create a new wider lane of locks.

WEATHER Warm and wet. Because it's close to the equator, temperatures vary little in Panama, with lows throughout the year around 75°F and highs around 90°F. Disney ships generally visit in May and September, which average 24–26 days of rain per month, with humidity above 90%. (On the upside, we hear big hair is coming back in style.)

TOURIST HIGHLIGHTS The ship moves through the canal without stopping to let off passengers. The highlight of the voyage is watching how the canal's locks fill and release water to move the ship up and down through the terrain. It takes 8–10 hours to get through all of the locks, so you have plenty of time to catch the action.

Port Canaveral, Florida   See page 182 for full profile.

Puerto Vallarta, Mexico

LANGUAGE Spanish

HISTORY The native settlers were the ancient Aztlán peoples. European influence began in the early 1500s, when Spaniards, including Hernán Cortés, took control of the region. During the 17th and 18th centuries, the area was a known shelter for pirates and smugglers. Organized trade began to blossom in 1859, when the Union en Cuale mining company started operating in the region. In the early 1900s, the mining trade gave way to fruit farming, which then ceded influence to the growing tourism industry. Since the 1950s, Puerto Vallarta has been a resort and cruise destination.

WEATHER Disney cruises visit Puerto Vallarta in May and September. Average daytime highs during those months are in the mid-80s to low

90s, with average nighttime lows in the low to mid-70s. Precipitation is typically low in May, averaging less than 2 inches per month. Late summer is much wetter, with September rainfall averaging about 10–11 inches per month.

TOURIST HIGHLIGHTS The beaches are the big draw here. Snooze by the waves or enjoy more-active pursuits such as snorkeling or biking. Animal lovers can enjoy dolphin excursions or watch whales and turtles. **El Centro,** Puerto Vallarta's downtown, features churches with charming colonial detail. Tequila manufacturing and tasting is a big draw to this area. Be sure to sample several varieties; you'll be amazed at the differences.

WHAT TO EAT Not surprisingly, Mexican food is prevalent in Puerto Vallarta. Look for tacos, taquitos, tostadas, and enchiladas. Fresh seafood is also on many local menus. Try red snapper or marlin served with spices and lime. Those in the mood for adult beverages will find no shortage of margaritas, daiquiris, and beer.

WHAT TO BUY Puerto Vallarta shopping caters to the tourist trade. You'll find silver, ceramics, leather, and woven goods in many forms, as well as the ubiquitous T-shirts and trinkets portside. Haggling is common with vendors by the beaches, so if you don't like the price you see, feel free to propose something lower. Several modern malls in the area sell major-brand cruise wear at typically reasonable prices. Foodies will want to bring home local chocolates or Mexican spices.

San Diego, California   See page 186 for full profile.

TRANSATLANTIC CRUISES

Barcelona, Spain   See page 189 for full profile.

Basseterre, Saint Kitts and Nevis   See page 173 for full profile.

Castaway Cay, Bahamas   See page 174 for full profile.

Funchal, Madeira, Portugal

LANGUAGE Portuguese

HISTORY Funchal is the capital of Portugal's Autonomous Region of Madeira, about 250 miles north of the Canary Islands in the Atlantic Ocean. Settlement began in the early 1400s, and Christopher Columbus was an early resident. During the late 15th century, the sugar industry expanded in Madeira, making this an important trading port. During the 16th century, Funchal was a stopping point for ships traveling from the Indies to the New World. The 1800s saw a period of upheaval, with control of the island of Madeira passing from the British to the Portuguese. In 1976 Portugal granted political autonomy to Madeira.

WEATHER Summers in Funchal are pleasant and mild. Average daytime highs are in the mid-70s, while average nighttime lows are in the mid-60s. Precipitation is typically low at this time of year, averaging less than 1 inch of rainfall per month May–August.

TOURIST HIGHLIGHTS For breathtaking vistas of the harbor, the **Monte Cable Car** will take you from the old town area to high hills. For outdoor strolling, try the **Jardins do Palheiro,** a British Colonial–style park. Many plantings here bloom virtually year-round. For a more strenuous hike, explore the *levadas,* a system of aqueducts, many with views of the natural wonders of the area. Museum lovers will enjoy the **Museum of Natural History** or the **Sacred Art Museum.** Animal enthusiasts will want to look into day trips for whale- and dolphin-watching.

WHAT TO EAT Garlic is present in nearly all savory dishes in the region. Try the local tomato-and-onion soup, espada (a native fish), codfish, scabbard fish served with banana, or *espetada* (grilled marinated beef). You'll also find rabbit and goat on many menus. Traditional pastries include the *bolo de mel,* or honey cake. And don't forget to try the locally produced sweet wines.

WHAT TO BUY Madeira is famous for its embroidery. You can find intricately decorated fabric and clothing throughout the area. Madeira dessert wine is often a prized purchase; bring home several of the local varieties. Wicker and baskets are also sold everywhere. Visit the **Mercado dos Lavradores** for handicrafts and local packaged treats.

Málaga, Spain

LANGUAGE Spanish

HISTORY The Phoenicians founded Málaga in about 770 BC. Later invasions resulted in periods of rule by the Carthaginians, Romans, Muslim Arabs, and Christian Spanish. Málaga had a period of rapid development in the 19th century, but the thriving commercialization stumbled when later rulers focused more energy in cities to the north. Today, the area is part of Spain's Autonomous Community of Andalusia.

WEATHER Average daytime highs in June, July, and August are in the 80s. Average nighttime lows during those months are in the mid- to high 60s. Precipitation is minimal during the summer, with average rainfall of less than 1 inch per month May–August.

TOURIST HIGHLIGHTS **La Alcazaba** is one of the best-preserved ancient Arab constructions, boasting more than 100 towers and wonderful views of the city. From **Gibralfaro Castle,** a Phoenician ruin, you can see Gibraltar in the distance. Uncovered in 1953, the **Roman Theater of Málaga** showcases architecture from the first century BC. Other popular sights are the **Málaga Cathedral,** the bullring, and the **Mercado Central.** Art lovers will enjoy the **Picasso Home Museum.** If you're in a theme park mood, try **Tivoli World,** with its rides and gardens.

WHAT TO EAT Food in Málaga is similar to that in other parts of Andalusia. Soups include gazpacho, *porra antequerana* (a sort of thick gazpacho with ham), *ajoblanco* (cold soup with ground almonds), and *sopa de ajo* (hot soup with garlic and bread), as well as various fish soups and chowders. Look also for grilled and fried fish, including anchovies, mackerel, hake, shrimp, and sardines. For dessert, try almond biscuits and honey-based pastries. For relaxation, be sure to indulge in the local sangria.

WHAT TO BUY Málaga is home to most major Spanish retailers. For local items try leather crafts, ceramics, woven shawls, or jewelry. Olive oil–based soaps are popular gifts. Also look for incense, candles, and replica religious statuary. Foodies will want to purchase sweet Málaga wine (similar to port), olive oil, and candy made with almonds and honey.

Philipsburg, Sint Maarten See page 181 for full profile.

Port Canaveral, Florida See page 182 for full profile.

San Juan, Puerto Rico See page 183 for full profile.

St. John's, Antigua and Barbuda See page 185 for full profile.

Tenerife, Canary Islands, Spain

LANGUAGE Spanish

HISTORY The Canary Islands are an autonomous community of Spain about 60 miles off the northwest coast of mainland Africa. The earliest recorded settlers on the island of Tenerife were the Guanches people, in about 200 BC. In AD 1494 the Spaniards conquered the island. Many of the native inhabitants were enslaved to work on sugarcane plantations, perished from European diseases, or emigrated to Latin America. In 1797 the Spanish withstood attacks by British invaders. Tourism became a major influence beginning in the 1890s.

WEATHER Average daytime highs in June, July, and August are in the high 70s to low 80s; average nighttime lows during those months are in the mid-60s to low 70s. Precipitation is minimal during the summer, with average rainfall of less than 1 inch per month June–August.

TOURIST HIGHLIGHTS Within Tenerife's boundaries you can find forests, deserts, mountains, volcanoes, and spectacular beaches. The **Old Quarter of Santa Cruz** offers historic architecture, museums, and monuments. Animal lovers will want to visit **Loro Parque,** a wildlife exhibit that houses one of the world's largest collections of parrots. For an active experience, visit **Aqualand** water park. **Mount Teide,** accessible by cable car, is the highest point in Spain, affording expansive views.

WHAT TO EAT Many dishes have a Spanish influence. Look for *rancho canario* (a soup of chicken, pork, cabbage, and noodles), *conejo* or *pollo en salmorejo* (rabbit or chicken with garlic), *baifo* (marinated goat), or *queso de cabra* (goat cheese). Fruit, including bananas, figs, mangoes, papayas, peaches, and avocados, is abundant. A typical dessert is *bienmesabe,* a puree of almonds, eggs, and sugar.

WHAT TO BUY Tenerife has numerous jewelry shops, with a particular focus on silver. Lacework here is often lovely. Also look for carved wood, pottery, and woven baskets. The cigars of Tenerife are said to be second in quality only to those of Cuba. Foodies will want to bring home jars of honey or bottles of wine. Jarred *mojos* (herb sauces) are also popular.

PART TWELVE

PORT ADVENTURES

DISNEY CRUISE LINE OFFERS more than 600 shore excursions—"port adventures," in Disney-speak—for families to experience while their ship is docked. While it's impossible for the authors to have tried them all, we've embarked on quite a few. We've also interviewed scores of families and DCL employees to learn which are the most popular and which ones they'd recommend to friends.

Because most Disney cruises stop at Castaway Cay (see Part Ten), this section includes detailed reviews of its port adventures. These generally last 1–3½ hours; others, such as snorkeling or biking, are self-guided. Disney staff leads most (but not all) of these excursions.

Beyond Castaway Cay, most port adventures last 3–6 hours, including transportation time, and all are designed to fit comfortably into the ship's schedule. Third-party companies based near the port run virtually all of the port adventures, except those on Castaway Cay. On the day of your activity, you'll be instructed to gather somewhere on the ship, such as a restaurant or lounge, at a predetermined time. Once you're there, a Disney cast member will ensure that you have the correct port-adventure tickets and identification to reboard the ship. You may also be asked to sign a liability waiver to participate in a particular activity.

When those tasks are complete, everyone signed up for the activity will be escorted by cast members off the ship to a meeting point on the port's docks. There, representatives of the third-party company running the port adventure will meet you. You'll be in their care until you're returned to the port after your activity.

OUR RECOMMENDATIONS
Beyond CASTAWAY CAY

DOLPHIN ENCOUNTERS

ACCORDING TO OUR SOURCES, dolphin encounters are the most popular shore-excursion choice for families. Every port in Mexico,

Dolphin Alternatives

IF $700 SOUNDS EXPENSIVE for a few minutes with any intelligent mammal, allow us to suggest some alternatives. One is **Castaway Ray's Stingray Adventure** (see page 215), which includes almost an hour of in-the-water time feeding and petting dozens of small, gentle stingrays in a special section of Castaway Cay's lagoon. Snorkel equipment is provided for your day on the island, where you may also see stingrays throughout the lagoon.

That said, if your kids have their hearts set on dolphins and your vacation schedule has room for an extra day, consider a visit to SeaWorld's **Discovery Cove** in Orlando (**discoverycove.com**). Prices for Discovery Cove's all-day Dolphin Swim Day package runs $229–$319 per person and includes a 30-minute dolphin experience, plus the following:

- Snorkeling equipment for SeaWorld's man-made Grand Reef, home to stingrays and dozens of fish species
- Access to an oasis-themed freshwater pool, where you can observe (but not touch) otters and marmosets
- An aviary where you can feed birds
- Access to a man-made beach and lazy river

Breakfast, lunch, and unlimited snacks and beverages (including alcohol) are included in the price, along with locker rentals, sunscreen, and admission to SeaWorld for the two weeks around your vacation dates.

---

along with Nassau, Falmouth, Grand Cayman, and St. Thomas, offers one. If your Caribbean or Bahamian cruise includes a port besides Castaway Cay, you'll almost certainly have a chance to book one.

Because of the dolphins' popularity, these port adventures aren't cheap, generally starting at around $180 for adults and $160 for children, or roughly $700 for a family of four.

Most dolphin-related port adventures last 4–7 hours, of which roughly 30 minutes are spent in the water with a dolphin and 10–20 other tourists. During our visits, we took turns with the rest of the group in petting, feeding, and taking photos with the dolphin. In hindsight, the remarkable thing is that we spent perhaps 1 minute each in direct contact with the animal.

The rest of the time is transportation to and from the port, a background class and instruction on how to interact with the dolphin, a short show during which the dolphins demonstrate their jumping skills and tricks, and some beach or pool time once your encounter is done.

NASSAU

THE BIG DRAW HERE is **Atlantis,** a Las Vegas–style resort about a 20-minute drive from the port (☎ 888-877-7525; **atlantis.com**). Activities available include golf, snorkeling, man-made beaches, a water park, and various dolphin encounters. Beyond those, Atlantis has a casino, spa, rock-climbing wall, and fishing charter boats. Atlantis's shore excursions start at $95 per adult and $59 per child for access to the beaches and grounds (but not the waterslides), including lunch.

Beyond Atlantis and the dolphin encounters, we've tried port adventures including harbor cruises, city tours, and chocolate and wine tastings. All were pleasant enough, but none of them was something we'd do again.

MAYAN PYRAMIDS

TOURS OF MAYAN RUINS take place in **Costa Maya** and **Cozumel, Mexico.** Those in Costa Maya cover Chacchoben and Kohunlich; Tulum ruins can be seen at Cozumel. Be aware that all three trips involve considerable transportation time: 4 hours of the Kohunlich's 6½-hour tour is spent on ferries or buses, as well as 4 of Tulum's 7½ hours; Chacchoben's transportation takes 2 of its 4½ hours. Prices are as follows: Chacchoben, $84 ages 10 and up, $69 ages 3–9; Kohunlich, $95 ages 10 and up, $75 ages 3–9; and Tulum, $129 ages 10 and up, $99 ages 5–9.

PORT ADVENTURES *on* CASTAWAY CAY

WE CONSIDER CASTAWAY CAY'S SHORE EXCURSIONS among the best values of any that DCL has to offer. Here's a quick rundown of what's available.

BICYCLE RENTALS

***unofficial* TIP**
The **Castaway Cay Getaway** and **Extreme Getaway Packages** include activities listed here and are cheaper than purchasing à la carte, but we don't recommend them—trying to fit all that adventure into one or two days seriously cuts into your relaxation (and eating!) time.

THESE SINGLE-SPEED ROAD BIKES with plump tires are good for getting some exercise while exploring the island. Men's and women's models are available, and the seats are designed for comfort. The seats can be adjusted up and down to suit your leg length, although years spent on the island have rusted many of the metal cams used to loosen the seats. Ask a cast member to help (they have wrenches!) if yours won't budge.

Pick up your bicycles just past the Pelican Point tram stop, near the middle of the family beaches. You can also rent bikes next to the Serenity Bay adult beach, just behind the Castaway Air Bar. Cost is $10–$13 per hour, though no one on the island seems to keep track of how long you've had your bike.

BOAT RENTALS

VARIOUS WATERCRAFT, including one- and two-seat kayaks, sailboats, and paddleboats, are available for rent in half-hour increments.

Costs range from $14 for a single-seat kayak to $27 for a Hobie Cat catamaran. The paddleboats require an extraordinary amount of leg power to get anywhere, and 30 minutes is going to be plenty for most people. Previous sailing experience is required to rent a sailboat.

CASTAWAY CAY 5K RUN

ONE OF THE BEST PORT ADVENTURES to start your day on Castaway Cay is fun, well organized, and absolutely free. Runners and walkers who wish to participate in the 5K meet around 8:15 on the morning the ship arrives at the island. The meeting location is almost always at one of the bars in the adult area of the ship because that's the way the best races begin; check your *Personal Navigator* the night before for details on when and where to meet.

There's no sign-up for the event—simply show up in the morning at the designated spot. Two cast members will meet you there and make sure you have your Key to the World Card and ID. They'll give you a runner's bib (a nice touch for this unchipped race) and safety pins; then you'll walk off the ship with the rest of the runners toward the start of the race, by the Pelican Point tram stop. Parents who need to drop their kids off at Scuttle's Cove will be given time to do so on the way.

Once you arrive at the start, everyone is given a chance to hit the restroom and drop anything they don't want to run with in the storage area by the bike rentals. This is unsecured, so don't leave your gold doubloons, but other stuff is fine.

Once everyone is ready, you're off and running. The route includes a trip up and down the airstrip and two loops out to the viewpoint. You'll be sharing the road with the trams as well as folks on bicycles, so be aware of your surroundings. One cast member will be at the entrance to the loop with water—take advantage of it, because this run is hot.

The other cast member will be by the digital timer at the end of the race to congratulate you on your spectacular finish and give you a medal. Wear it proudly for the other folks who were still at the breakfast buffet while you were out running 3 miles in the heat.

The 5K and snorkeling are the two port adventures that we always do on the island. They're a fantastic bargain and great ways to enjoy your day.

5K RUN FAQS

What should I pack? Don't forget your running shoes and clothes.

Can my kid join me? Sort of. Disney officially restricts participants to folks age 12 and older, so your child won't get a bib or medal. Because of the informal setup of the race, though, there's no way to stop kids under 12 from running along with you. Parents are given time during the walk to the race start to drop off kids at Scuttle's Cove.

Is it a race? This 5K brings out people of all abilities and seriousness about their running. Take it at your own pace and just enjoy it.

Is there a time limit? Not officially, but the cast members would probably appreciate it if you're done within 40–45 minutes. (There's also a Castaway Cay Power Walk if that's more your speed.)

5K RUN FAQS (continued)

Can I buy a souvenir? Yes. When RunDisney began sponsoring this event, we got "medals" (plastic) and the opportunity to purchase T-shirts at the end (in addition to the race bibs you receive). The T-shirts, while attractive, are cotton instead of tech material.

Can I shower after the race? There are no private showers on the island, just the ones by the restrooms for knocking off the sand. If you didn't bring a swimsuit with you and don't plan to get right into the water, you'll need to walk back to the ship to shower in your cabin.

How's the weather? Hot. Drink lots of water. Wear sunscreen. Eating at Remy or Palo the night before probably isn't the best idea. Did we mention that it's hot?

What about itineraries with two stops at Castaway Cay? You get two opportunities to run. Yay! You can do both or either.

Is water available? Yes. Not only does a cast member offer water on the course, but the 5K also begins and ends by a regular water stop for the island. Drink lots!

BOTTOM FISHING

A 3-HOUR CATCH-AND-RELEASE fishing excursion ($139 per person) takes place in the waters around Castaway Cay, with Disney-provided fishing rods and bait. Your boat's captain will take you into the waters around the island; the most commonly caught species are yellow jack, grouper, various porgies, and snapper. It's not unheard of to hook a barracuda or small shark, too. Most charters leave around 9 a.m. and are back in time for lunch. Readers prone to seasickness shouldn't take this excursion, and kids must be age 6 or older to participate.

CASTAWAY RAY'S STINGRAY ADVENTURE

THIS IS YOUR CHANCE to pet and feed small- and medium-size stingrays in a supervised, structured setting on the shore of the Stingray Lagoon. Disney keeps dozens of these stingrays in a sectioned-off part of Castaway Cay's lagoon, and the stingrays are trained to use a special feeding platform at mealtimes. The cost is $45 for guests age 10 and up, $36 for kids ages 5–9.

Holding a specially formulated pellet of food between two fingers, you'll place your hand, palm down, on the platform. A stingray will swim up to the platform, glide over your hand, and grab the food in its mouth. You'll also have the chance to pet each ray as it swims by. There's plenty of food and plenty of stingrays for everyone. Besides the feeding, you'll get a brief introduction to stingrays, skates, and sharks before you begin, when a cast member reviews rules and procedures.

Many children are worried about being bitten by the stingrays, and let's face it: The word *sting* in their name doesn't exactly make rays the poster children for cuddly animals. But the rays don't have teeth, and the only thing that seems to get them excited is the prospect of feeding time. Calling them rays may help your kids find these animals more approachable. Kid fears might also be assuaged by a mention of the friendly Mr. Ray in *Finding Nemo*.

FLOAT AND TUBE RENTALS

INNER TUBES AND RECTANGULAR FLOATS are available for $10 for one day or $13 for two days. You can swap out one type for the other during the day.

GLASS-BOTTOM-BOAT EXCURSION

GUESTS BOARD A SMALL MOTORIZED WATERCRAFT that holds about 25 people and that ventures about 15 minutes out into the ocean. You can observe sea life below through several "windows" in the floor of the boat. During the trip, you're accompanied by a local guide who discusses the fish and other natural elements you'll encounter.

The highlight of the tour takes place at approximately the mid-point of the journey: Guests are given a cup filled with about 1 ounce of oatmeal, which they toss overboard to attract fish. During the feeding portion of the tour, several hundred tropical fish of various species surround the boat, and the guide points out the characteristics of as many fish as possible. The feeding lasts about 5 minutes, after which the fish will disappear quickly. Sightings of fish at other points of the tour are sporadic.

The trip takes about 45 minutes to an hour (about 15 minutes out, 15 minutes back, and around 15 minutes parked at viewing spots along the reef adjacent to Castaway Cay). Cost is $37 for adults and $25 for kids age 0–9. Guests must be able to climb five steps to board and debark the boat to participate, and guests will stand aboard the boat for the duration of the excursion.

PARASAILING

GUESTS LOOKING FOR A BIRD'S-EYE VIEW of paradise should check out this excursion. Floating hundreds of feet in the air, you're master of all you survey, or at least it seems that way for several minutes.

You board a speedboat and travel several hundred yards away from land. Then, in singles or pairs, you stand at the back of the boat and are harnessed to a line-bound parachute that is slowly let out until you and the parachute are 600–1,000 feet above the water. Enjoy panoramic views of your ship, Castaway Cay, and beyond.

Each excursion takes about 10 people onto the boat. There are no ride-alongs; every guest on the boat must pay. Your actual parasail event will last about 5–7 minutes. Depending on the number of other guests, the entire experience lasts 45 minutes–1 hour.

Open to guests age 8 and up, parasailing excursions cost $95 for both adults and kids. Guests must weigh between 90 and 375 pounds; those who weigh less than 90 pounds may be able to ride if they fly in tandem with another guest, but their combined weight may not exceed 375 pounds. Determination of single or tandem rides is fully at the discretion of the staff.

Kids under age 13 must be accompanied by a paying adult age 18 or older. Guests ages 13–17 may go on the excursion unaccompanied but must be escorted to the Marge's Barges excursion meeting site by an adult age 18 or older. All guests must sign a safety waiver.

You must leave your shoes on the dock and are strongly discouraged from wearing a hat or glasses during your sail; there is a storage area on the boat for your personal belongings. Wheelchairs and other wheeled mobility devices cannot be accommodated.

No photography service is provided during the excursion—you're welcome to bring cameras onto the boat, but you assume all liability for the loss of anything you bring up with you. Understandably, anything dropped into the ocean can't be retrieved.

SNORKELING

THIS IS ONE OF THE LEAST EXPENSIVE, most rewarding shore excursions offered on a Disney cruise. We recommend it for every family. Cost is $14 for kids ages 5–9 for one day, $18 for two days; $29 for age 10 and up for one day, $36 for two days.

First, find some chairs on the family beach, where you can store your stuff while you're in the water. If possible, choose something near a vertical landmark such as a tree; it will be easier to find when you come back to shore.

Next, pick up your snorkeling gear at Gil's Fins and Boats, a short walk from Scuttle's Cove, the island's first tram stop. You'll be given a mask, snorkel, fins, and an inflatable buoyancy vest to make swimming easier. Also pick up a blue-mesh gear bag, which makes it easier to haul your stuff back to your beach chairs.

Put on your vest before you get in the water, but don't inflate it just yet. Wait until you're in hip-high water to put on your flippers because it's impossible to walk in them on shore (and they'll get sandy). Keep your mask off until you get into the water.

If you're snorkeling with younger children, plan on spending 10–15 minutes adjusting the fit of masks and vests. Inflate their vests by blowing into the vertical tube on the left side of the vest, adding just enough air to keep the top of their heads above water. (If you overinflate the vests, they'll have trouble getting their masks below the surface.) Also practice using the flippers, which work best with slow, deliberate leg movements.

Once everyone's gear is working, take one last look at the lagoon to get your bearings. Disney has placed orange-and-white buoys above the underwater sites, so head for those.

There usually aren't a lot of fish in the first 30–40 yards nearest the shore, though it's possible to see almost anything once you're in the water. Fish species in the lagoon include yellowtail snapper, sergeant major, banded butterfly fish, blue tang, and barracuda. Obviously, you shouldn't try to catch any of these fish with your hands.

If you've snorkeled before and you enjoy it, Castaway Cay offers another snorkeling excursion in the waters off the island. You board the *Seahorse*, a large catamaran, and head for the northwest side of the island, about a mile offshore from the Serenity Bay adult beach, where you're able to snorkel in the open ocean for 2–2½ hours. Cost is $55 for adults, $36 for kids ages 5–9.

WALKING AND KAYAK NATURE ADVENTURE

THIS PORT ADVENTURE BEGINS at Marge's Barges, where everyone boards a tram to the Serenity Bay adult beach. Next you walk behind the adult beach cabanas to a nature trail, which leads to the beach beyond. During the walk, your guide will point out interesting plants and animals and talk about the history of the Bahamas.

Upon reaching the beach, participants don their life jackets and head out in their kayaks. This is the part where you're at Mother Nature's whim. We took this tour after a friend raved about it. She headed out in the morning and was able to kayak to the interior of the island. Our own tour was later in the afternoon as the tide was going out. The interior of the island was inaccessible by kayak, and the tides made piloting our single kayak very difficult. We wouldn't book this adventure in the afternoon again, even if it were the only time available.

Even if you're able to book this in the morning, however, the tour is 3–3½ hours long—time you could spend snorkeling, biking, or lazing on the beach. Ideally, you would book this on the morning of the second stop of a five-night Castaway Cay cruise.

Be sure to bring walking shoes, sunglasses, a hat, sunscreen, and an underwater or water-resistant camera; consider gloves for paddling to avoid blisters. Wear a swimsuit under your clothes for swimming. You must stow your belongings on the beach for the kayaking, so leave the doubloons in the cabin. Water is provided. Cost is $64 for guests age 10 and up.

PERSONAL WATERCRAFT ADVENTURE

BOOKING THIS PORT ADVENTURE is the only way that guests can use WaveRunner watercraft on Castaway Cay, and that fact alone makes it worth your while if you're willing to spend the money.

Riders begin at the Boat Beach (the beach closest to where the ship docks), where they're given life jackets and a safety briefing. While you must be at least 18 years old to drive the WaveRunner, kids as young as 8 may ride along. Our advice for two adults is for each to ride as singles unless one is truly afraid of piloting a craft alone—a single rider will go much faster than two adults due to the weight difference. If you've never piloted a WaveRunner before, don't worry; it's fairly easy. It's actually easier to maneuver once you get up to speed than when you're idling or going slowly at the beginning of the excursion.

If you're familiar with driving a motorcycle or Vespa, you've got this down. Most participants get the hang of things quickly.

As you head out, riders will start in single file with a guide leading and one more assistant bringing up the rear. Try to avoid hitting the wake of the craft in front of you because the bumpiness can be a little scary when you're up to speed, which tops out at a little more than 30 mph at full throttle.

Unless you choose to swim or tip your craft, you won't get especially wet, though you will want to wear waterproof shoes or sandals or go barefoot. Flip-flops aren't allowed, as they're likely to come off in the water (along with hats). You may store anything that you don't want to take with you in an unlocked chest at the beginning of the tour. We recommend taking a waterproof camera for photos on the beach; just secure it around your neck for the trip out.

Disney says the hour-long tour may have two stops, but ours had one—the same beach you visit on the Walking and Kayak Nature Adventure. The fact that you can visit this beach on the WaveRunner without having to kayak there is a plus, but perhaps we're still bitter about the blister we got kayaking. The other stop is an island opposite the beach.

When you arrive, your tour guide will give you a very brief history of the islands and point out any interesting flora and fauna, much like an abbreviated version of the Walking and Kayak tour. Then you can swim in the ocean for a bit before heading back to the Boat Beach to end your port adventure. The piloting of the WaveRunners, not the nature talk or the beach visit, is the real highlight.

Would we book this again? *Maybe.* This is one of the more expensive port adventures for its length. The WaveRunners are fun, but the Boat Beach is far enough away that just getting there and back will cut into your time on the island. If you have the chance, you may want to book this for earlier in the day as you're just getting off the ship, or late as you're heading back. Price is $95 for a single rider, $160 for two riders.

ITINERARIES INDEX

DISNEY CRUISE LINE'S FOUR SHIPS serve five main geographic areas: Alaska, the Bahamas, the California coast, the Caribbean, and the Mediterranean. DCL also offers "repositioning" cruises when it needs to move a ship between the United States and Europe or from the Atlantic to the Pacific.

To appeal to as wide an audience as possible, Disney cruises vary in length (and price) within each geographic area. Guests interested in visiting the Bahamas, for instance, can choose from cruises of three, four, or five nights.

There's even more variation, however, since Disney's ships visit the same ports as every other cruise line's ships, and the destination ports can't dock every line's ship at the same time. (Disney's Castaway Cay is a good illustration—it can dock only one ship at a time.)

To help fit its ships into the ports' schedules, DCL offers multiple versions of most itineraries, each of which visits exactly the same ports, but in different order. As an example, consider a four-night Bahamian cruise out of Port Canaveral, which visits Nassau and Castaway Cay and usually includes a day at sea. Disney offers at least six separate itineraries:

SHIP AND ITINERARY VERSION	NIGHT 1	NIGHT 2	NIGHT 3	NIGHT 4
Dream A	Port Canaveral	Nassau	Castaway Cay	At Sea
Dream B	Port Canaveral	Nassau	At Sea	Castaway Cay
Dream C	Port Canaveral	At Sea	Nassau	Castaway Cay
Magic C	Port Canaveral	Castaway Cay	Nassau	At Sea
Wonder C	Port Canaveral	Nassau	Castaway Cay	Castaway Cay
Dream H	Port Canaveral	Castaway Cay	Castaway Cay	At Sea

Taking these variations into account, Disney's four ships sail nearly 50 distinct itineraries, listed in the following section. We've also included maps of the ports for each geographic area. To keep things simple, the maps show only the ports visited along the ships' routes, not the order in which each port is visited.

See Part Twelve for detailed port information.

ONLINE FARE TRACKER

OUR WEBSITE has an interactive tool that demonstrates how Disney Cruise Line fares vary by date, stateroom type, and the size of your party. Access it here: **touringplans.com/disney-cruise-line/tools/fare-tracker.**

By viewing this data, you can get a sense of the best time(s) to book a cruise, and you can see which cruises are likely to have last-minute discounts. Full access to the Fare Tracker and other Disney Cruise Line content is available as an add-on to a **touringplans.com** subscription; the fees are nominal, and owners of the current edition of *The Unofficial Guide to Disney Cruise Line* get a substantial subscription discount. If you aren't satisfied for any reason, we offer a 45-day money-back guarantee.

ALASKAN CRUISES [see map opposite]

Disney Wonder

7-NIGHT ALASKAN CRUISE: ITINERARY A

ITINERARY Day 1 Vancouver, British Columbia; Day 2 at sea; Day 3 Tracy Arm, Alaska; Day 4 Skagway, Alaska; Day 5 Juneau, Alaska; Day 6 Ketchikan, Alaska; Day 7 at sea; Day 8 Vancouver, British Columbia.

2014 SAIL DATES June 2–9, June 9–16, June 16–23, June 23–30, June 30–July 7, July 7–14, July 14–21, July 21–28, July 28–August 4, August 4–11, August 11–18, August 18–25, August 25–September 1, and September 1–8.

9-NIGHT ALASKAN CRUISE: ITINERARY A

ITINERARY Day 1 Vancouver, British Columbia; Days 2 and 3 at sea; Day 4 Sitka, Alaska; Day 5 Tracy Arm, Alaska; Day 6 Skagway, Alaska; Day 7 Juneau, Alaska; Day 8 Ketchikan, Alaska; Day 9 at sea; Day 10 Vancouver, British Columbia.

2014 SAIL DATES May 24–June 2.

BAHAMIAN AND CARIBBEAN CRUISES [see map next page]

Disney Magic

3-NIGHT BAHAMIAN CRUISE: ITINERARY A

ITINERARY Day 1 Port Canaveral, Florida; Day 2 Nassau, Bahamas; Day 3 Castaway Cay, Bahamas; Day 4 Port Canaveral, Florida.

2014 SAIL DATES April 4–7, April 11–14, April 18–21, April 25–28, May 9–12, May 16–19.

3-NIGHT BAHAMIAN CRUISE: ITINERARY D

ITINERARY Day 1 Port Canaveral, Florida; Day 2 at sea; Day 3 Castaway Cay, Bahamas; Day 4 Port Canaveral, Florida.

2014 SAIL DATES May 2–5.

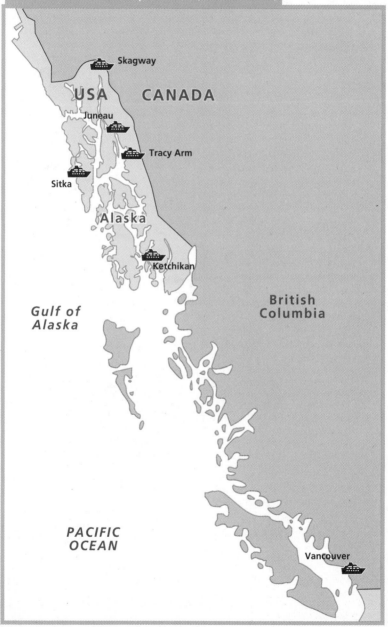

Alaska Ports of Call (Wonder)

Bahamian and Caribbean Ports of Call

USA

Port
Canaveral

Florida

Gulf of
Mexico

Key
West

Miami

Grand Cayman

Cozumel

Costa Maya

MEXICO

PACIFIC
OCEAN

3-NIGHT SAN JUAN–PORT CANAVERAL CRUISE
ITINERARY Day 1 San Juan, Puerto Rico; **Day 2** at sea; **Day 3** Castaway Cay, Bahamas; **Day 4** Port Canaveral, Florida.
2014 SAIL DATES October 18–21.

4-NIGHT BAHAMIAN CRUISE: ITINERARY B
ITINERARY Day 1 Port Canaveral, Florida; **Day 2** Nassau, Bahamas; **Day 3** Castaway Cay, Bahamas; **Day 4** at sea; **Day 5** Port Canaveral, Florida.
2014 SAIL DATES March 31–April 4, April 7–11, April 14–18, April 21–25, April 28–May 2, May 5–9, May 12–16.

7-NIGHT EASTERN CARIBBEAN CRUISE: ITINERARY A
ITINERARY Day 1 Port Canaveral, Florida; **Days 2 and 3** at sea; **Day 4** Philipsburg, Sint Maarten; **Day 5** St. John–St. Thomas, US Virgin Islands; **Day 6** at sea; **Day 7** Castaway Cay, Bahamas; **Day 8** Port Canaveral, Florida.
2014 SAIL DATES October 26–November 2, November 9–16.

7-NIGHT SOUTHERN CARIBBEAN CRUISE: ITINERARY A
ITINERARY Day 1 San Juan, Puerto Rico; **Day 2** at sea; **Day 3** St. John's, Antigua and Barbuda; **Day 4** Castries, Saint Lucia; **Day 5** Saint George's, Grenada; **Day 6** Bridgetown, Barbados; **Day 7** Basseterre, Saint Kitts and Nevis; **Day 8** San Juan, Puerto Rico.
2014 SAIL DATES September 20–27, September 27–October 4, October 4–11, October 11–18.

7-NIGHT WESTERN CARIBBEAN CRUISE: ITINERARY A
ITINERARY Day 1 Port Canaveral, Florida; **Day 2** Key West, Florida; **Day 3** at sea; **Day 4** Grand Cayman, Cayman Islands; **Day 5** Cozumel, Mexico; **Day 6** at sea; **Day 7** Castaway Cay, Bahamas; **Day 8** Port Canaveral, Florida.
2014 SAIL DATES November 2–9, November 23–30, December 7–14, December 21–28.
2015 SAIL DATES January 4–11, January 18–25, February 1–8, February 15–22, March 1–8, March 15–22, March 29–April 5, April 12–19, April 26–May 3.

7-NIGHT WESTERN CARIBBEAN CRUISE: ITINERARY B
ITINERARY Day 1 Port Canaveral, Florida; **Day 2** at sea; **Day 3** Cozumel, Mexico; **Day 4** Grand Cayman, Cayman Islands; **Day 5** Falmouth, Jamaica; **Day 6** at sea; **Day 7** Castaway Cay, Bahamas; **Day 8** Port Canaveral, Florida.
2014 SAIL DATES November 16–23, November 30–December 7, December 14–21.
2014–15 SAIL DATES December 28, 2014–January 4, 2015.
2015 SAIL DATES January 11–18, January 25–February 1, February 8–15, February 22–March 1, March 8–15, March 22–29, April 5–12, April 19–26.

Disney Wonder
4-NIGHT BAHAMIAN CRUISE: ITINERARY B

ITINERARY Day 1 Miami, Florida; Day 2 Castaway Cay, Bahamas; Day 3 Nassau, Bahamas; Day 4 Key West, Florida; Day 5 Miami, Florida.

2014 SAIL DATES April 9–13, April 23–27, November 19–23, December 3–7, December 17–21.

2015 SAIL DATES January 14–18, January 28–February 1, February 11–15, February 25–March 1, March 11–15, March 25–29, April 8–12, April 22–26.

4-NIGHT BAHAMIAN CRUISE: ITINERARY C
ITINERARY Day 1 Port Canaveral, Florida; Day 2 Nassau, Bahamas; Days 3 and 4 Castaway Cay, Bahamas; Day 5 Port Canaveral, Florida.
2014 SAIL DATES October 6–10.

4-NIGHT BAHAMIAN CRUISE: ITINERARY D
ITINERARY Day 1 Miami, Florida; Day 2 Castaway Cay, Bahamas; Day 3 at sea; Day 4 Key West, Florida; Day 5 Miami, Florida.
2014 SAIL DATES October 22–26, November 5–9.

4-NIGHT BAHAMIAN CRUISE: ITINERARY E
ITINERARY Day 1 Miami, Florida; Day 2 at sea; Day 3 Nassau, Bahamas; Day 4 Castaway Cay, Bahamas; Day 5 Miami, Florida.
2014 SAIL DATES December 26–30.

5-NIGHT BAHAMIAN CRUISE: ITINERARY A
ITINERARY Day 1 Port Canaveral, Florida; Day 2 Castaway Cay, Bahamas; Day 3 at sea; Day 4 Key West, Florida; Day 5 Castaway Cay, Bahamas; Day 6 Port Canaveral, Florida.
2014 SAIL DATES October 1–6.

5-NIGHT BAHAMIAN CRUISE: ITINERARY B
ITINERARY Day 1 Port Canaveral, Florida; Day 2 Key West, Florida; Days 3 and 4 Castaway Cay, Bahamas; Day 5 Nassau, Bahamas; Day 6 Port Canaveral, Florida.
2014 SAIL DATES September 26–October 1.

5-NIGHT BAHAMIAN CRUISE: ITINERARY C
ITINERARY Day 1 Miami, Florida; Day 2 Castaway Cay, Bahamas; Day 3 Nassau, Bahamas; Day 4 at sea; Day 5 Key West, Florida; Day 6 Miami, Florida.
2014–15 SAIL DATES December 30, 2014–January 4, 2015.

5-NIGHT WESTERN CARIBBEAN CRUISE: ITINERARY A
ITINERARY Day 1 Miami, Florida; Day 2 at sea; Day 3 Cozumel, Mexico; Day 4 at sea; Day 5 Castaway Cay, Bahamas; Day 6 Miami, Florida.
2014 SAIL DATES March 30–April 4, April 13–18, April 27–May 2, October 26–31, November 9–14, November 23–28, December 7–12, December 21–26.
2015 SAIL DATES January 4–9, January 18–23, February 1–6, February 15–20, March 1–6, March 15–20, March 29–April 3, April 12–17, April 26–May 1.

5-NIGHT WESTERN CARIBBEAN CRUISE: ITINERARY B

ITINERARY Day 1 Miami, Florida; Day 2 at sea; Day 3 Grand Cayman, Cayman Islands; Day 4 Cozumel, Mexico; Day 5 at sea; Day 6 Miami, Florida.

2014 SAIL DATES April 4–9, April 18–23, October 17–22, October 31–November 5, November 14–19, November 28–December 3, December 12–17.

5-NIGHT WESTERN CARIBBEAN CRUISE: ITINERARY C

ITINERARY Day 1 Miami, Florida; Day 2 at sea; Day 3 Grand Cayman, Cayman Islands; Day 4 at sea; Day 5 Castaway Cay, Bahamas; Day 6 Miami, Florida.

2015 SAIL DATES January 9–14, January 23–28, February 6–11, February 20–25, March 6–11, March 20–25, April 3–8, April 17–22.

6-NIGHT WESTERN CARIBBEAN CRUISE: ITINERARY A

ITINERARY Day 1 Miami, Florida; Day 2 at sea; Day 3 Grand Cayman, Cayman Islands; Day 4 Cozumel, Mexico; Day 5 at sea; Day 6 Castaway Cay, Bahamas; Day 7 Miami, Florida.

2014 SAIL DATES October 11–17.

Disney Dream

3-NIGHT BAHAMIAN CRUISE: ITINERARY A

ITINERARY Day 1 Port Canaveral, Florida; Day 2 Nassau, Bahamas; Day 3 Castaway Cay, Bahamas; Day 4 Port Canaveral, Florida.

2014 SAIL DATES April 3–6, April 10–13, April 17–20, April 24–27, May 1–4, May 8–11, May 15–18, May 22–25, May 29–June 1, June 5–8, June 12–15, June 19–22, June 26–29, July 3–6, July 10–13, July 17–20, July 24–27, July 31–August 3, August 7–10, August 14–17, August 21–24, August 28–31, September 4–7, September 11–14, September 18–21, September 25–28, October 2–5, October 9–12, October 16–19, October 31–November 3, November 14–17, November 21–24, November 28–December 1, December 5–8, December 12–15, December 19–22, December 26–29.

2015 SAIL DATES January 2–5, January 9–12, January 16–19, January 23–26, January 30–February 2, February 6–9, February 13–16, February 20–23, February 27–March 2, March 6–9, March 13–16, March 20–23, March 27–30, April 3–6, April 10–13, April 17–20, April 24–27.

3-NIGHT BAHAMIAN CRUISE: ITINERARY H

ITINERARY Day 1 Port Canaveral, Florida; Day 2 at sea; Day 3 Castaway Cay, Bahamas; Day 4 Port Canaveral, Florida.

2014 SAIL DATES November 7–10.

4-NIGHT BAHAMIAN CRUISE: ITINERARY A

ITINERARY Day 1 Port Canaveral, Florida; Day 2 Nassau, Bahamas; Day 3 Castaway Cay, Bahamas; Day 4 at sea; Day 5 Port Canaveral, Florida.

2014 SAIL DATES March 30–April 3, April 6–10, April 13–17, April 20–24, April 27–May 1, May 4–8, May 11–15, May 25–29, June 1–5, June 8–12, June 15–19, June 22–26, June 29–July 1, July 6–10, July 13–17, July 20–24, July 27–31, August 3–7, August 10–14, August 17–21, August 31–September 4,

September 7–11, September 14–18, September 21–25, September 28–October 2, October 5–9, October 12–16, October 19–23, October 27–31, November 3–7, November 17–21, November 24–28, December 1–5, December 8–12, December 15–19, December 22–26.

2015 SAIL DATES January 5–9, January 12–16, January 19–23, January 26–30, February 2–6, February 9–13, February 16–20, February 23–27, March 2–6, March 9–13, March 16–20, March 23–27, March 30–April 3, April 6–10, April 13–17, April 20–24, April 27–May 1.

4-NIGHT BAHAMIAN CRUISE: ITINERARY B

ITINERARY Day 1 Port Canaveral, Florida; Day 2 Nassau, Bahamas; Day 3 at sea; Day 4 Castaway Cay, Bahamas; Day 5 Port Canaveral, Florida.

2014–15 SAIL DATES December 29, 2014–January 2, 2015.

4-NIGHT BAHAMIAN CRUISE: ITINERARY F

ITINERARY Day 1 Port Canaveral, Florida; Day 2 Nassau, Bahamas; Days 3 and 4 Castaway Cay, Bahamas; Day 5 Port Canaveral, Florida.

2014 SAIL DATES October 23–27.

4-NIGHT BAHAMIAN CRUISE: ITINERARY H

ITINERARY Day 1 Port Canaveral, Florida; Days 2 and 3 Castaway Cay, Bahamas; Day 4 at sea; Day 5 Port Canaveral, Florida.

2014 SAIL DATES November 10–14.

Disney Fantasy

7-NIGHT EASTERN CARIBBEAN CRUISE: ITINERARY A

ITINERARY Day 1 Port Canaveral, Florida; Days 2 and 3 at sea; Day 4 Philipsburg, Sint Maarten; Day 5 St. John–St. Thomas, US Virgin Islands; Day 6 at sea; Day 7 Castaway Cay, Bahamas; Day 8 Port Canaveral, Florida.

2014 SAIL DATES April 5–12, April 19–26, May 3–10, May 17–24, May 31–June 7, June 14–21, June 28–July 5, July 12–19, July 26–August 2, August 9–16, August 23–30, September 6–13, September 20–27, October 4–11, October 18–25.

7-NIGHT EASTERN CARIBBEAN CRUISE: ITINERARY B

ITINERARY Day 1 Port Canaveral, Florida; Days 2 and 3 at sea; Day 4 St. John–St. Thomas, US Virgin Islands; Day 5 San Juan, Puerto Rico; Day 6 at sea; Day 7 Castaway Cay, Bahamas; Day 8 Port Canaveral, Florida.

2014 SAIL DATES November 1–8, November 15–22, November 29–December 6, December 13–20.

2014–15 SAIL DATES December 27, 2014–January 3, 2015.

2015 SAIL DATES January 10–17, January 24–31, February 7–14, February 21–28, March 7–14, March 21–28, April 4–11, April 18–25.

7-NIGHT EASTERN CARIBBEAN CRUISE: ITINERARY C

ITINERARY Day 1 Port Canaveral, Florida; Days 2 and 3 at sea; Day 4 Philipsburg, Sint Maarten; Day 5 San Juan, Puerto Rico; Day 6 at sea; Day 7 Castaway Cay, Bahamas; Day 8 Port Canaveral, Florida.

2014 SAIL DATES November 22–29, December 6–13, December 20–27.

2015 SAIL DATES January 3–10, January 17–24, January 31–February 7, February 14–21, February 28–March 7, March 14–21, March 28–April 4, April 11–18, April 25–May 2.

7-NIGHT WESTERN CARIBBEAN CRUISE: ITINERARY B
ITINERARY Day 1 Port Canaveral, Florida; **Day 2** at sea; **Day 3** Grand Cayman, Cayman Islands; **Day 4** Costa Maya, Mexico; **Day 5** Cozumel, Mexico; **Day 6** at sea; **Day 7** Castaway Cay, Bahamas; **Day 8** Port Canaveral, Florida.
2014 SAIL DATES March 29–April 5, April 12–19, April 26–May 3.

7-NIGHT WESTERN CARIBBEAN CRUISE: ITINERARY C
ITINERARY Day 1 Port Canaveral, Florida; **Day 2** at sea; **Day 3** Cozumel, Mexico; **Day 4** Grand Cayman, Cayman Islands; **Day 5** Falmouth, Jamaica; **Day 6** at sea; **Day 7** Castaway Cay, Bahamas; **Day 8** Port Canaveral, Florida.
2014 SAIL DATES May 10–17, May 24–31, June 7–14, June 21–28, July 5–12, July 19–26, August 2–9, August 16–23, August 30–September 6, September 13–20, September 27–October 4, October 11–18, October 25–November 1, November 8–15.

CALIFORNIA COAST CRUISES *[see map opposite]*
Disney Wonder
2-NIGHT WEEKEND GETAWAY CRUISE
ITINERARY Day 1 San Diego, California; **Day 2** at sea; **Day 3** San Diego, California.
2014 SAIL DATES May 17–19.

4-NIGHT VANCOUVER–SAN DIEGO CRUISE *(Repositioning)*
ITINERARY Day 1 Vancouver, British Columbia; **Day 2** Victoria, British Columbia; **Days 3 and 4** at sea; **Day 5** San Diego, California.
2014 SAIL DATES September 8–12.

5-NIGHT SAN DIEGO–VANCOUVER CRUISE *(Repositioning)*
ITINERARY Day 1 San Diego, California; **Day 2** at sea; **Day 3** San Francisco, California; **Days 4 and 5** at sea; **Day 6** Vancouver, British Columbia.
2014 SAIL DATES May 19–24.

EUROPEAN CRUISES *[see map next page]*
Disney Magic
4-NIGHT MEDITERRANEAN CRUISE: ITINERARY B
ITINERARY Day 1 Barcelona, Spain; **Day 2** Palma, Spain; **Day 3** Ibiza, Spain; **Day 4** at sea; **Day 5** Barcelona, Spain.
2014 SAIL DATES August 7–11.

Continued on page 234

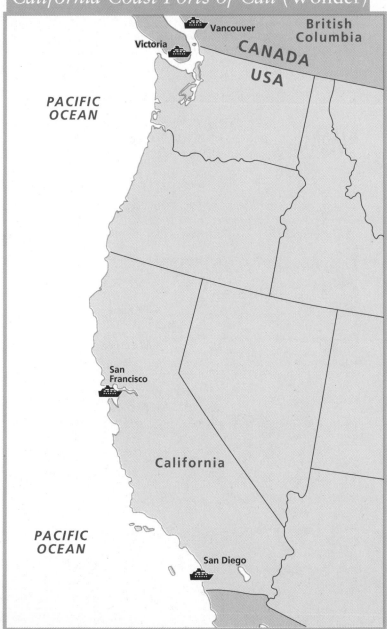

California Coast Ports of Call (Wonder)

European Ports of Call (Magic)

Continued from page 230

5-NIGHT MEDITERRANEAN CRUISE: ITINERARY A

ITINERARY Day 1 Barcelona, Spain; Day 2 Villefranche, France; Day 3 La Spezia, Italy; Day 4 Civitavecchia, Italy; Day 5 at sea; Day 6 Barcelona, Spain.
2014 SAIL DATES August 11–16.

7-NIGHT MEDITERRANEAN CRUISE: ITINERARY A

ITINERARY Day 1 Barcelona, Spain; Day 2 at sea; Day 3 Villefranche, France; Day 4 La Spezia, Italy; Day 5 Civitavecchia, Italy; Day 6 Naples, Italy; Day 7 at sea; Day 8 Barcelona, Spain.
2014 SAIL DATES May 31–June 7, June 7–14, August 16–23, August 23–30, August 30–September 6.

9-NIGHT MEDITERRANEAN CRUISE: ITINERARY A

ITINERARY Day 1 Venice, Italy; Day 2 at sea; Day 3 Katakolon, Greece; Day 4 Piraeus, Greece; Day 5 Kusadasi, Turkey; Day 6 Rhodes, Greece; Day 7 Mykonos, Greece; Day 8 at sea; Days 9 and 10 Venice, Italy.
2014 SAIL DATES June 26–July 5, July 5–14.

12-NIGHT MEDITERRANEAN CRUISE: ITINERARY A

ITINERARY Day 1 Barcelona, Spain; Day 2 Villefranche, France; Day 3 La Spezia, Italy; Day 4 Civitavecchia, Italy; Days 5 and 6 at sea; Day 7 Piraeus, Greece; Day 8 Kusadasi, Turkey; Day 9 Mykonos, Greece; Day 10 at sea; Day 11 Valletta, Malta; Day 12 at sea; Day 13 Barcelona, Spain.
2014 SAIL DATES July 26–August 7.

12-NIGHT MEDITERRANEAN CRUISE: ITINERARY C *(Repositioning)*

ITINERARY Day 1 Barcelona, Spain; Day 2 at sea; Day 3 Villefranche, France; Day 4 La Spezia, Italy; Day 5 Civitavecchia, Italy; Day 6 Naples, Italy; Day 7 at sea; Day 8 Catania, Italy; Day 9 Corfu, Greece; Day 10 Dubrovnik, Croatia; Day 11 at sea; Days 12 and 13 Venice, Italy.
2014 SAIL DATES June 14–26.

12-NIGHT MEDITERRANEAN CRUISE: ITINERARY D *(Repositioning)*

ITINERARY Day 1 Venice, Italy; Days 2 and 3 at sea; Day 4 Piraeus, Greece; Day 5 Kusadasi, Turkey; Day 6 Rhodes, Greece; Day 7 Heraklion, Greece; Day 8 Mykonos, Greece; Day 9 Santorini, Greece; Day 10 at sea; Day 11 Valletta, Malta; Day 12 at sea; Day 13 Barcelona, Spain.
2014 SAIL DATES July 14–26.

PANAMA CANAL CRUISES [see map pages 236–237]

Disney Wonder

14-NIGHT EASTBOUND PANAMA CANAL CRUISE:
ITINERARY C *(Repositioning)*

ITINERARY Day 1 San Diego, California; Day 2 at sea; Day 3 Cabo San Lucas, Mexico; Day 4 Puerto Vallarta, Mexico; Days 5–8 at sea; Day 9 Panama Canal, Panama; Day 10 Cartagena, Colombia; Days 11 and 12 at sea; Day 13 Cozumel, Mexico; Day 14 at sea; Day 15 Port Canaveral, Florida.
2014 SAIL DATES September 12–26.

15-NIGHT WESTBOUND PANAMA CANAL CRUISE *(Repositioning)*
ITINERARY Day 1 Miami, Florida; Day 2 Key West, Florida; Day 3 at sea; Day 4 Cozumel, Mexico; Days 5 and 6 at sea; Day 7 Cartagena, Colombia; Day 8 Panama Canal, Panama; Days 9–12 at sea; Day 13 Puerto Vallarta, Mexico; Day 14 Cabo San Lucas, Mexico; Day 15 at sea; Day 16 San Diego, California.
2014 SAIL DATES May 2–17.

TRANSATLANTIC CRUISES *[see map pages 238–239]*
Disney Magic
12-NIGHT EASTBOUND TRANSATLANTIC CRUISE: ITINERARY A
ITINERARY Day 1 Port Canaveral, Florida; Day 2 Castaway Cay, Bahamas; Days 3–8 at sea; Day 9 Funchal, Portugal; Day 10 at sea; Day 11 Málaga, Spain; Day 12 at sea; Day 13 Barcelona, Spain.
2014 SAIL DATES May 19–31.

14-NIGHT WESTBOUND TRANSATLANTIC CRUISE
ITINERARY Day 1 Barcelona, Spain; Day 2 at sea; Day 3 Málaga, Spain; Days 4 and 5 at sea; Day 6 Tenerife, Spain; Days 7–11 at sea; Day 12 St. John's, Antigua and Barbuda; Day 13 Philipsburg, Sint Maarten; Day 14 Basseterre, Saint Kitts and Nevis; Day 15 San Juan, Puerto Rico.
2014 SAIL DATES September 6–20.

Panama Canal Ports of Call (Wonder)

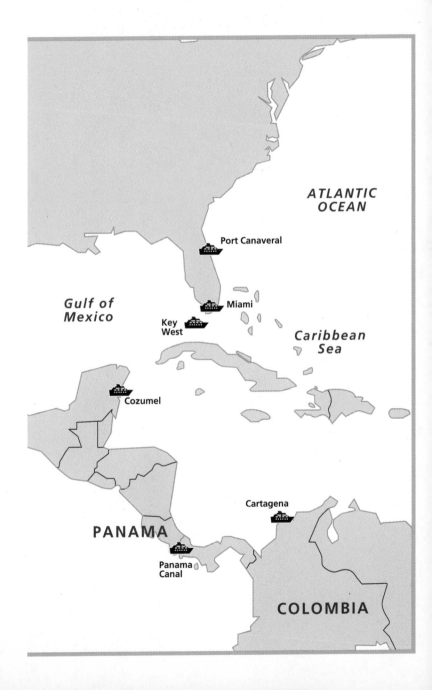

ATLANTIC OCEAN

Port Canaveral

Gulf of Mexico

Miami

Key West

Caribbean Sea

Cozumel

Cartagena

PANAMA

Panama Canal

COLOMBIA

Transatlantic Ports of Call (Magic)

USA

ATLANTIC
OCEAN

Gulf of
Mexico

Port Canaveral

Castaway Cay

San Juan

Philipsburg

Basseterre

St John's

Caribbean
Sea

PACIFIC
OCEAN

SUBJECT INDEX